ILLUSTRATED ATLAS
OF THE
WORLD

Consultant
TREVOR MARCHINGTON M.A.

This edition published in 1992 by Blitz Editions,
an imprint of Bookmart Limited, Registered Number 2372865.
Trading as Bookmart Limited, Desford Road, Enderby,
Leicester LE9 5AD

© 1992 Vallardi Industrie Grafiche SpA
ISBN 1 85605 117 X

Printed in Italy by Vallardi Industrie Grafiche - Lainate (Mi)
June 1992

Photographic Sources: Arch. Vallardi: 9cr, 10l, 13r, 16l, 19t,bl, 23l, 30t,cl,blr, 33l,c, 34t, 35t, 41cl, 42-43. Archivio 2P: 34b. Barone: 27t. Coleman: 33cr, 40t,cbr, 41t,cr. G. Costa: 35cr. Fiore: 15. Marka: 2-3, 4-5, 6-7, 9cl,b, 10c,r, 11, 12, 13l,c, 16c,r, 17c, 18b,c,r, 19c,r, 21l,cb,rb, 22c,r, 25, 26, 28c, 29, 31, 32, 40cl. Michelin: 33t. Pedone: 20ct, 21tr. A. Pellegrini: 30c. Prato Previde: 18t, 20l,cb,r, 28lr. Publiaerfoto: 27c. Regaldi: 17r, 21ct. Ricatto: 17l, 18bl, 22l, 30cr. Sauli: 9t. Titus: 35cl.

Contents

The Earth

Volcanic and seismic phenomena give the strongest indications that the Earth's surface is changing, something which, to the casual observer, does not seem to happen. However, if we consider the crust of our Earth in terms of geological time, it becomes clear that our planet is in a continuous process of evolution, with mountain chains rising out of the sea, oceans being swallowed up, and ice caps forming and dispersing. For us, all these are landmarks in Earth chronology, taking place over millions of years.

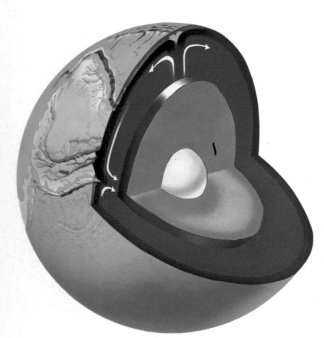

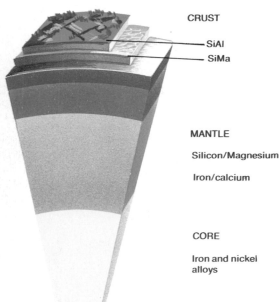

CRUST
- SiAl
- SiMa

MANTLE

Silicon/Magnesium

Iron/calcium

CORE

Iron and nickel alloys

Inside the Earth

The various natural phenomena, and what we know about them from geology, géophysics and geochemistry, lead us to suppose that Earth's structure takes the form of a series of concentric shells (see diagram on the left). There is a marked difference between the density in the core of the planet (12-13 g/cm²) and that of the solid crust (2-7 g/cm². Temperature increases by 3°C per 100 metres of depth. Seismic waves are deflected and change speed according to the depths they reach. Three fundamental areas may be distinguished – the continental crust, designated SiAl because of the abundance of silicon and aluminium, and the oceanic crust called SiMa, because of the presence of silicon and magnesium; the mostly rigid mantle; and the core, the inside of which is thought to be solid due to the very high pressures prevailing, while the outer part is liquid. The Earth's crust and upper part of the mantle form a rigid band, known as the lithosphere. This covers a lower, plastic layer called the asthenosphere.

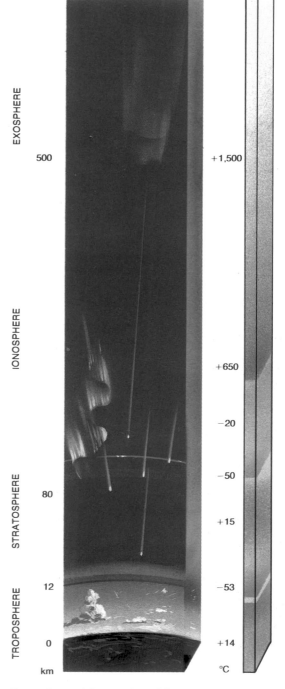

The atmosphere

The atmosphere is made up of a series of gaseous zones encircling our planet. The layer in immediate contact with the crust and known as the troposphere, varies in height from 8 kilometres above the Poles to about 18 kilometres above the Equator. It is from here that rain, snow and hail originate. The troposphere is made up of certain known gases in constant percentages: nitrogen, 78.09 per cent; oxygen, 20.95 per cent; and carbon dioxide, 0.03 per cent, along with argon (0.93 per cent) and other rare gases and specks of salt and dust. Above the troposphere lies the stratosphere, where density and humidity are considerably reduced. The temperature, which drops in the troposphere down to −50°C, remains constant at first but then tends to rise in the stratosphere, forming the so-called warm layer. This stratosphere contains an ozone layer, which is responsible for filtering much of the potentially harmful solar radiation. At more than 90 kilometres up, is the ionosphere, consisting of electrically-charged particles. Above the ionosphere is the exosphere which merges into space.

Formation and destruction of the crust

The lithosphere, consisting of the crust and the upper stratum of the mantle, has an average thickness between 30 kilometres beneath the continents to 5 kilometres beneath the oceans. Its main feature is that it is split vertically into rigid plates or blocks which are able to move over the more flexible underlying asthenosphere, probably as a result of convective movements (indicated by arrows in the diagram below) within the asthenosphere itself. It is along the edges of the plates that the main phenomena of the Earth's crust occur: the expansion of ocean beds along the oceanic ridges where plates diverge; orogenesis, or mountain building, with the formation of ridges and mountain chains; and volcanic and seismic activity, where plates converge and pile on top of or slide alongside one another.

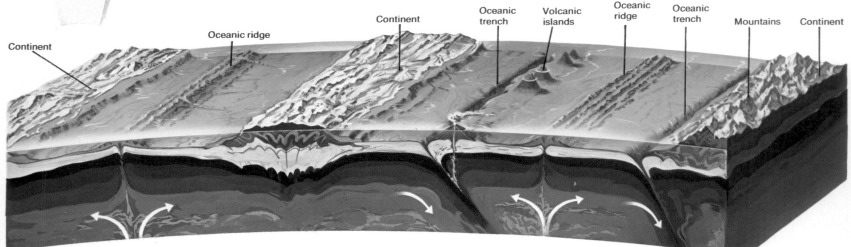

Continent · Oceanic ridge · Continent · Oceanic trench · Volcanic islands · Oceanic ridge · Oceanic trench · Mountains · Continent

The origin of the continents

The rigid plates or blocks of the lithosphere are able to move over the soft asthenospheric layer beneath. The plates which support the continents have moved around with the passage of geological time. The German scientist Alfred Wegener postulated his theory of the origin of the continents in the early part of this century, though he was not able to identify their true origin on account of the limited scientific equipment available at the time. It is only recently that geologists have obtained reliable evidence of the Earth's structure, and have evolved the theory of 'global tectonics'. They have, for instance, found evidence of considerable heat-flow along the oceanic ridges, and a reduced heat-flow along the trenches, which in all probability indicates convection currents within the mantle. Palaeomagnetic anomalies have been discovered on the ocean beds, providing conclusive proof of their expansion.

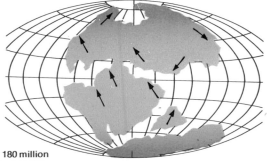

180 million years ago

65 million years ago

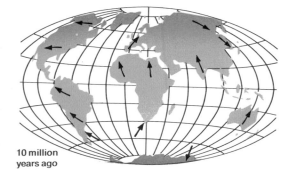
10 million years ago

Erosion

The Earth's landscape is shaped by a complex series of physical and chemical phenomena. This shaping of the landscape is known as erosion. One of the most powerful eroding agents is water, in its various physical states: in rivers, in glaciers, which erode mountains, and in sea waves, which eat into coastlines. The wind too erodes the land in dry areas, forming rocky peaks and arches.

Volcanic activity

The map below enables us to compare the distribution of seismic activity with that of volcanic areas. There is obviously a considerable degree of coincidence. Earthquakes and volcanoes are in fact two phenomena linked with the dynamics of the Earth's crust. The areas of greatest incidence, as recorded since the 1950s, coincide with the distribution of plate edges, namely oceanic ridges, transform faults and oceanic trenches. Volcanoes are situated mainly near the edges of the plates, and these volcanoes are evidence both of the formation of fresh crustal rock (along the oceanic ridges, as the ocean beds expand) and of the destruction of the crust, by melting, within the mantle. This occurs in the subduction zone, where one plate slides beneath its neighbour. The diagram on the far right shows a section through an active volcano. The magma collects in a pocket between lithosphere and asthenosphere, and comes to the surface through fissures or areas of low resistance. On contact with the atmosphere, it solidifies along with ash and other types of ejecta to form a volcanic cone.

Stromboli type (right)
Small flows of lava, accompanied by intermittent eruptive activity.

Hawaiian type (left)
Characterised by a continuous flow of very liquid lava.

Vulcanic type (right)
Violent eruptions of volcanic ash and small stones, accompanied by a characteristic plume of smoke.

DISTRIBUTION OF VOLCANIC AND SEISMIC AREAS

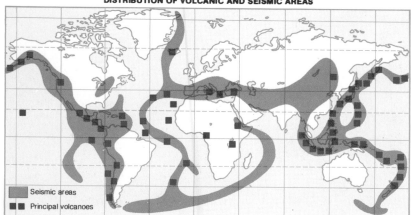

Seismic areas
Principal volcanoes

Earthquakes (right)
Earthquakes are caused by movements of rocks along faults, and by friction along the edges of the plates. They are thus located in the regions characterised by instability in the Earth's crust (ridges, trenches and recent mountain chains). Tremors are violent also along the edges of two plates running sideways in opposite directions (transform faults).

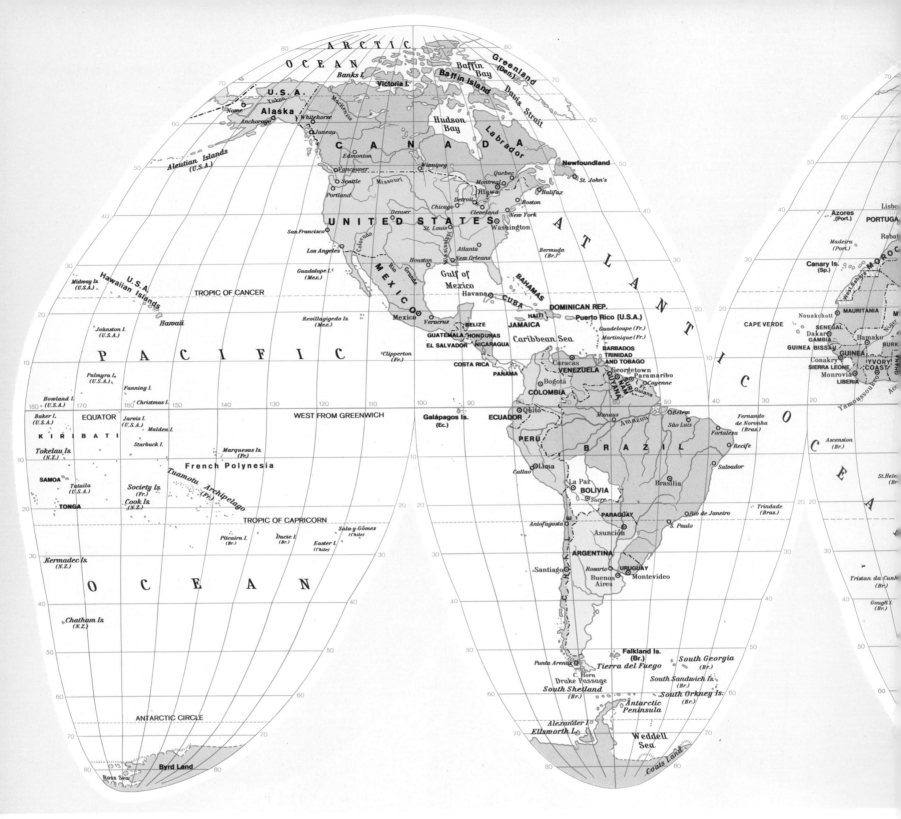

North America
A country of widely contrasting climates, North America has both polar and tropical zones. Its vast open spaces (more than 24 million square kilometres) and enormous agricultural and mineral resources are enjoyed in the central northern area by a population largely of European origin, which has reached an advanced stage of industrial development and prosperity.

South America
Traversed lengthwise by the majestic mountain range of the Andes, South America also has considerable variations in climate. The population (more than 264 million inhabitants) is greatly influenced by Latin (Portuguese and Spanish) culture. Considerable economic and social inequalities persist. Below, a South American Indian village near Lake Titicaca.

Africa
The Sahara separates white Africa, influenced since ancient times by the economic development of the Mediterranean, and black Africa, where the population is predominantly Negroid. This area was dominated by European colonialism until the Second World War, but most African countries have now gained their independence from the colonial powers. Below, an Egyptian pyramid.

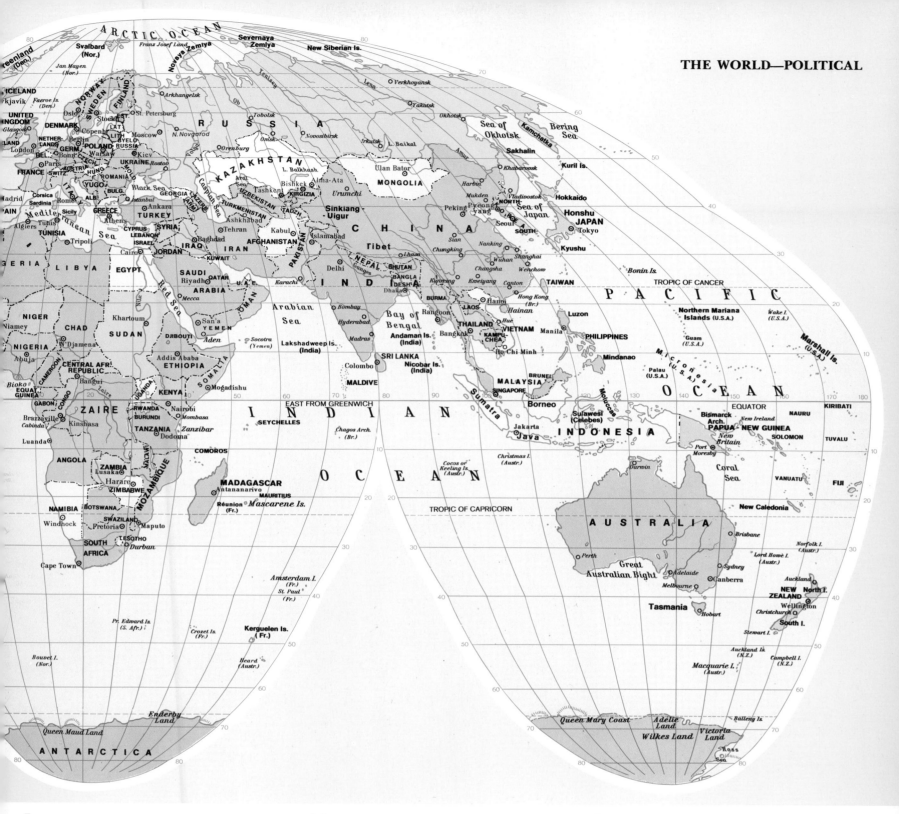

Europe
Although not very extensive (occupying little more than 10.5 million square kilometres) Europe constitutes a vital centre for international trading. It is densely populated (66 inhabitants per square kilometre) and its ancient cultural traditions, linked with the Mediterranean, have given place to the industrial revolution and the age of technology. Below, the Parthenon in Greece.

Asia
Asia is the largest of the continents, covering an area of more than 44 million square kilometres and accounting for about 60 per cent of the world's population. It is the home of ancient civilisations and religions, and much of it was subjected to European colonialism up to the end of the Second World War. Below, the magnificent carvings and statues at a Buddhist temple.

Oceania
The smallest continent in area and, apart from Antarctica, the least densely populated of the continents (with 24 million inhabitants), Oceania was not fully discovered until the 18th century, and its population has been predominantly Anglo-Saxon up to now. Large areas of Australia lie waste, but rapid economic development is now taking place, due to its considerable mineral resources.

The oceans

The Earth's system of seas and oceans is known as the hydrosphere. It covers about 70 per cent of the surface area of the planet. In fact, of the Earth's total area of 510 million square kilometres more than 360 million square kilometres are covered by sea. Although there are notable differences in temperatures and degrees of salinity, the seas and oceans constitute a continuous system, as distinct from the continents, so that it is possible to move from one to another without interruption. It is only through geographical conventions and historical developments that the sea masses have been divided into three oceans, the Atlantic, the Pacific and the Indian, which are enclosed between continental masses, and into numerous seas. The latter fill the inlets and surround the promontories of the continental coastlines, such as the Mediterranean Sea, the Baltic Sea, and the Red Sea; then there are the coastal waters which form the China and Arabian seas, and the island seas, such as the Celebes Sea.

Oceans and seas vary considerably in depth. The continental shelf stretches along almost all the continental coastlines. This is a gently sloping underwater area at a depth ranging from sea level to about 180 metres. The greatest depths have been found to correspond with the oceanic trenches: 11,033 metres in the Marianas Trench and the trenches of Tonga, Curili and the Philippines, all in the Pacific Ocean and all descending to more than 10,000 metres. The deepest Atlantic rift is that of Puerto Rico (9,212 metres), and in the Indian Ocean that of Java (7,450 metres).

One of the most considerable and obvious differences between seas is their degree of salinity. Sea water is in fact a salt solution. The percentage of salt is about 3·5 per cent and consists mainly of sodium chloride. Hence 1 kilogramme of sea water contains about 35 grammes of dissolved elements. Sea water also contains magnesium chloride, calcium sulphate and potassium chloride. The salinity varies according to evaporation (4·2 per cent in the Red Sea) and with the influx of fresh water from the continental rivers.

The temperature of the sea surface also varies in relation to latitude and seasonal heat patterns. In the ocean depths, it is more or less uniform, varying between 2°C in Equatorial areas and −2°C in polar. There are three types of movement in oceanic sea water masses. The waves are determined mainly by wind. The tides are governed by the gravitational pull of the Sun and Moon. Ocean currents are caused by chemical and physical variations in the various water masses.

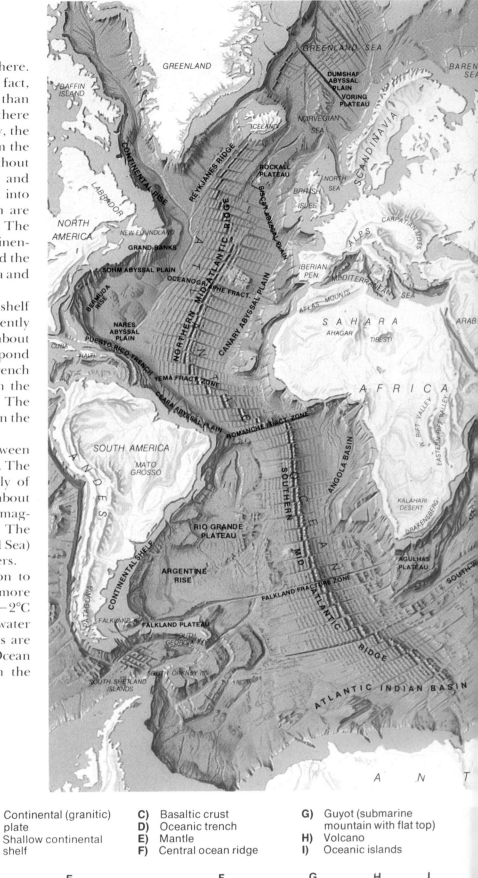

Submarine landscape
Science and modern technology have revealed to us the complex morphology of the ocean depths, where majestic mountain chains (ridges) alternate with the trenches and the continental shelf.

A) Continental (granitic) plate
B) Shallow continental shelf
C) Basaltic crust
D) Oceanic trench
E) Mantle
F) Central ocean ridge
G) Guyot (submarine mountain with flat top)
H) Volcano
I) Oceanic islands

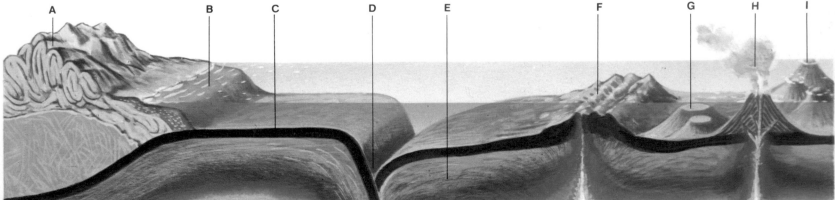

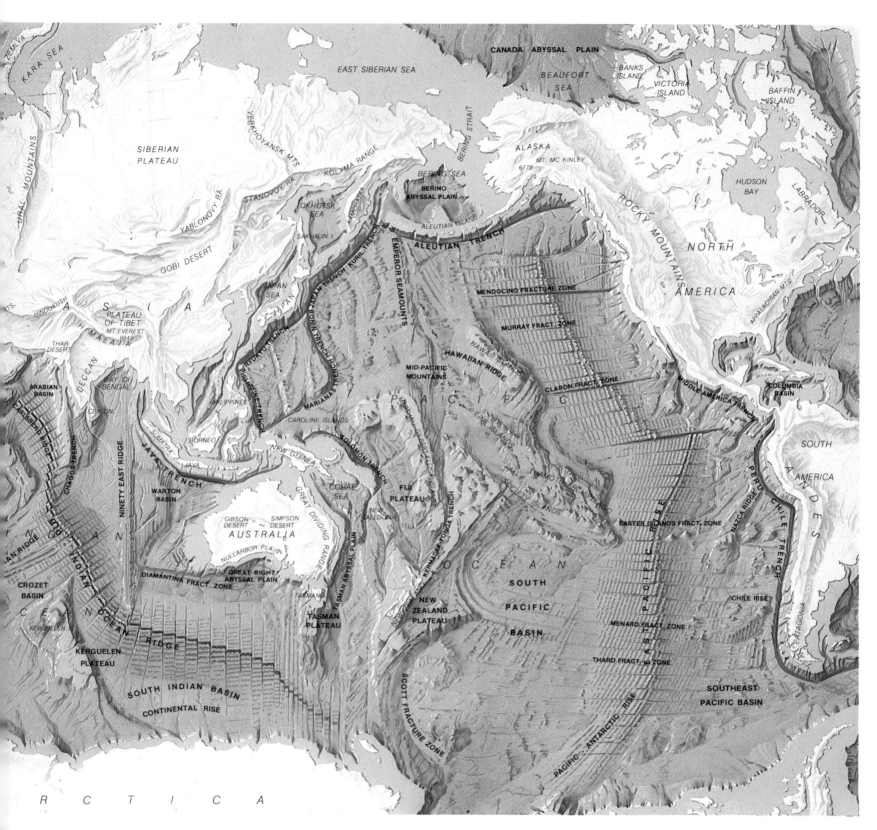

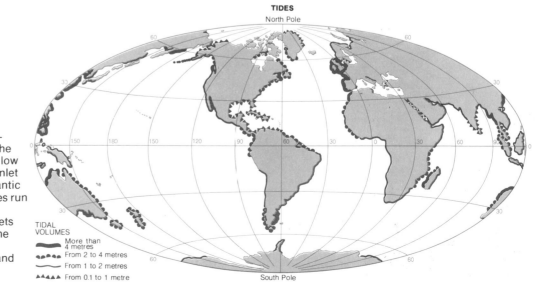

Tides

The photograph on the left shows low tide in an inlet on the Atlantic coast. Tides run highest in narrow inlets because the water is confined and funnelled.

TIDES
North Pole

South Pole

TIDAL VOLUMES
More than 4 metres
From 2 to 4 metres
From 1 to 2 metres
From 0.1 to 1 metre

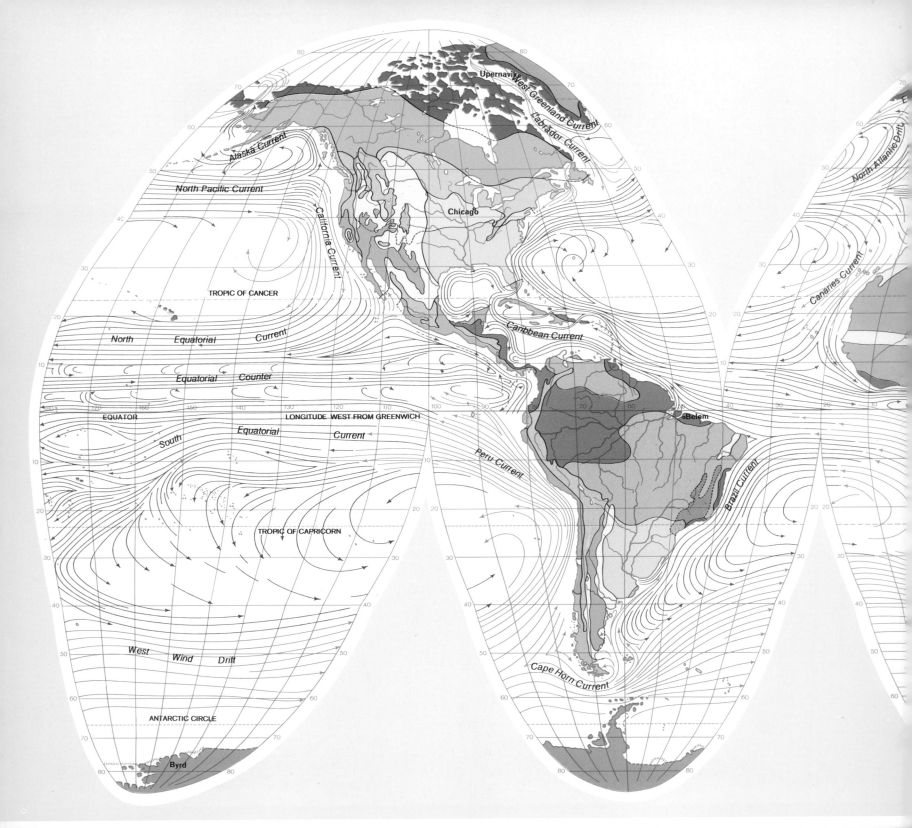

Upernavik

West Greenland Current

Labrador Current

Alaska Current

North Pacific Current

California Current

Chicago

North Atlantic Drift

Canaries Current

Caribbean Current

TROPIC OF CANCER

North Equatorial Current

Equatorial Counter

EQUATOR

LONGITUDE WEST FROM GREENWICH

South Equatorial Current

Belem

Peru Current

Brazil Current

TROPIC OF CAPRICORN

West Wind Drift

Cape Horn Current

ANTARCTIC CIRCLE

Byrd

TROPICAL CLIMATES

Hot and humid

Hot with summer rains

The hot and humid (Equatorial) climates and hot climates with summer rains are prevalent in the inter-tropical zones, such as the Amazon and Zaïre basins, the islands of the Indonesian archipelago and New Guinea. The annual rainfall here is about 2,000 millimetres, while daily temperatures may vary widely.

ARID CLIMATES

Steppes

Deserts

Arid climates prevail in the hot and cold desert zones. It is in the former that the Earth's highest temperatures are recorded (59°C in the Dasht e Lut, a desert in eastern Iran), and in the latter there is a clearly defined cold season, with temperatures below many degrees below zero.

TEMPERATE CLIMATES

Mediterranean

Continental

Oceanic

Temperate climates vary according to latitude and to proximity to the sea, the sea having a moderating effect. Temperate climates are of three kinds, Mediterranean, continental and oceanic, and they have four distinct seasons. Europe has a temperate climate.

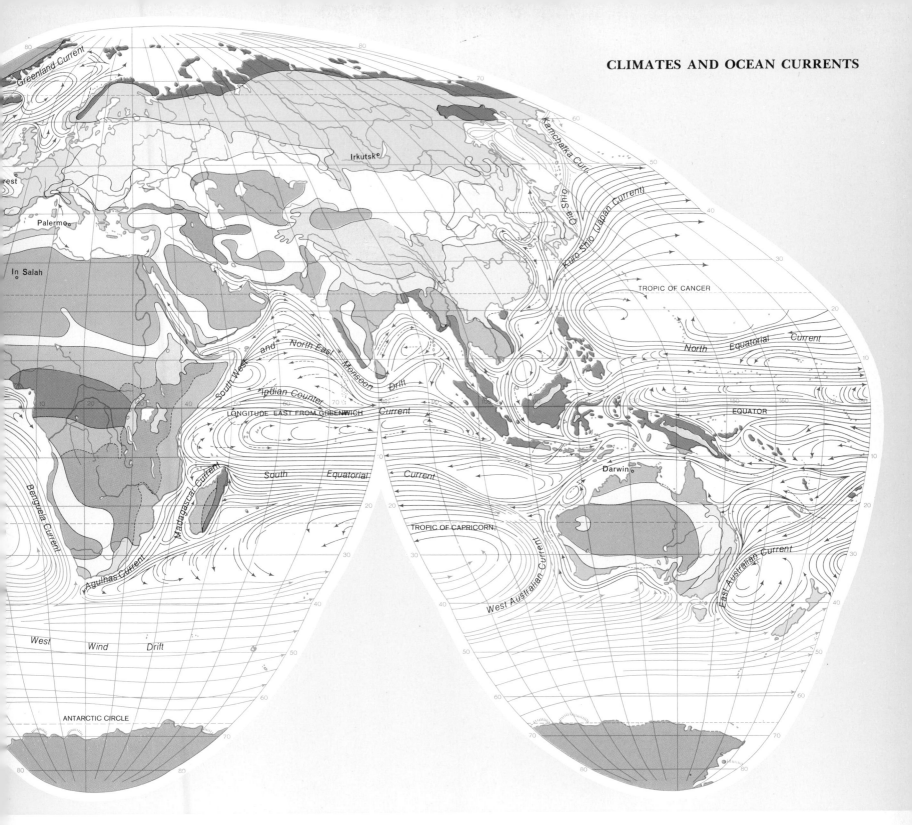

Greenland Current

Irkutsk

Palermo

rest

In Salah

Benguela Current

Madagascar Current

South West and North East Monsoon Drift

Indian Counter

LONGITUDE EAST FROM GREENWICH

Current

South Equatorial Current

Aguihas Current

West Wind Drift

ANTARCTIC CIRCLE

Kamchatka Curr.

Oia-Shio

Kuro-Sivo (Japan Current)

TROPIC OF CANCER

North Equatorial Current

EQUATOR

Darwin

TROPIC OF CAPRICORN

West Australian Current

East Australian Current

COLD CLIMATES

Continental (hot summers)

Continental (cool summers)

Sub-arctic

Continental masses also strongly influence cold climates, which may be differentiated from one another on the basis of their average summer temperatures, which are sometimes higher than 20°C.

COLD CLIMATES IN HIGH MOUNTAIN AREAS

Altitude, latitude and exposure are the factors which largely characterise the cold high mountain climates, where in the hottest month the average temperature is less than 10°C. The temperature drops with the altitude, in the Alps by 0.5°C per 100 metres on the north face, and by 0.6°C on the south. Above a certain height there is permanent snow.

POLAR CLIMATES

Tundra

Ice all the year round

Areas of polar climate, with a covering of tundra and constant ice, have temperatures in the hottest month between 0 and 10°C, whilst winter temperatures can fall to −30°C or even lower. Very few people live in these areas.

Rainfall

Atmospheric humidity, or the amount of water vapour contained in the air, derives from evaporation from the ocean and lake surfaces. The quantity is not infinite but is a function of the temperature. In fact at 0°C the air can contain a maximum of 4.8 grammes of water vapour per cubic metre, whilst at 25°C, the figure is 32.8 grammes per cubic metre. Rainfall depends on the condensation of water, and has a very varied distribution. Maximum annual rainfall occurs along the Equator, where hot and humid air masses occur. Rainfall is lowest at a latitude of about 30°, due to the presence of permanent tropical anticyclones. The highest annual rainfall ever recorded was in Assam (26,401 millimetres) in the monsoon region.

ANNUAL PRECIPITATION

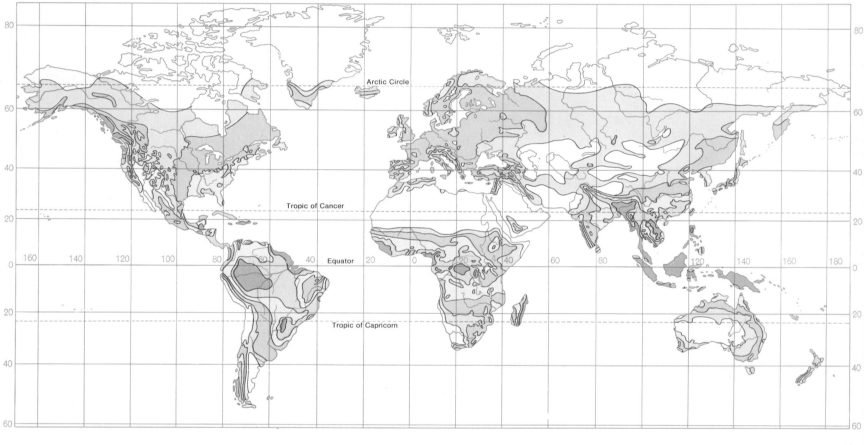

- 0 to 250 mm
- 250 to 500 mm
- 500 to 1,000 mm
- 1,000 mm to 1,500 mm
- 1,500 to 2,000 mm
- Over to 2,000 mm

Areas of scanty rainfall (between 0 and 500 millimetres) are found in two belts around the tropics. There is also low precipitation in the polar regions, where high pressure prevails as a result of cold air masses containing little moisture.

Areas with annual rainfall between 500 and 1,500 millimetres are found at central latitudes, where tropical and polar air masses converge. The land relief has a considerable influence on the distribution of rainfall.

Areas with the heaviest rainfall (between 1,500 and more than 2,000 millimetres) are found at a latitude of 10° north and 5° south, where intense heating by the sun causes moisture-laden air to rise in fast upward currents, causing heavy rain.

The soil

Soil is formed as rock decomposes through chemical and physical processes, to create a soft topsoil, consisting of mineral particles, decomposed organic materials, water, air and living organisms. The type of soil, and therefore its suitability for farming purposes, depends, apart from the type of climate, upon the type of mother rock. In tropical rainy areas, for example, the soil is heavily leached, that is the rain dissolves various minerals. The red colour of these soils is caused by the presence of iron. Such soils are often infertile. The best types of soil are chernozems (black earths) which occur in steppes and prairies. They are coloured by humus formed from dead grass and are organically rich.

TYPES OF SOIL

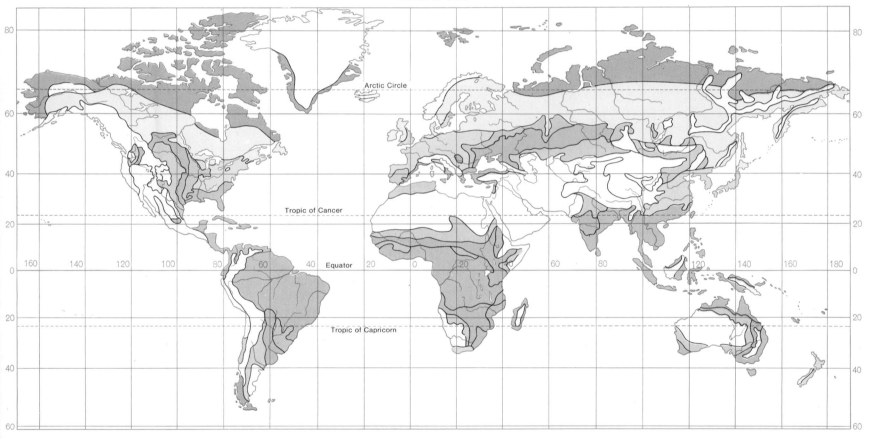

▨	Periglacial soils
☐	Podsols
▨	Greyish-brown podsolic soils
▨	Red earth and laterite, tropical and sub-tropical soils
▨	Neutral prairie soils
▨	Chernozems
▨	Rendzina and brown soils of the steppes
☐	Sandy desert soils
☐	Rendzina and other mountain soils

The grey ash soils of the taiga are known as podsolic soils. Bacterial activity in these soils is very much restricted by the low temperatures.

The red soils of the tropical zones, sometimes called laterites, are high in iron and aluminium. They derive from the leaching of elements in the soil.

The high temperatures and exceptionally low rainfall of deserts render the formation of proper soil almost impossible.

TROPIC OF CANCER

EQUATOR   LONGITUDE WEST FROM GREENWICH

TROPIC OF CAPRICORN

ANTARCTIC CIRCLE

Rain forest

Semi-deciduous tropical forest

Woodland

Plentiful rainfall and its even distribution throughout the year give rise in Equatorial regions to an abundance of natural vegetation. These are the rain forests, characterised by the wide variety of plant species, some of which are of high economic value. They include the *Hevea brasiliensis*, providing rubber, and ebony, rosewood, mahogany, oil and coconut palms, and banana plants.

Broad-leaved and mixed forests

Beech, chestnut and oak are the most typical and most widespread species in broad-leaved forests in the temperate regions, where trees are interspersed with undergrowth.

Mediterranean maquis

Maquis is characterised by its low growth – shrubs and drought-resistant bushes, olive trees, umbrella pines and vines are the main species.

Coniferous forests

Coniferous trees with needle-shaped leaves predominate in the coniferous forest zone, or taiga, sometimes along with birch and poplar. The undergrowth is scanty, consisting of herbaceous plants such as bilberries.

Tundra

The tundra vegetation is sparse Only mosses, lichens, some flowering plants and a few stunted trees survive the harsh conditions.

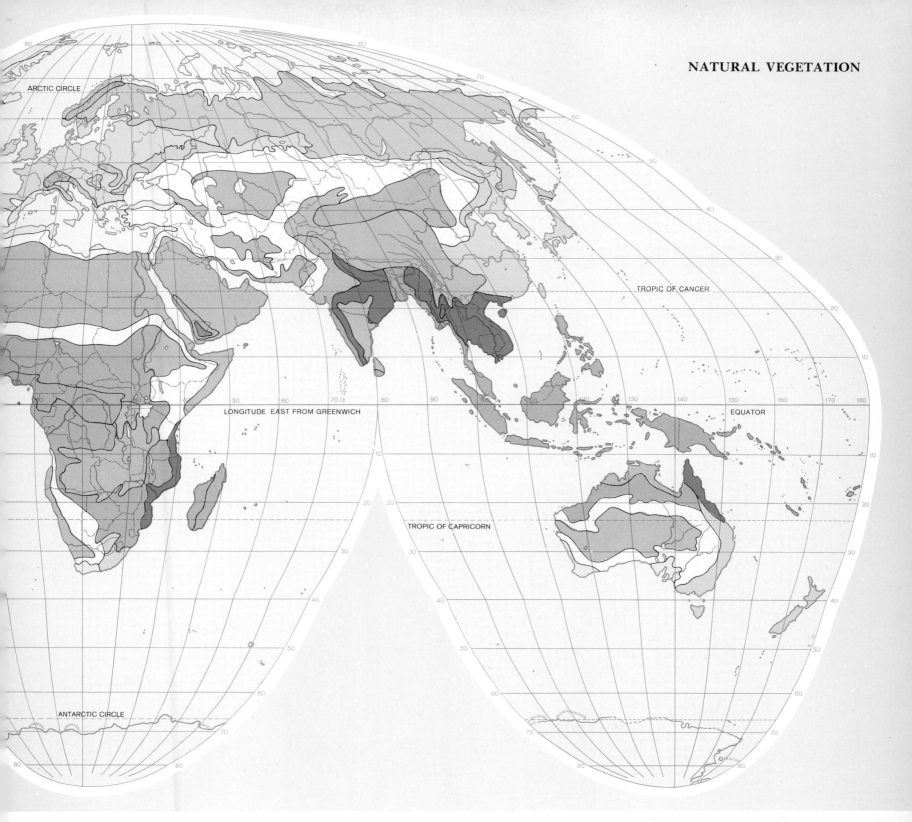

ARCTIC CIRCLE

TROPIC OF CANCER

LONGITUDE EAST FROM GREENWICH

EQUATOR

TROPIC OF CAPRICORN

ANTARCTIC CIRCLE

Herbaceous savannah

Prairie

Trees are few and far between among the grasses of the prairies. The moisture is concentrated in a shallow layer, and only plants with roots extending horizontally can thrive.

The savannah is made up of tropical grasses, which can reach a height of two metres in the rainy season. There are scattered trees, such as the baobab.

Steppes in the tropics and at central latitudes

The steppes are more barren than the prairies and have fewer trees.

Deserts

Only drought-resistant plants (xerophyles) with long roots are able to thrive in desert regions.

High mountain vegetation

The period of plant growth in mountain regions is short. Broad-leaved trees in the Alps are found up to 1,700 metres, though coniferous trees grow up to over 2,000 metres. Then there is grass, mosses and lichens

Ice caps

Obviously plant growth is not possible where the land is permanently covered with ice. Mosses, lichens and sparse woody bushes are found in the small open spaces, but their growth is severely limited.

Map labels (North and South America):

Vancouver
Seattle
Portland
Minneapolis
St Paul
Milwaukee
Toronto
Buffalo
Montreal
Boston
Detroit
Cleve
New York
Denver
Chicago
Pittsb
Sacramento
Kansas City
Cincin
Philadelphia
St Louis
Louisville
Baltimore
San Francisco
Memphis
Washington
Los Angeles
Birmingham
Atlanta
San Diego
Phoenix
Ft. Wort
Dallas
Houston
San Antonio
New Orleans
Miami
Monterrey
Havana
Guadalajara
Mexico
San Juan
Caracas
Medellin
Bogota
Recife
Lima
Salvador
Brasilia
Belo Horizonte
Rio de Janeiro
Sao Paulo
Cordoba
Porto Alegre
Rosario
Santiago
Buenos Aires
Montevideo

Lisbo
Rab
Casabla

TROPIC OF CANCER
EQUATOR
LONGITUDE WEST FROM GREENWICH
TROPIC OF CAPRICORN
ANTARCTIC CIRCLE

180 170 160 150 140 130 120 110 100 90 80 70 60 50 40 30 20 10

Legend:

| ▨ Uninhabited regions | ☐ 0–1 inhabitants per square kilometre | ☐ 1–10 inhabitants per square kilometre | ☐ 10–25 inhabitants per square kilometre |

Population

About 27 million square kilometres of the Earth's land surface are totally and permanently uninhabited. These are areas where the special climatic conditions are hostile to Man, except where he can create very small microclimates in which to survive, as scientists do in research establishments in Antarctica. Such areas are the polar and circumpolar regions (17 million square kilometres) and, within the habitable world, the deserts, dense forests and high mountains.

The sub-polar regions of Canada, the Amazon forest, the cold deserts of Asia, the hot deserts of Australia and Africa – these are areas of very low population density. Below, desert dwellers in Africa.

The areas which are almost uninhabited are usually surrounded by areas where the population is greater, and where climatic and physical conditions are less harsh. Some of these are the semi-desert, steppe and heathland regions, where there are no more than 10 inhabitants per square kilometre.

Areas where the population density is between 10 and 25 inhabitants per square kilometre are often isolated pockets of land surrounded by less inhabited regions. Some areas of South America, for example, come into this category, as well as large tracts of the eastern USA.

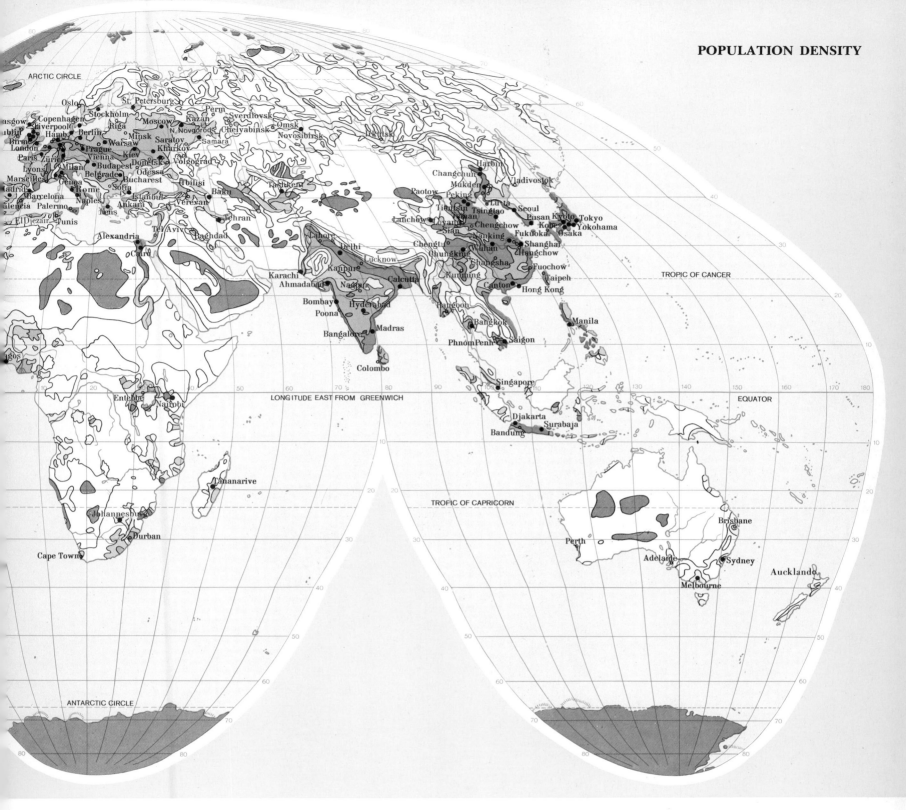

(Map of Europe, Asia, Africa and Australasia showing population density, with cities labelled including:) ARCTIC CIRCLE, Oslo, St. Petersburg, Stockholm, Moscow, Kazan, Perm, Sverdlovsk, Glasgow, Copenhagen, Riga, Minsk, N. Novgorod, Chelyabinsk, Omsk, Novosibirsk, Irkutsk, Liverpool, Hamb., Berlin, Warsaw, Saratov, Kharkov, Samara, London, Prague, Kiev, Donetsk, Volgograd, Paris, Zürich, Vienna, Budapest, Lyons, Milan, Belgrade, Bucharest, Odessa, Tbilisi, Tashkent, Changchun, Harbin, Vladivostok, Marseilles, Genoa, Rome, Sofia, Istanbul, Baku, Paotow, Mukden, Peking, Madrid, Barcelona, Naples, Ankara, Yerevan, Tientsin, Lu ta, Seoul, Valencia, Palermo, Tehran, Tanchow, Loyang, Tsingtao, Pusan, Kyoto, Tokyo, El Djezair, Tunis, Baghdad, Sian, Chengchow, Nanking, Fukuoka, Kobe, Yokohama, Alexandria, Tel Aviv, Chengtu, Wuhan, Shanghai, Osaka, Cairo, Chungking, Hangchow, Delhi, Changsha, Fuochow, Lahore, Lucknow, Kunming, Kanpur, Karachi, Nagpur, Calcutta, Canton, Taipeh, Ahmadabad, Hong Kong, TROPIC OF CANCER, Bombay, Hyderabad, Rangoon, Poona, Bangalore, Madras, Bangkok, Manila, Phnom Penh, Saigon, Colombo, Lagos, Entebbe, Nairobi, LONGITUDE EAST FROM GREENWICH, Singapore, EQUATOR, Djakarta, Surabaja, Bandung, Tananarive, TROPIC OF CAPRICORN, Brisbane, Johannesburg, Perth, Adelaide, Sydney, Auckland, Durban, Cape Town, Melbourne, ANTARCTIC CIRCLE

| ▨ | 25–50 inhabitants per square kilometre | ▨ | 50–100 inhabitants per square kilometre | ▨ | Over 100 inhabitants per square kilometre |

Parts of Europe, mainly in the east, have a population density of between 25 and 50 inhabitants per square kilometre. In other continents, if we exclude some Asian countries such as India and China, a population of this density is rather unusual. Below, horse-drawn transport is still widely used in eastern Europe.

Between 50 and 100 inhabitants per square kilometre is the average population density in most of Europe, including countries such as France, Austria and Spain. Vast areas in India and China also have a comparable figure.

There are a few areas of high population density, in the northern hemisphere and in temperate zones. This high concentration is made possible either by the climatic and land conditions, such as in the fertile delta regions of China and India, or by economic, political and social factors. For example in Europe, the Industrial Revolution, and, in North America, immigration from Europe have created areas of high population density.

The evolution of Man

The origin and development of early Man is a fascinating but problematical area of research. We have only some fragments of bone, mainly jawbones and teeth, on which to base our theories as to the nature and evolution of our forebears.

Their first beginnings are lost in a period which, though geologically quite recent, is historically almost beyond our powers to imagine, millions of years ago. Scientists at present favour the theory that our species and that of the great apes have a common origin, going back between 15 and 20 million years. From fossils discovered in Africa, India and Europe, they believe that these creatures were very different both from the great apes of today and from Man as we know him. It is however highly probable that, from these tree-dwelling hominids, the group emerged which left the forest, started to walk on two legs and looked to the soil for its source of food. They evolved into modern Man.

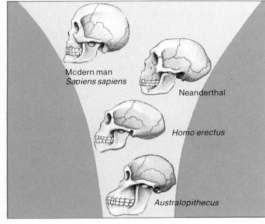

Early Man
Homo erectus may have descended from *Australopithecus*, which lived in Africa between 4 and 1 million years ago. The remains of *Homo erectus* discovered in the Old World are between 1,000,000 and 5,000,000 years old. *Homo erectus* used tools fashioned from stone, could make fires, and banded into groups which survived by hunting game. He is regarded as the direct ancestor of *Homo sapiens*, of which we know of various forms at various times, thanks to numerous discoveries in Africa, Asia and Europe. *Homo sapiens* is divided into several sub-species, the most notable being *Homo sapiens neanderthalensis*, who lived in the last Ice Age, during which, about 40,000 years ago, *Homo sapiens sapiens*, or modern Man, first appeared.

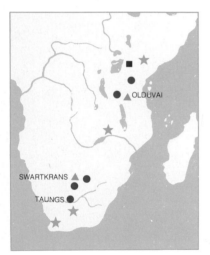

Discoveries
Pre-hominoid discoveries are restricted almost exclusively to central South America and Africa *(Australopithecus, Ramapithecus)*, whilst quantities of remains of the genus *Homo* have been discovered in Europe. Few traces have been found of *Homo erectus*, but remains of various sub-species of *Homo sapiens* *(Homo sapiens steinheimensis, Homo sapiens neanderthalensis, Homo sapiens sapiens)* have been discovered in many places, notably in Tanzania. Fossils of Neanderthal, Steinheim and Cro-Magnon Man have been found in Europe.

■ Ramapithecus   ▲ Homo erectus
● Australopithecus   ★ Homo sapiens

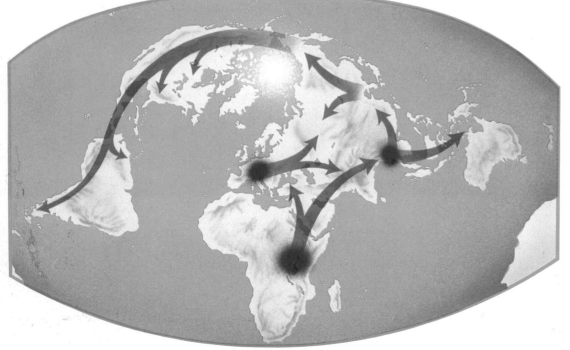

Man the hunter who populates the world
His ability to hunt in groups, and to move around or travel considerable distances permitted *Homo erectus* to move from Central Africa, probably along the valley of the Nile, to the tropical regions of India and south-east Asia, and from there into Europe. During a period of hot climate, about 150,000 to 200,000 years ago, a sub-species of *Homo sapiens, Homo sapiens steinheimensis*, populated the plains of northern Europe. After a period of intense cold, accompanied by glaciation, this people was succeeded by another, with different cranial structure, known today by the name Neanderthal. These people occupied western Europe until the final Ice Age, the Pleistocene, and was in its turn replaced by modern Man, about 35,000 to 40,000 years ago. The New World was populated by *Homo sapiens* much later on. The earliest people in North America arrived there around 20,000 years ago. Probably groups of hunters moved into Alaska from Siberia during the final Ice Age, when the two countries were linked by an ice bridge. The population of North and South America was due to the alternation of glaciation and interglacial warmth, causing hunting populations to move in pursuit of migrating fauna and flora, their sources of food.

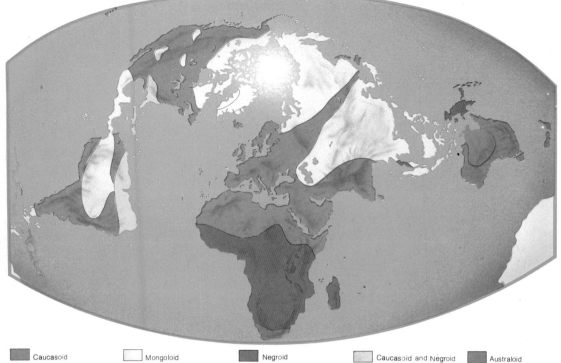

Mongoloids
The classic mongoloids have yellowish skin, straight hair and slanting eyes. They are found throughout Asia (with the exception of part of India and the Middle East) and in the eastern part of Madagascar.

Negroids
Living in central and southern Africa, the western part of Madagascar, Australia, the Philippines and the Indonesian islands, they usually have dark skins and curly hair.

Caucasoids
Found throughout Europe, Arabia, India and northern Africa, the caucasoids have many different outward appearances. For example, the colour of their skin varies from whitish to brown.

 Caucasoid   Mongoloid   Negroid   Caucasoid and Negroid   Australoid

Races

Whilst belonging to the same species *(Homo sapiens)*, human beings differ considerably in their physical characteristics. At one end of the spectrum are the tall Nordic types, with pale eyes and blond hair, at the other the African pygmies, small in stature, with dark skin and black hair. Taking account of the physical and psychological aspects, anthropologists tend to sub-divide the human species into three large groups or races: Caucasoid, Mongoloid and Negroid, whose distribution in the various continents is shown in the map above. This is not, however, a rigid classification. In fact many peoples fall into categories somewhere between these groupings, and there are also considerable variations within the groups themselves.

Migrations

The distribution of groups of human beings has altered considerably over the centuries, and noticeable changes are still taking place. Large movements of populations have taken place on political, economic and religious grounds, and these have sometimes changed the ethnic picture of entire continents. The map on the right shows the main migration patterns from the 16th century to the present day. The European influence is clearly shown. Europeans came several times to settle in North and South America, Africa and Australia. There has also been a great deal of movement within the continent of Europe itself.

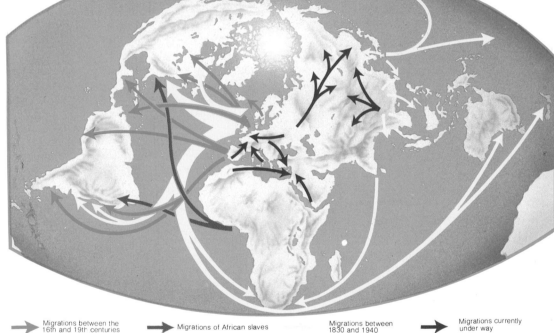

→ Migrations between the 16th and 19th centuries   → Migrations of African slaves   Migrations between 1830 and 1940   → Migrations currently under way

LANGUAGES

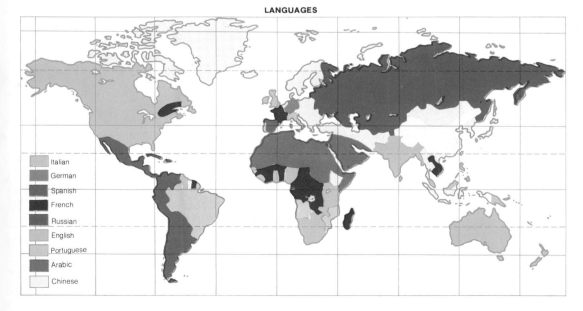

Italian
German
Spanish
French
Russian
English
Portuguese
Arabic
Chinese

Languages

Along with race and religion, there is one other element which distinguishes the inhabitants of Earth from one another – their language. It is hard to say how many languages there are, and not always possible to distinguish between language and dialect. The theory is, however, that more than 2,500 tongues are spoken on Earth; some, like Basque, by only small groups of people, some, like English, by millions every day. Generally, classification may be made on historical grounds – languages of common origin being grouped at various levels. Italian, Spanish, Portuguese and French, for instance, are grouped together as the Romance languages, because all derive from the same Latin root. Historical factors also contribute to the spread of language, this being particularly evident with some European tongues, which have spread to many continents. The most obvious example is that of English, which was taken to North America in the early migrations, and then spread to many parts of the world, such as Africa and Australia, as a result of colonialism.

25

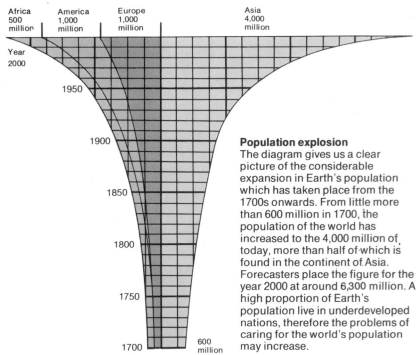

| Africa 500 million | America 1,000 million | Europe 1,000 million | Asia 4,000 million |

Population explosion
The diagram gives us a clear picture of the considerable expansion in Earth's population which has taken place from the 1700s onwards. From little more than 600 million in 1700, the population of the world has increased to the 4,000 million of today, more than half of which is found in the continent of Asia. Forecasters place the figure for the year 2000 at around 6,300 million. A high proportion of Earth's population live in underdeveloped nations, therefore the problems of caring for the world's population may increase.

Population

The world's total population, its distribution into areas and its numerical and geographical evolution provide us with data indispensable to the analysis of our major political and economic problems of present-day life. In only a few centuries, the Earth's population has increased dramatically, from about 500 million in 1650 to more than 4,000 million today, and according to the forecasts, there will be no reversal of this trend in the short term.

At first sight, population increase is linked with shifts in the balance of natural and social development. National populations are, in fact, determined by the relative difference between birth and death rates, and are sometimes also influenced by emigration and immigration figures. Clearly such variations depend in their turn upon economic, social and political factors. The recent population explosion on a worldwide scale, for instance, is largely linked with technical and scientific progress, which has improved the standard of living, caused a drop in the infant and child mortality rates, and an increased life expectancy.

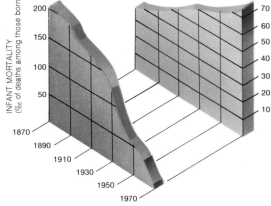

LIFE EXPECTANCY (average age)

Infant mortality and life expectancy
The graph above contrasts the figures for infant mortality with those for life expectancy over the last hundred years. On a world level, the rate of infant mortality, which was about 200 per 1,000 births in 1870, has shown a marked reduction. Life expectancy, and thus the average age obtained, is now more than 70 years in Western Europe. These figures vary considerably, however, according to geographical location. In southern Africa, the average life expectancy is around 53 years.

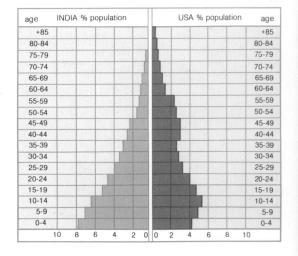

Distribution of populations by age
The graph above compares the percentage distribution of the population by age in a country of advanced economic development (United States) and in an underdeveloped country (India). It is obvious that in India the percentage drops steadily with advancing age, and the people do not generally live beyond 80. In the USA, the variations are more marked. Numbers are declining at the lower age levels, due to the drop in the birth rate which is a feature in all industrialised countries today.

POPULATION INCREASE

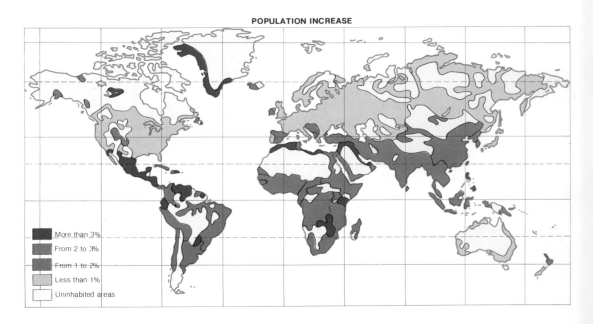

More than 3%
From 2 to 3%
From 1 to 2%
Less than 1%
Uninhabited areas

Rate of population increase
In the industrialised countries which already have a high population density (large areas of Europe and the United States), the annual rate of population increase has shown a marked reduction and is currently less than 1 per cent. Major increases (between 2 and 3 per cent and over) are recorded in underdeveloped areas, where the economy is in a period of transition. This is true in particular of large areas of Africa, Asia, and South and Central America, where a limited improvement in living conditions has brought about a drop in the mortality rate, especially among new-born babies.

Urbanisation

Urbanisation is not a development exclusive to the twentieth century, nor is it confined to the more advanced countries. The first urban development took place in Sumeria, in the 4th century before Christ, whilst at the height of its splendour, the city of Rome had more than half a million inhabitants. However, it is certainly only since the Industrial Revolution, which began in the late 18th century, that urbanisation has assumed its present form – perhaps the most representative feature of twentieth-century society.

The development of the city, and the attraction is exerts, on people in surrounding districts, is in porportion to its industrial development, the facilities it provides, and the importance of the city itself. In some areas of Europe, such as Belgium, Holland and France, the urban population currently exceeds 70 per cent. In areas of lesser economic development, the percentages are lower (Egypt 45 per cent, India 22 per cent), but the exodus from the country to the city continues. However, the problems created by rapid urbanisation, which have emerged in recent times, appear common to cities both in industrialised and also in under-developed regions.

The city
In many countries, Italy for example (above, a photograph of Florence), cities have grown up around small pockets of habitation whose history is lost in the mists of antiquity. The impact of an industrial civilisation upon urban structures which go back to the Middle Ages and beyond, naturally poses some serious problems. Access is one, pollution another, along with high population density and lack of free space. These problems also affect the suburbs. Right, an aerial photograph of the suburbs of Milan.

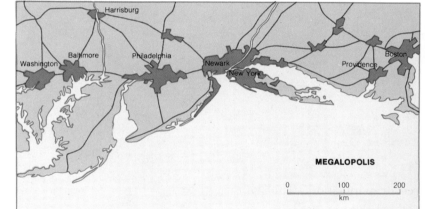

The megalopolis
In some countries, towns keep on growing until they join up with other towns, forming an almost uninterrupted urban sprawl, heavily built upon and with high population density. An area of this type is designated a megalopolis, the largest of which is on the east coast of America and extends from Boston to Washington, taking in New York City.

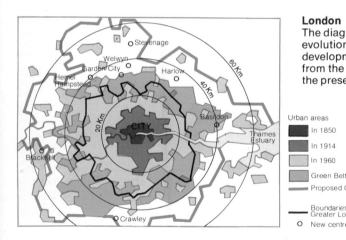

London
The diagram shows the evolution and urban development of London, from the mid 1800s up to the present day (left).

Urban areas
- In 1850
- In 1914
- In 1960
- Green Belt
- Proposed Green Belt extension
- Boundaries of the Greater London area
- ○ New centres

MEGALOPOLIS

THE CITIES WITH THE LARGEST POPULATIONS IN EACH CONTINENT			
EUROPE:		**AFRICA**	
Moscow	8,769,000	Cairo	13,300,000
Paris	8,707,000	Alexandria	2,917,000
London	6,735,000	Kinshasa	2,653,000
Madrid	4,925,000	Casablanca	2,904,000
Leningrad	4,456,000	Lagos	1,243,000
Rome	3,784,000	Johannesburg	1,609,000
Berlin	3,339,000	**AMERICA**	
Athens	3,027,000	Mexico City	18,748,000
Kiev	2,587,000	New York	18,054,000
Budapest	2,104,000	São Paulo	10,997,000
Vienna	1,480,000	Buenos Aires	9,766,000
ASIA		Los Angeles	8,296,000
Shanghai	12,320,000	Chicago	8,116,000
Tokyo	11,680,000	Lima	6,053,000
Seoul	9,646,000	Rio de Janeiro	6,011,000
Beijing	9,579,000	San Francisco	5,878,000
Calcutta	9,165,000	Santiago	5,913,000
Bombay	8,227,000	Philadelphia	4,826,000
Tientsin	8,190,000	Detroit	4,601,000
Djakarta	7,829,000	**OCEANIA**	
Tehran	6,022,000	Sidney	3,430,000
Delhi	5,714,000	Melbourne	2,942,000

MAJOR URBAN AREAS

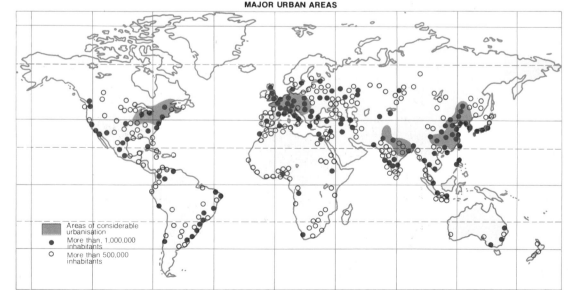

- Areas of considerable urbanisation
- ● More than 1,000,000 inhabitants
- ○ More than 500,000 inhabitants

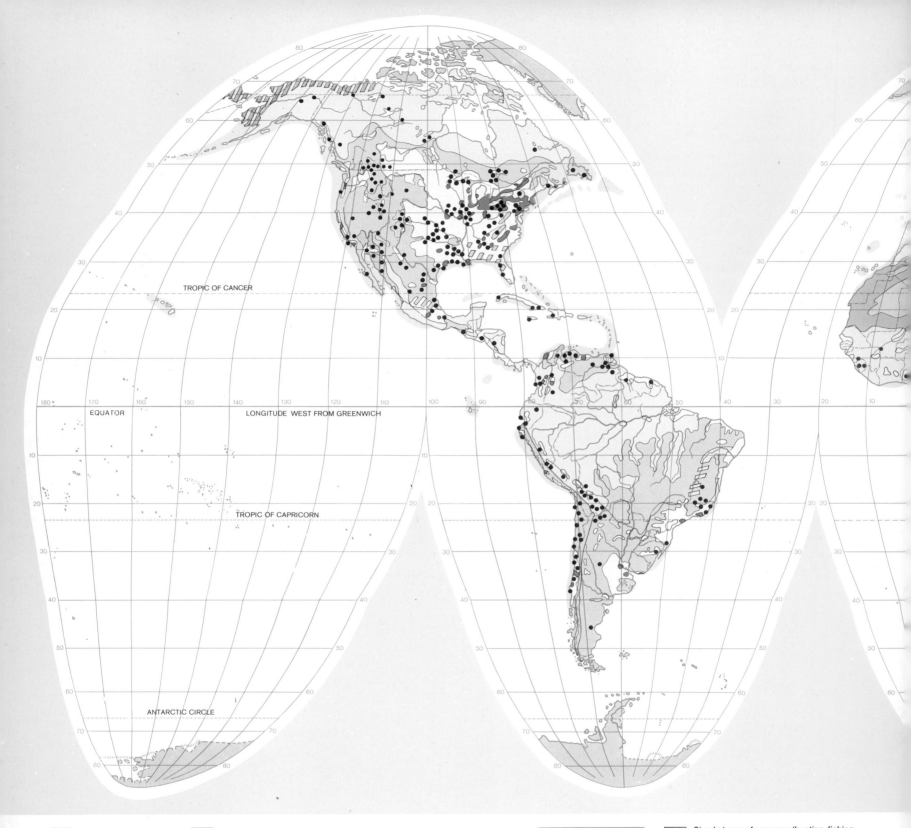

TROPIC OF CANCER

EQUATOR   LONGITUDE WEST FROM GREENWICH

TROPIC OF CAPRICORN

ANTARCTIC CIRCLE

Coastal fishing areas

More than 70 million tonnes of fish are taken from these waters annually, mainly along the continental shelf.

 **Mining areas**

These are found both in areas with a high standard of living and in the underdeveloped regions, where minerals form valuable natural resources.

Areas without an organised economy

These are the areas where there are no stable centres of settlement.

Nomadic pastoralists

The numbers of nomadic pastoralists are dwindling all the time, though they were formerly characteristic features of the vast desert areas and steppe heathlands of Africa and Asia. Some such peoples are the Tuareg in the Sahara, the Bedouins of Arabia and the Mongols of Central Asia, and they move periodically in search of fresh pasture land and water for their flocks. Urban development and industry, followed by oil extraction in desert areas of this type, are now causing people to stay much more in one place.

Simple types of economy (hunting, fishing, gathering, primitive agriculture)

Areas where the population engages in hunting, fishing, simple harvesting and very primitive agriculture are those which are sparsely inhabited, such as the Amazon Forest, the Zaire Basin and New Guinea. Small groups of people in these types of areas continue to live at bare subsistence level. The pygmies, for example, are hunters, and also collect fruit, roots and other things which they have not cultivated.

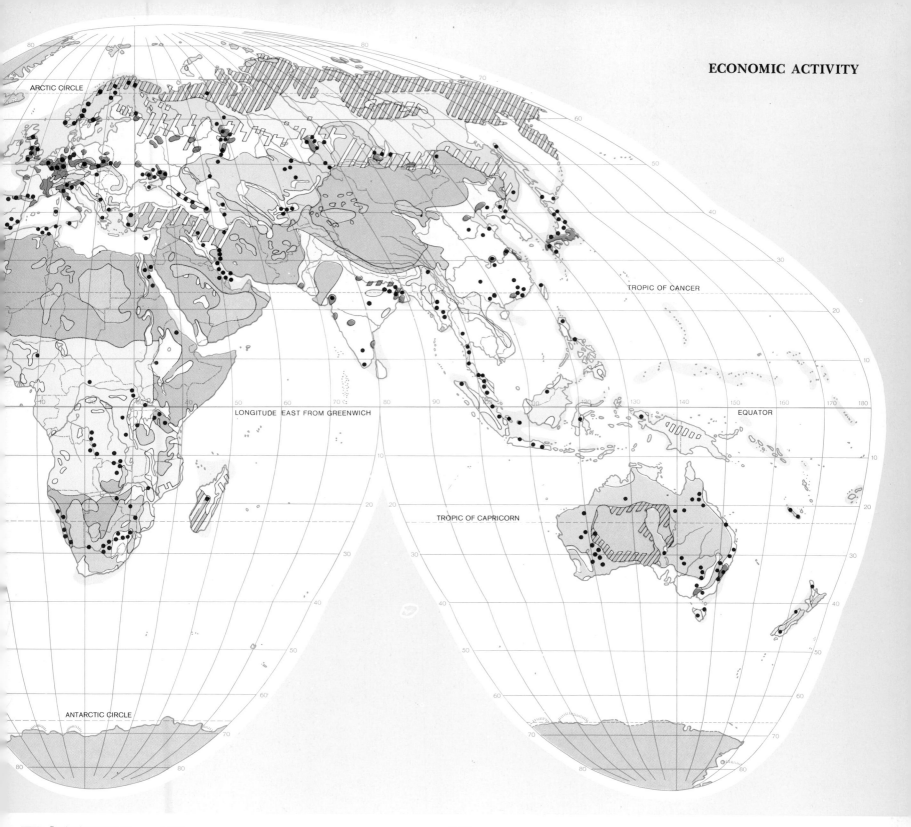

Predominantly forest economy

Large-scale animal husbandry

Predominantly agriculture (large-scale and intensive)

Industrial economy

A predominantly forest economy occurs only in the central northern belt of the temperate zone, where use is made of coniferous timber (pine, conifer and larch) and of birchwood. There is no forest belt in the southern hemisphere.

Traditional animal husbandry is practised on a large scale in vast tracts of central Asia, the Americas and Africa, although the methods are often technically and economically backward.

There are two main kinds of agricultural activity. The type practised in Europe, part of the United States and other countries of high economic development involves the use of modern techniques and a high yield is obtained with low manpower. The other type, using traditional methods, is expensive in terms of labour and productivity is comparatively low.

Many countries now have a highly developed economy based primarily on industry as in Europe, North America and Japan. A high degree of industrial development is accompanied by complex financial and commercial activity.

Food resources

The first men lived by hunting, fishing and the gathering of wild fruit. This is the most primitive form of economy and is found today only in the most isolated and inaccessible regions of the world (Amazonia, Indonesia and equatorial Africa). When, about 10,000 years ago, man first discovered that animals could be reared and the soil cultivated a process was begun which has literally changed the face of the Earth.

Pastoralism developed for the most part in the marginal areas near the hot and cold deserts of Africa and Asia. Nowadays there are very few completely nomadic populations; most have settled or practice only seasonal nomadism.

Agricultural practice has made continual improvement over the centuries, progressing from primitive cultivation with a hoe, to ploughing with a plough pulled by animals, to modern mechanised agriculture.

From the beginning of this process a large part of the planet has been cultivated. First were the tropical areas along the large fluvial basins, favoured with heat all year round and with abundant rainfall. However, the most productive areas now are in the temperate zones, both because of the natural conditions and because the agriculture is at a high level of technological development.

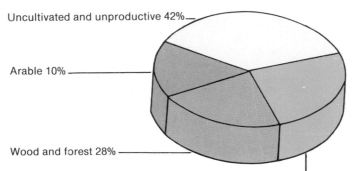

Uncultivated and unproductive 42%

Arable 10%

Wood and forest 28%

Grazing land 20%

Land use
The graph shows the current situation, the result of man's transformation of the environment; for example the forests which covered nearly half of the Earth's surface have been destroyed to make room for cultivation. The ratio percentages show in fact a dangerous imbalance: most of the uncultivated and unproductive land is desert, which is increasing to the consequent loss of grazing land (the phenomenon of desertification).

Basic economy
The three main activities of a basic economy: (left) subsistence agriculture still practised by the Tarahumara Indians, using primitive tools, in the Western Sierra Madre in Mexico; (above) fishing on the Atlantic coast of Sierra Leone; (below) goat rearing in the arid steppelands of the Sahel in Africa.

Agriculture
The rice field (above) is typical of the monsoon countries of Asia, which are also the most highly populated countries in the world. Like rice, sugar cane plantations (below) need a large number of manual workers, which fact gave rise in the past to the African slave trade.

Percentage of active populations employed in agriculture
The graph below shows the percentage of active population employed in agriculture in various countries. The more developed and industrialised the economy the less the number of people involved in agriculture This is because agricultural productivity is not proportional to the number of workers but to the amount of technology (machines,

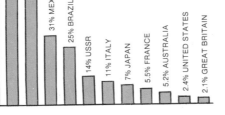

chemical fertilizers etc.) in use. Nepal, with 92% of its population involved in agriculture, has only a subsistence-level economy, while the USA, with only 2.4% employed in agriculture, is the biggest exporter of certain cereals in the world.

92% NEPAL
81% MALI
71% CAMBODIA
68% CHINA
67% INDIA
31% MEXICO
25% BRAZIL
14% USSR
11% ITALY
7% JAPAN
5.5% FRANCE
5.2% AUSTRALIA
2.4% UNITED STATES
2.1% GREAT BRITAIN

Nutrition

A useful indication of a population's living standard is found in the type and quantity of food it consumes, and inadequate nourishment is in fact a fundamental characteristic of many of the developing countries of the so-called Third World. Recent studies have shown that today almost 2,000 million people do not have enough to eat, and that there is always a connection between food consumption and level of income. It has in fact been established that both total protein consumption and total calorie consumption increase with increasing income. The developing countries not only have a lower protein consumption in terms of quantity but also in terms of quality. Their diet is rarely varied, consisting mainly of staple foods, rice perhaps, or cereals. Yields are usually low as fields are poorly irrigated and agricultural machinery and methods are outdated.

Malnutrition
The effects of malnutrition and starvation, constituted by a prolonged reduction in diet to a point below the minimum required to sustain life, are evident amongst large populations and in vast tracts of our Earth. Many people among the populations of India, numerous African countries, Latin America and the Far East display such symptoms as loss of weight, hypertension, swellings caused by starvation and, particularly in children, retarded growth and conditions such as rickets.

- Fats
- Eggs
- Cereals
- Sugar
- Meat or fish
- Milk
- Fruit and vegetables

American labourer's diet
2,110 grammes a day

Different foodstuffs available
The diagrams (below and left) serve to illustrate the quantity and quality of the food available daily to an American labourer and to an Indian peasant respectively. In the American diet, the food, apart from being plentiful, is varied, with fruit, milk and vegetables predominating; in the Indian diet, however, the staple ingredient is rice.

- Fats
- Meat or fish
- Vegetables
- Rice

Indian peasant's diet
560 grammes a day

Daily calorie consumption per inhabitant
The map on the right shows the amount of food available daily to each inhabitant of the countries of the world. It should be noted that, according to the Food and Agriculture Organisation's estimates, an intake of 1,600 calories per day is required in order to sustain a minimum amount of physical activity. It is clear from the map that the regions of greatest food shortage coincide with the underdeveloped or developing areas, which are often densely populated. This applies to large areas of Africa and Asia, and many of the Andean countries of South America.

PER CAPITA CALORIE CONSUMPTION

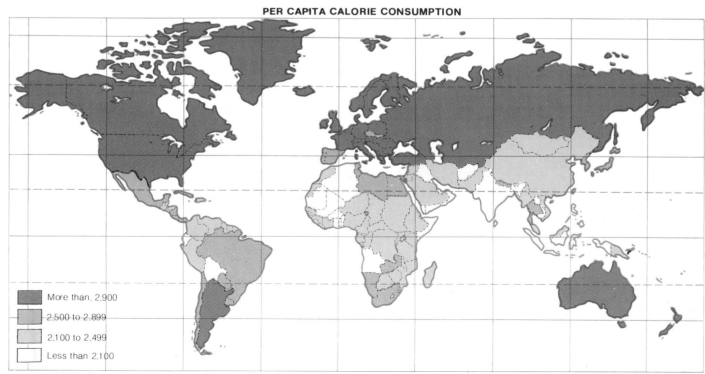

- More than 2,900
- 2,500 to 2,899
- 2,100 to 2,499
- Less than 2,100

Energy

For centuries the muscle power of man and beast was the type of energy most commonly in use, along with the forces of wind and water. It was from the 18th century onwards that, thanks to technical and scientific developments, coal began to be used on a large scale to provide mechanical power and heat. Then electrical energy came to the fore, produced either in power stations or in hydroelectric installations, opening the way to industrial development for many countries which did not have their own raw materials. Then it was the turn of hydrocarbons, especially oil. This was easy to extract and, until recently, was relatively cheap, so that it became the source of energy most widely used.

Continued expansion of industry, the increased use of motor vehicles, political tensions, and the danger that the hydrocarbon resources will soon be exhausted have encouraged research and development into other energy sources, such as nuclear energy and solar energy.

Energy consumption
The amount of energy consumed annually per head of population can be a good indication of the level of any country's development. As we see from the map the highest consumption of energy is found in mainly industrialised areas, where income per capita is high (the USA, for example).

The same applies to almost all the countries of Europe, and to the USSR and Canada, where consumption is only slightly less. Industry, especially the metal and chemical industries, along with the domestic consumption, account for this accentuated energy use. Consumption is considerably lower in most other regions, but is increasing all the time.

CONSUMPTION OF ENERGY

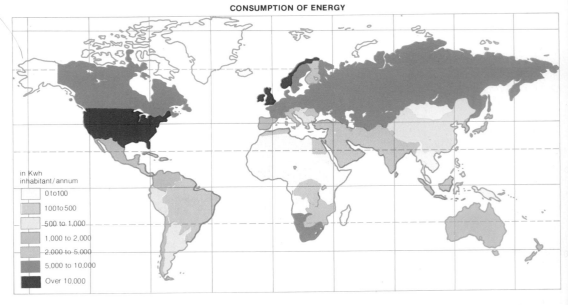

in Kwh inhabitant/annum
- 0 to 100
- 100 to 500
- 500 to 1,000
- 1,000 to 2,000
- 2,000 to 5,000
- 5,000 to 10,000
- Over 10,000

Producer and consumer countries (below)
The map illustrates the fact that, throughout the world, oil-producer and oil-consumer countries are rarely one and the same. The most striking instance is that of the Arab countries, which produce almost one third of the world's total oil supplies, and export the entire amount. The USSR is a special case, there being a balance between production and consumption. The USA, although it has abundant reserves, consumes more oil than it produces.

WORLD ENERGY CONSUMPTION

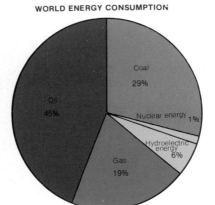

Coal 29%
Oil 45%
Nuclear energy 1%
Hydroelectric energy 6%
Gas 19%

Categories of world energy consumption
As we see from the illustration on the left, more than half the energy now consumed in the world is obtained from hydrocarbons (oil and natural gas). The percentage increase in the use of these energy sources goes back to the early decades of the twentieth century. Coal, which up to about 1910 accounted for almost 70 per cent of total consumption, is now reduced to less than 33 per cent. The percentage of nuclear energy in use is at the moment quite small, as its production involves high costs and an advanced technology.

WORLD OIL PRODUCTION AND CONSUMPTION

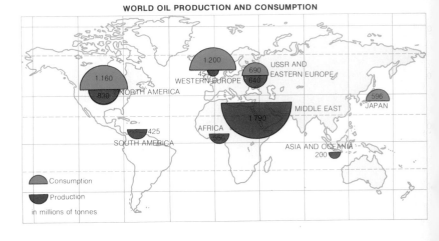

NORTH AMERICA 1.160 / 830
WESTERN EUROPE 1.200 / 45
USSR AND EASTERN EUROPE 690 / 640
JAPAN 596
MIDDLE EAST 1.790
SOUTH AMERICA 425
AFRICA
ASIA AND OCEANIA 200

- Consumption
- Production
in millions of tonnes

Economy and society

The size and development of population, increased urbanisation and industrialisation, technical and scientific development, the distribution of lines of communication, the efficiency of methods of transport and availability of resources — all these factors condition to some degree our economic development, and thus also the standard of living of the peoples of the world.

There is a stark contrast today between those few countries with an abundance of natural resources which are sometimes wasted, and the many countries whose populations struggle for survival. The disparities between countries are enormous, and are only partly attributable to the presence of natural resources. It is easy to see that many countries in the process of development have an abundance of resources but that their exploitation has limited advantages for the producer countries.

Iron mines in the USA
Along with coal and oil, iron is the other raw material essential to industry. It is extracted from various minerals including lodestone and haematite. Often, as seen in the illustration, it is produced from open-cast mines. At present about 550 million tonnes of iron are produced every year.

The copper mines of Chuquicamata (Chile)
Another important raw material is the mineral copper. It is indispensable in various sectors of industry, above all that of electricity, being both a thermal and electrical conductor. It is extracted in large quantities from mines in the USA, the USSR, and Chile.

Steel production
The main producers of the world's 770 million tonnes of steel a year are USSR, Japan and ECSC (European Coal and Steel Community).
The drop in consumption over recent years has meant a necessary restructuring of the industry, which is still in progress today.

GROSS NATIONAL PRODUCT

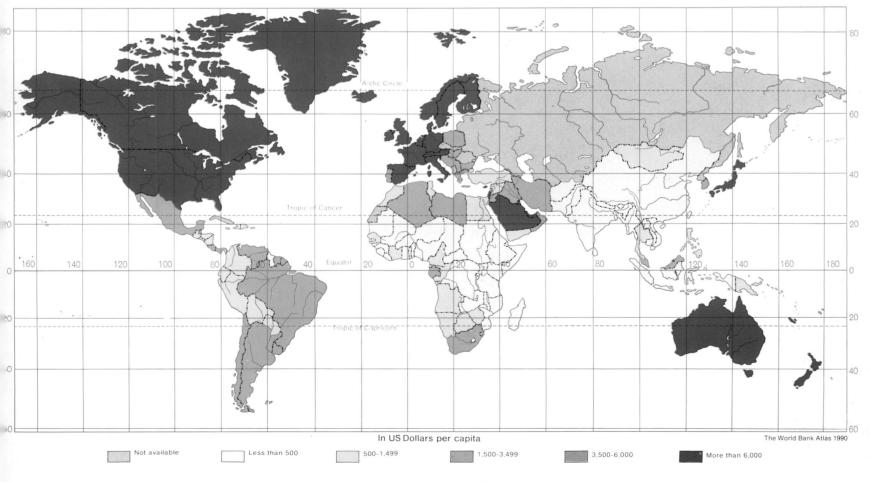

In US Dollars per capita

The World Bank Atlas 1990

| | Not available | | Less than 500 | | 500-1,499 | | 1,500-3,499 | | 3,500-6,000 | | More than 6,000 |

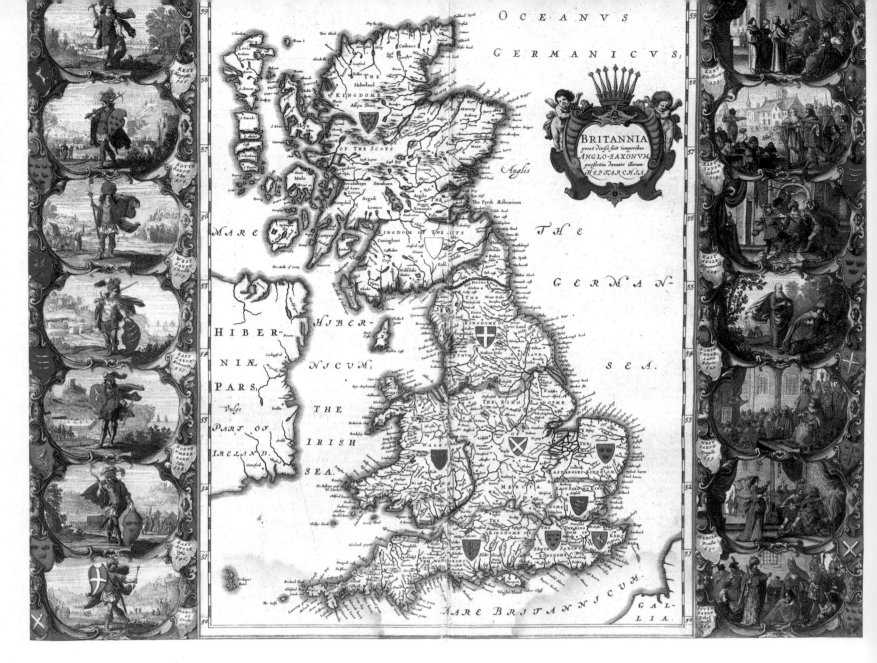

The British Isles

For many centuries, the British Isles took little part in commercial and cultural exchanges with other nations.

During the 15th century, Britain began to develop as a powerful sea-going nation. The south-coast and Atlantic-facing ports developed, and Englishmen explored and traded throughout the known world and Britain became a great commercial sea power.

With the Industrial Revolution of the 18th century, Great Britain became the world's major power in both political and economic terms. This changed following the two World Wars, and the growing influence and industrialisation of the United States and the USSR, which became the two superpowers. The British Empire was broken up and the United Kingdom began to strengthen its links with the European continent. In 1973 it became part of the E.E.C.

Stonehenge
When the sea level rose with the melting of the great Pleistocene ice cap, it transformed Britain into an island. Britain's few inhabitants were hunters, using weapons of stone and bone. Stonehenge was erected in about 2000 BC. It is one of the major examples of primitive architecture in Great Britain, and consists of concentric circles of colossal stones, often forming a three-stoned arch. Stonehenge may have been a temple for sun-worshippers.

The great invasions
Britain was invaded many times between the 1st and the 11th centuries, and this influenced its language, customs and the civilisation of its peoples. The Romans were the first to conquer the island in 55 and 54 BC under the leadership of Julius Caesar. The Romans were followed in succession by Saxons, Jutes, Vikings, Danes and Normans.

THE MANY INVASIONS OF BRITAIN

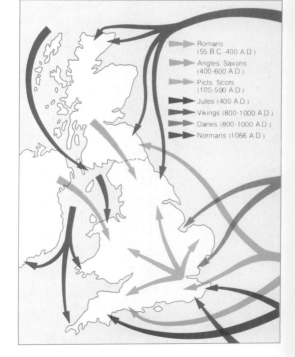

Romans (55 B.C.-400 A.D.)
Angles, Saxons (400-600 A.D.)
Picts, Scots (100-500 A.D.)
Jutes (400 A.D.)
Vikings (800-1000 A.D.)
Danes (800-1000 A.D.)
Normans (1066 A.D.)

Castle and fortifications

The civil and religious architecture of Great Britain reflects the styles and tastes not only of the native Saxons, but also of the numerous peoples who came to settle in succession in the island, right up to the end of the Middle Ages, such as Normans, Vikings and Danes. One area which has particularly diverse architecture is south-east England. Romans, Vikings and Normans all passed through it. Each of these peoples left behind them a number of fortifications to add to the castles erected for defence purposes in successive eras. There are also many castles in Wales and Scotland. The photograph (right) shows Richmond Castle in Yorkshire, one of the earliest Norman castles.

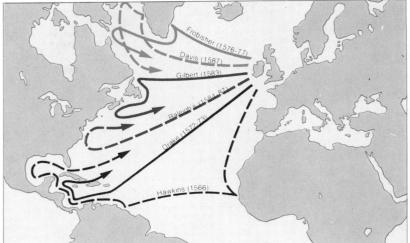

THE GREAT VOYAGES OF DISCOVERY

Conquests and discoveries

For Great Britain, the 16th century meant the splendour of the Elizabethan era. Elizabeth I understood that the destiny of her country was indissolubly linked with the sea. She therefore did all she could to promote the development of her fleet and to encourage explorations and maritime trading. Elizabeth made use in her service of the most able navigators of the time, Sir Walter Raleigh, Sir Francis Drake, Sir Martin Frobisher, and others. Frobisher made many voyages in the northern Atlantic looking for the North West Passage; however he got no farther than Baffin Island. John Davis also looked for the North-West Passage; he was stopped by the ice floes off the coast of Greenland, close to the strait which bears his name and which is the entry to the passage he was looking for.

The British Empire

The British Empire reached its greatest extent following the First World War. Its bases had already been established during the reign of Queen Victoria, however, and it was at the height of its power in the second half of the 19th century. In Africa, Britain colonised Egypt, Nigeria, Kenya, Uganda and the Sudan, in an effort to establish a continuous route linking the Mediterranean to South Africa. Links with the colonies frequently took on the character of dominions, allowing a greater degree of autonomy to the native peoples. Examples of this are Canada, Australia, New Zealand and South Africa.

The Victorian era

The Victorian era had a profound effect on the history of Great Britain. Queen Victoria (right) reigned from 1837 to 1901. She was a great monarch, although her powers were restricted by her prime ministers, Palmerston, Disraeli and Gladstone. One of the things that made her popular was the effect she had on the spread of education.

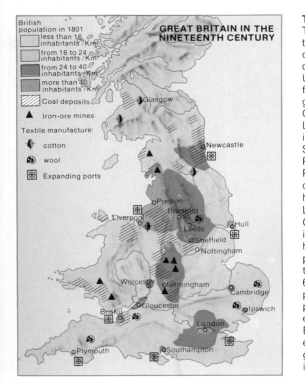

GREAT BRITAIN IN THE NINETEENTH CENTURY

British population in 1801
- less than 16 inhabitants /Km²
- from 16 to 24 inhabitants /Km²
- from 24 to 40 inhabitants /Km²
- more than 40 inhabitants /Km²
- Coal deposits
- ▲ Iron-ore mines

Textile manufacture:
- cotton
- wool
- ⊞ Expanding ports

Glasgow
Newcastle
Preston
Bradford
Liverpool
Leeds
Hull
Sheffield
Nottingham
Worcester
Birmingham
Cambridge
Bristol
Gloucester
Ipswich
London
Plymouth
Southampton

The British Constitution

The British Constitution has seen many changes down the centuries. Today the United Kingdom, is in fact ruled by its government in the Queen's name. Legislative power rests in the hands of the Sovereign and Parliament. The Parliament (left) is divided into two houses: the House of Lords and the House of Commons. The former is made up of hereditary and life peers and peeresses; the second consists of 635 members of parliament, elected by popular vote once every five years. Executive power is exercised by the government, through its prime minister.

THE BRITISH EMPIRE 1919

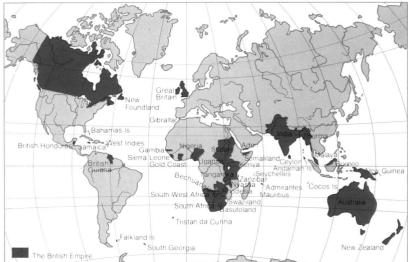

The British Empire

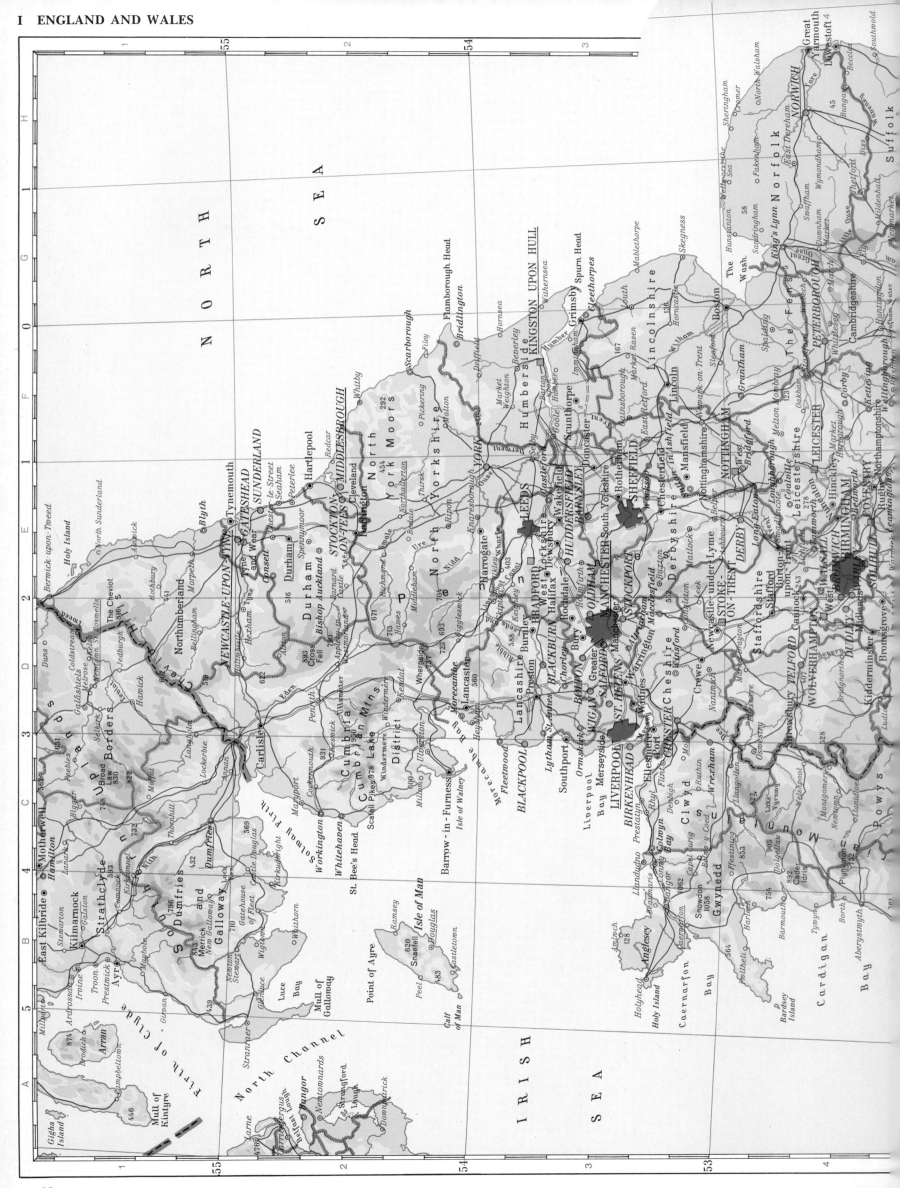

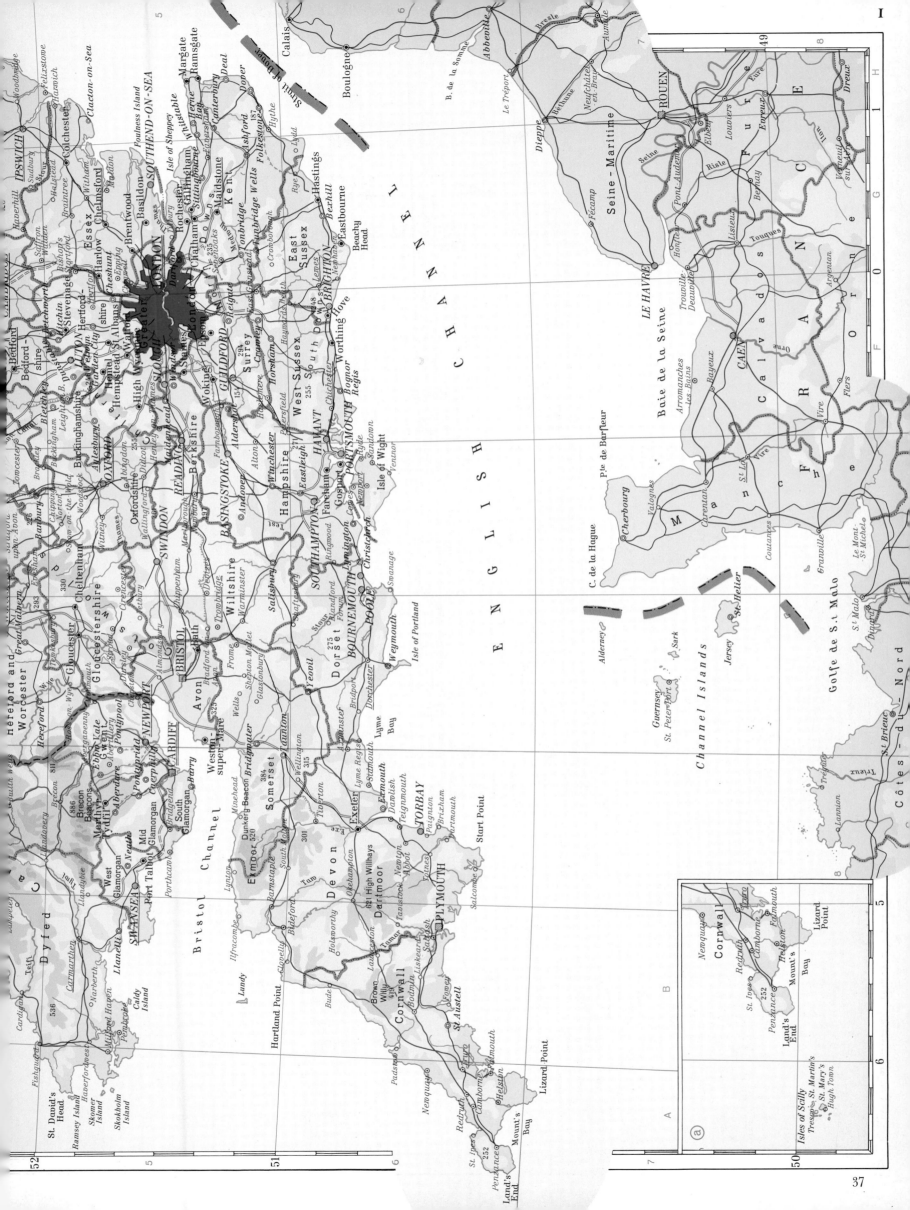

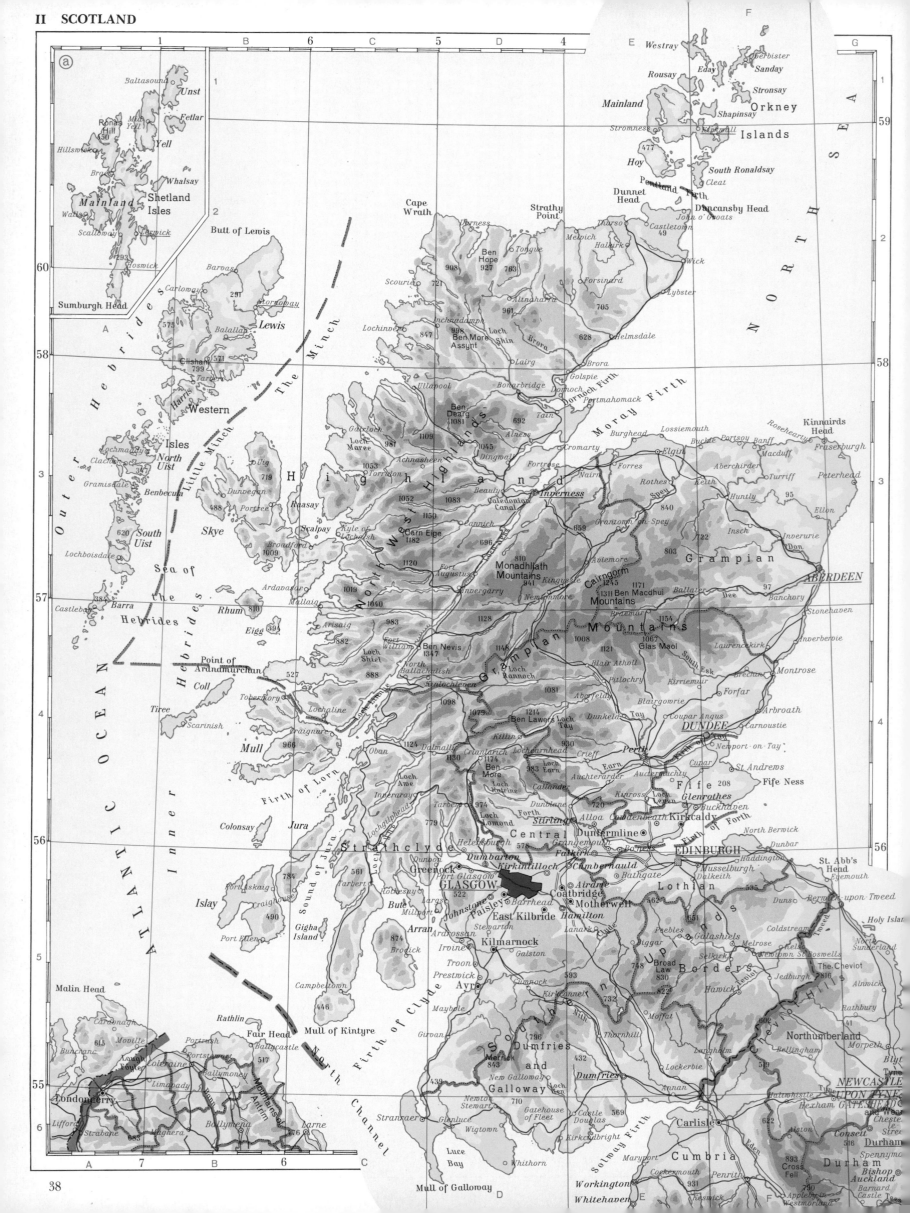

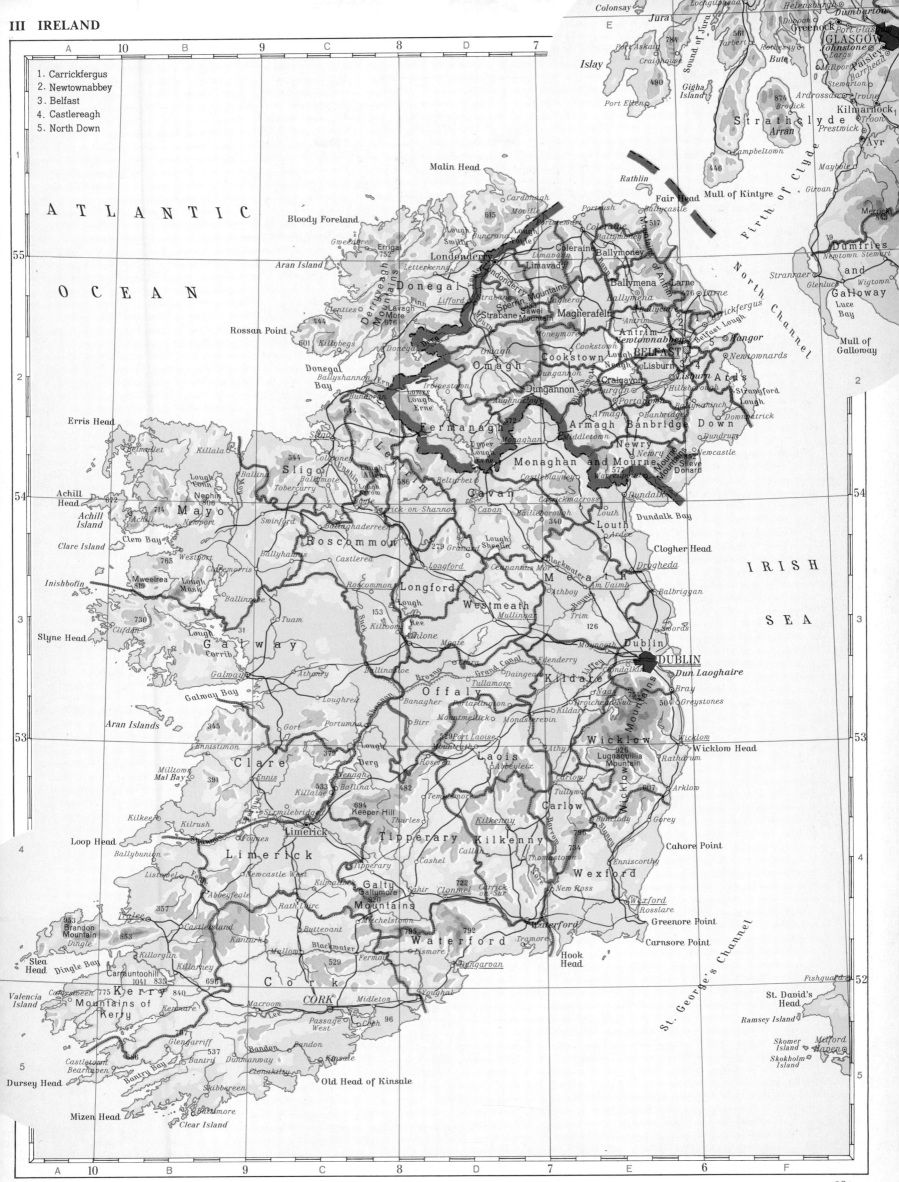

1. Carrickfergus
2. Newtownabbey
3. Belfast
4. Castlereagh
5. North Down

A T L A N T I C

O C E A N

Malin Head

Bloody Foreland

Aran Island

Errigal 752

Rossan Point

Killybegs 601

Donegal Bay

Erris Head

Ballyshannon

Belmullet Killala

Achill Head 672

Achill Island

Clare Island

Inishbofin

Slyne Head

Clew Bay

Nephin 806

Mweelrea 819

Lough Mask

Clifden 730

Aran Islands

Loop Head

Ballybunion

Milltown Mal Bay 391

Kilkee

Kilrush

Dingle Bay

Stea Head

Dursey Head

Mizen Head

Clear Island

Old Head of Kinsale

Malin Head

Londonderry

Donegal

Sligo 544

Mayo 714

Roscommon

Galway 345

Clare

Limerick

Mountains of Kerry

Kerry 1041 775 840

Brandon Mountain 953 835

Carrauntoohill

Cork

CORK

Waterford

Tipperary

Kilkenny

Wexford

Wicklow

Laois

Offaly

Kildare

Dublin

DUBLIN

Dun Laoghaire

Westmeath

Longford

Meath

Louth

Cavan

Monaghan

Fermanagh

Armagh Banbridge Down

Newry

Monaghan and Mourne

Dundalk Bay

Clogher Head

Drogheda

Balbriggan

Swords

Bray

Greystones

Wicklow Head

Arklow

Gorey

Cahore Point

Wexford Rosslare

Greenore Point

Carnsore Point

Hook Head

I R I S H

S E A

Firth of Clyde

North Channel

GLASGOW

Strathclyde

Arran

Mull of Kintyre

Mull of Galloway

Dumfries and Galloway

St. George's Channel

Fishguard

St. David's Head

Ramsey Island

Skomer Island

Milford Haven

39

Climate

The climate of Great Britain is temperate and oceanic. This means that it is strongly influenced by the sea, and in particular by the warm Gulf Stream which flows north past its west coast. There are four distinct seasons, and the winters are mild, especially in the south, and the summers fairly cool. The rainfall is quite high, in some areas it exceeds 2,000 mm a year, and falls frequently at all seasons. Snow falls occasionally in winter, particularly on high ground, although heavy snow falls are infrequent in the southern areas. The weather is extremely variable and may change radically from one day to the next, or from morning to afternoon. Rainfall is usually highest in Scotland (left) and Wales.

RAINFALL

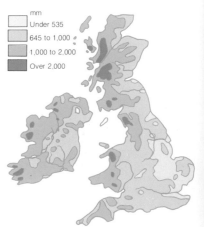

mm
Under 535
645 to 1,000
1,000 to 2,000
Over 2,000

JULY TEMPERATURE

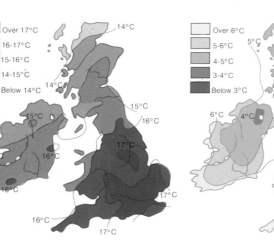

Over 17°C
16-17°C
15-16°C
14-15°C
Below 14°C

JANUARY TEMPERATURE

Over 6°C
5-6°C
4-5°C
3-4°C
Below 3°C

Climate and insularity

There are many factors which influence the special characteristics of the British climate, two of which are its ocean location and its insularity. It is sited between the Eurasian continental land mass and the Atlantic Ocean. It is the latter which creates a blanket of humid air, causing rainfall almost all the year round. A factor which helps to mitigate the English climate is the warm ocean current, the Gulf Stream. Its influence is particularly evident in Cornwall (left).

AGRICULTURE AND ANIMAL HUSBANDRY

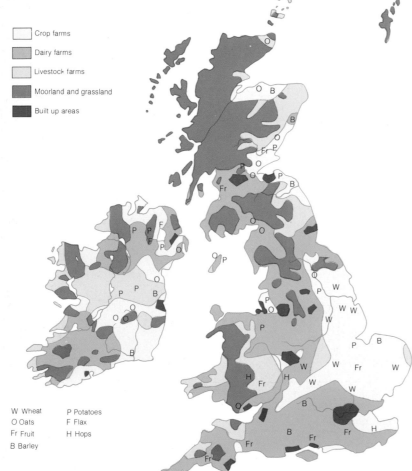

Crop farms
Dairy farms
Livestock farms
Moorland and grassland
Built up areas

W Wheat   P Potatoes
O Oats   F Flax
Fr Fruit   H Hops
B Barley

Agriculture and animal husbandry

Due to the favourable climate, almost 50 per cent of the land is used for cultivation and permanent grazing. Less than 2 per cent of the active population is employed in agriculture and animal husbandry, but the degree of mechanisation makes for high productivity. Major crops are cereals (above), potatoes and sugar beet. The main farming sector is animal husbandry, cattle (right) and sheep.

Industry

The presence of mineral resources (coal and iron in particular), the influx of raw materials from the colonies, an already existing trading structure, and technical and scientific innovations, all helped to bring about the so-called Industrial Revolution in the second half of the 18th century. Many areas of Great Britain became intensely industrialised, with a consequent increase in population in many centres such as London, Manchester, Liverpool and Birmingham. The 18th and 19th centuries saw a marked development in the textile industry (below, a mechanical loom dating from the end of the 18th century), involving in particular the cotton mills of Lancashire, which processed cotton coming in from the colonies, and the woollen mills of Yorkshire. Steel and engineering works grew up in the areas of coal and iron deposits, contributing to the process of specialisation by area, which for many years has been characteristic of the English industrial structure. The industries of any country are affected by repercussions of the world's economic evolution, and this, as well as internal factors, have caused the decline of some traditional industries. Because of foreign competition, textile industries (particularly the cotton industry) have been restructured, and the mechanical industries have come to the fore, both in the traditional sectors (railway construction, machine tools, shipyards) and above all in the more modern sectors (the car industry, the aeronautical industry and electronics). Considerable progress has also been made in the chemicals sector (petrochemicals).

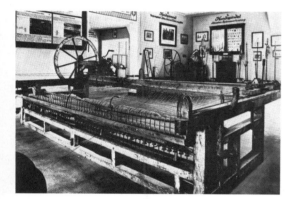

Iron and steel

This was a major sector in British industry up to a few decades ago (right, a blast furnace), but today the British iron and steel industry is struggling to compete as regards quantity with the production of the great industrial powers such as the United States and the Soviet Union. The industry is centred mainly in Wales, Lincolnshire, Scotland and Lancashire, but it has recently been contracting in order to become more efficient and competitive.

	Coalfields
	Working Coalfields
×	Early Iron Ore Mines
▲	Blast furnaces Steelworks and Rolling Mills
Hull	Industrial Centres

Coal

The principle coal mining areas of Great Britain are situated in Scotland, Northumberland, Yorkshire and Wales, and correspond to the ancient rock strata of the Upper Palaeozoic era. Annual production currently exceeds 130 million tonnes. Below, the pit-head of a coal mine in South Wales.

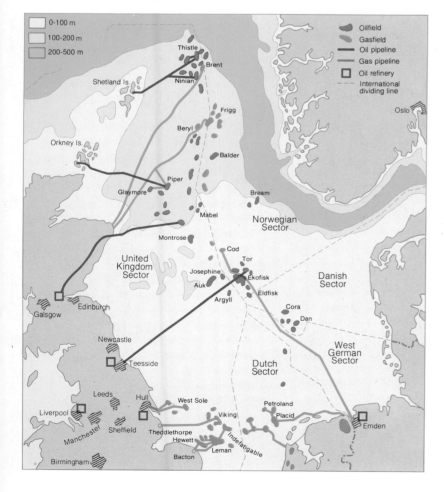

Oil

Dependence on foreign sources for the bulk of her energy needs, accentuated after the Second World War, spurred Great Britain to intensify the search for oil in her own territorial waters. Oil and natural gas deposits discovered in the continental shelf of the North Sea have been exploited since the mid-1970s by both British and American companies. In 1981 crude oil production reached 89 million tonnes.

41

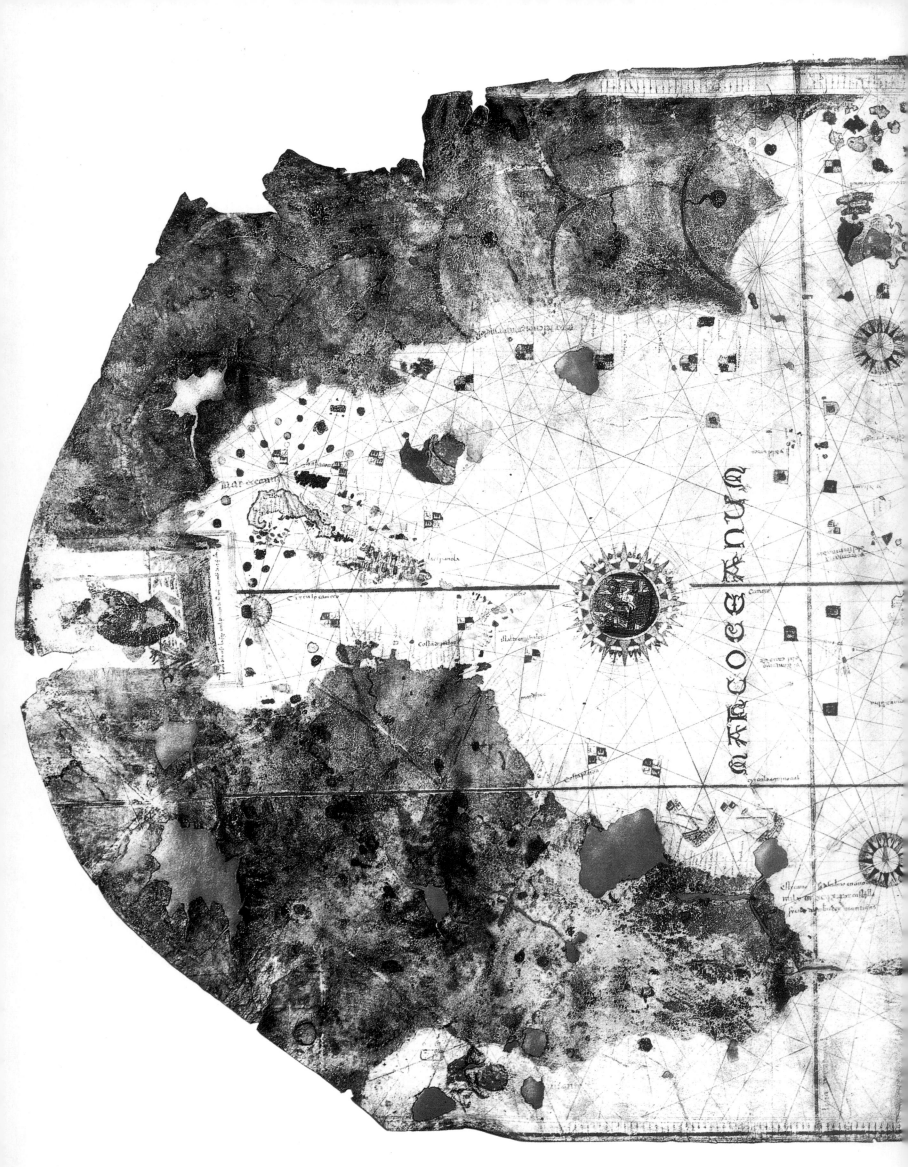

WORLD ATLAS

Scale 1:14 000 000

ALTITUDES
Metres Feet
4000 13123
3000 9843
2000 6562
1000 3281
500 1640
200 656
0
Sea level
Depression

DEPTHS
0
200 656
1000 3281
2000 6562
4000 13123
Over 4000

ATLANTIC OCEAN

ARCTIC OCEAN

Iceland
Vatnajökull 2119
Öraefajökull 1666

Horn
Breidhi Fd.
Rifstangi
Rauna Bay
Fara Bay
Reykjanes

Arctic Circle

3745
3970

Norwegian Sea

Vesterålen
Lofoten Is.
Kebnekaise 2122
2090
Svartisen 1600
419 Uddjaur
Vega Røsvatn Norrland
Vikna
2306 Dovrefjell
Trondheim Fjord
Hitra Trondheim Storsjön Indal
Stadlandet Galdhøpiggen 2469
Sogne Fj. 124 Mjøsa
Hallingdal Siljan Dal Gävle
Bergen Oslo 132
Lindesnes Skagerrak Skagen (The Skaw) Mälaren Stockh.
Svealand
Vänern
Vättern Gotland 83
Denmark Copenhagen
Öland

Strömö Faeroe Is.
Syderö

Rockall 21
British Isles
Hebrides
Lewis N.Minch
North West Highlands
Ben Nevis 1343 Mull Islay
Grampian Mts.
3142
Donegal B. L.Neagh Belfast
L.Corrib Central Plateau
Galway Bay Shannon Dublin
Dunmore Hd. Ireland 1042
C.Clear
St.George's Ch.
Cambrian Mts. 1085
Bristol Channel
Land's End 82
Scilly Is. Cornwall 621
Pte.de St.Mathieu

Orkney Is.
Pentland Firth
Fair I. 268
Moray Firth
Edinburgh
Merrick 842
Firth of Forth 238
Pennines
I.of Man 620
Irish Sea Anglesey
Snowdon 926
Humber 18
The Wash
Bristol London Thames 294
Ouse
I.of Wight Strait of Dover

North Sea

Shetland Is. Mainland 450
1159

Bokna Fjord

Fyn Zealand 162
Kiel Lübeck Bay Rügen Bornholm
Heligoland Frisian Is.
Netherlands Friesland Weser Elbe
Amsterdam Berlin
Waal Westphalia Rhine Oder
Flanders Brussels Mittelland Canal
Picardy Meuse Harz Mts. 1142
Normandy Ardennes Eifel 700 Rhön 950
Seine Lorraine Hunsrück 816 Central German Highlands
Paris Basin Champagne Marne Black Forest Erz Gebirge 1244
Brittany Meuse Vosges 424 Schwabian Jura Bohemian Forest
Belle I. Loire Loir Burgundy Jura Mts. L.Constance Danube Bohemia Prague
Nantes Poitou Cher Saône Geneva St.Gotthard Pass Brenner P. Bavaria Moravia
I.d'Oléron Vienne 2108 1372 Inn Austria Vienna
Gironde Dordogne Mt.Dore 1896 Mt.Blanc 4810 Mte.Rosa 4634 Bernina Dolomites Styria
5048 Guyenne Massif Central Lyon Bernina 3342 Julian Alps Semmering P. 980
Gascogne Garonne Cevennes 3541 4049 2863 Brenta Mur L.Balaton 713
C.Finisterre Tarn Languedoc Mte.Viso Milan Dinaric Alps Bakony 106
Galicia Asturias Picos de Europa 2615 Provence Genoa Venice Po Trieste Croatia Drava
Cantabrian Mts. Cevennes G.of Lion Nice Ligurian Sea Venice Bosnia
Oporto Valladolid Ebro Marseille Mte.Cimone 2163 Bologna Adriatic Hercegovina
Douro Old Castile C.Creus Corsica Arno Florence Gran Sasso 2914 Durmitor 2522
Sa.da Estrela 1991 Iberian Mts. Moncayo 2315 C.Creus Ajaccio Apennines 270 Gargano 1222
Alagón Sa.de Guadarrama 2430 Aragón Barcelona Str.of Bonifacio Elba 2710 Mte.Cinto 1056
Tagus Madrid Sa.de Gredos 2592 New Castile Catalonia Sassari 1362 Rome Vesuvius 1277
Lisbon 1601 Iberian Peninsula Segre Sardinia Naples
Guadiana Sierra Morena G.of Valencia Jucar Balearic Is. Mallorca Gennargentu 1834 Tyrrhenian Sea
C.St.Vincent Sa.de Monchique Sevilla Murcia Menorca 1445 3840
150 Guadalquivir La Sagra 2382 Ibiza C.Nao Cagliari
5402 Andalusia Malaga Sa.Nevada 3478 C.de Palos 3151
C.da Roca Str.of Gibraltar C.de Gata
4958 Gibraltar Alborán I.
Rabat C.Tres Forcas Algiers
C.Cantin El Rif 2452 C.de Fer C.Blanc
Morocco Schou Ouer Rbia Maritime Atlas Annaba G.of Tunis
Marrakech Middle Atlas 3190 Chelif 2308 Medjerda Tunis
Dj.Toubkal 4165 Algeria Chott ech Chergui 987 Chott el Hodna Aurès 2329
High Atlas 3737 Saharan Atlas Djedi Tunisia
Sous Anti Atlas Chott Melrhir Chott Djerid G.of Gabès Djerba I.

MEDITERRANEAN SEA

Bay of Biscay

Great Britain

English Channel
Channel Is.

Pyrenees
Maladeta 3404
Pic.de Aneto

Lipari Is. 1929 Sila
Ustica
Egadi Is. Palermo 1956
Sicily Etna 3263
Trapani Catania
Str.of Messina
C.Passero Ionian Sea
Pantelleria C.Spartivento
G.of Hammamet
Linosa 258 Malta
Lampedusa 4115
Kerkennah Is.
G.of Djerba

West from Greenwich 0 East from Greenwich 5

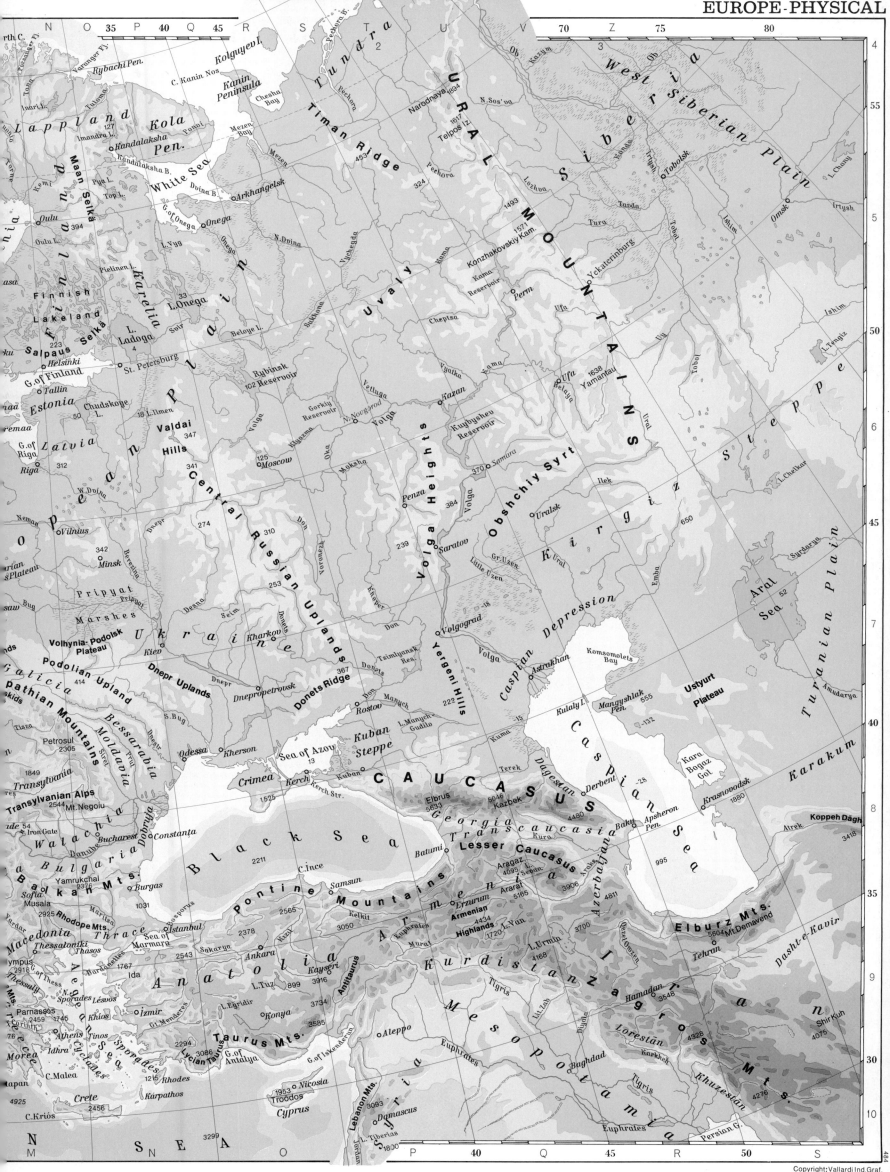

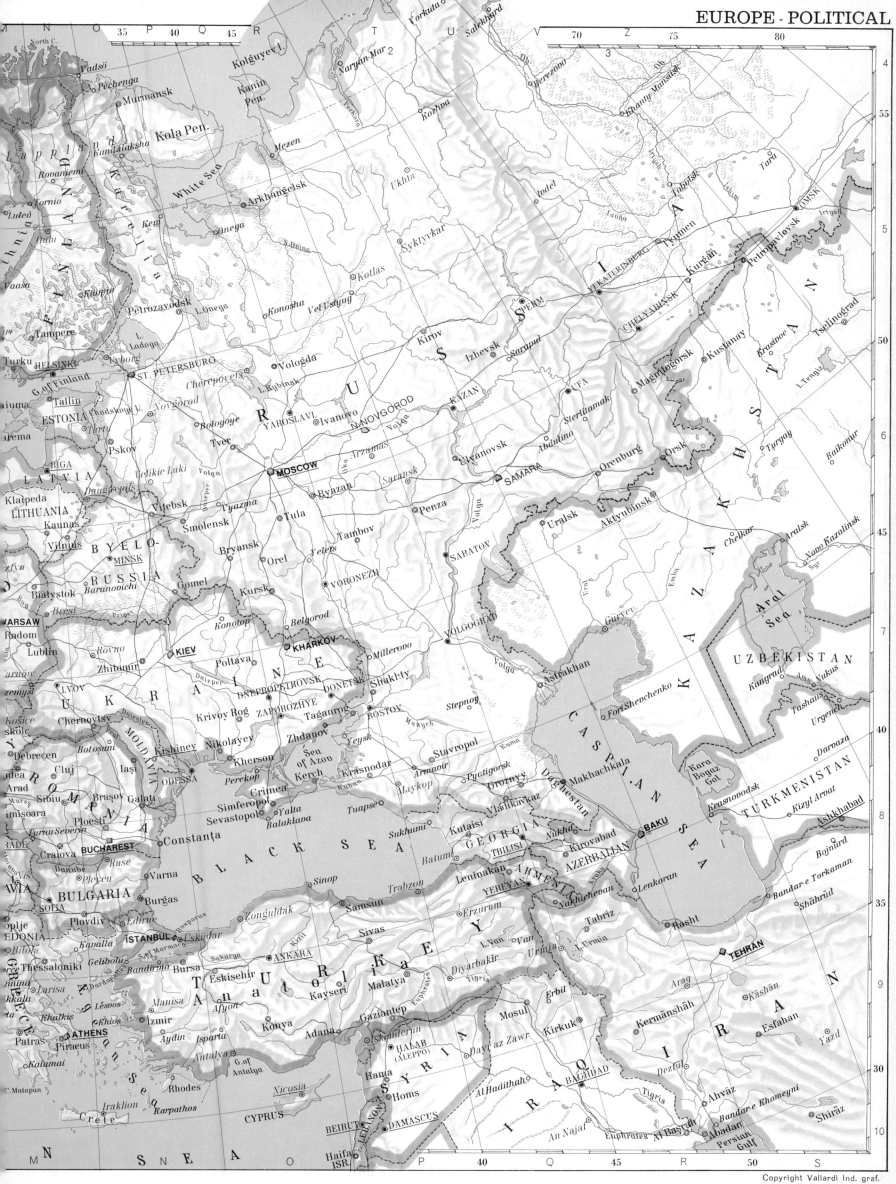

ATLANTIC OCEAN

ARCTIC OCEAN

Greenland

Iceland

Reykjavik

North Pole
4290

British Isles

Norwegian Sea

Jan Mayen
2545

Faeroe Is.
3970

Ireland

Dublin

Great Britain

Shetland Is.

London

English Channel

North Sea

Scandinavia

West Spitsbergen

North East Land

Svalbard

Bear I.

Barents Sea

Franz Josef Land

Novaya Zemlya

Komsomoletsl.
Oct.Revolution I.
Bolshevik I.

C.Chelyuskin

Severnaya Zemlya

Kotelny I.

New Siberian Is.

De Long Is.

Laptev Sea

Str.of Gibraltar

Lisbon

Tagus

Iberian Peninsula

Madrid

Ebro

Pyrenees

Barcelona

Loire

Paris

Amsterdam

Berlin

Rhine

Jutland

Copenhagen

Oslo

Stockholm

Baltic Sea

Riga

St.Petersburg

L.Ladoga

Lake Onega

Vychegda

Pechora

Timani Ridge

Taymyr Pen.

Byranga Mts.

Corsica

Sardinia

Balearic Is.

Algiers

Atlas

Mediterranean

Alps

MtBlanc
4810

Apennines

Vienna

Budapest

Carpathians

Warsaw

Vistula

Dvina

L.Ladoga

Moscow

Volga

Kama

West Siberian Plain

Ob

Putorana Mts.
2037

Central Siberian Plateau

Narodnaya
1894

Tobol'sk

Lower Tunguska

Stony Tunguska

Tunisia

Atlas

Algeria

Mediterranean Sea

Sicily

Adriatic Sea

Rome

Tyrrhenian Sea

Balkans

Pindus Mts.
2925

Belgrade

Danube

Rhodope

Black Sea

Crimea

Dnepr

Don

Central-Russian Uplands

Kiev

Volga Heights

Uvaly

Moscow

Volga

Ural

Uralsk

Kirgiz Steppe

Ishim

Omsk

L.Chany

Tomsk

Eastern Sayan

Irkutsk

L.Bay

Tripoli

Tripolitania

G.of Sidra

Benghazi

Ionian Sea

Morea

Crete

Aegean Sea

Istanbul

Bosporus
2217

Ankara

Pontine Mts.

Anatolia

Caucasus Mts.
5633

Elbrus

Tbilisi

Caspian Depression

Astrakhan

Caspian Sea

Ustyurt Plateau

Aral Sea

Syrdarya

Mugunkun

Turanian Plain

L.Balkhash
340

Kazakh Uplands

L.Zaysan

Belukha
4506

Altai

Hangay Mts.
4030

Plateau

Ulan Bator

Mongolia

Fezzan

Libyan Desert

Taurus Mts.
3347

Cyprus

Lebanon Mts.

Damascus

Syrian Desert

L.Urmia

L.Van

Kurdistan

Araks

Ararat
5165

Elburz Mts.
5633

Tehran

Demavend

Dasht-i-Kavir

Plateau of Iran

Karakum

Amudarya

Kyzylkum

Hari

Alai Ra.

Communism Peak
7495

Pamirs

Hindu Kush Ra.
7700

Kabul

Khyber P.

Kashgar

Tien Shan
7439

Dzungaria

Turfan Depression
5485

Tarim

Tarim Basin

Takla Makan Desert

Altyn Tagh

Lop Nor

Nan Shan

Tsaidam

Koko Nor

Hwang-Ho

Lanch

Kufra Oasis

Tropic of Cancer

J.Uwaynat
1934

Egypt

Cairo

Sinai Pen.
2637

Jerusalem

Dead Sea

Damascus
1307

Mesopotamia

Baghdad

Euphrates

Tigris

Zagros Mts.

Nafud Desert
1500

Arabian

Nile

2nd Cat.

3rd Cat.

L.Nasser
2217

Nubian Desert

Dakhla Des.

Riyadh

Persian Gulf

Qatar

Dasht-i-Lut
4420

Makran

Baluchistan

Kirthar Ra.

Khyber P.

Indus

Karakoram Ra.
8611

Kunlun Shan
7723

Plateau of Tibet

Bayan Kara Shan

Trans-Himalaya

Nam Tso

Salween

Mekong

Minya

Yangtze Kiang

1st Cat.

Mecca

Port Sudan

Red Sea

Arabian Peninsula

Rub al Khali

G.of Oman
3107

Muscat

Ras al-Hadd

Al Masirah I.

G.of Oman

Str.of Hormuz

Indus Plain

Karachi

Great Indian (Thar) Desert
1721

Delhi

Ganges

Aravalli Ra.

India

Himalaya

Mt.Everest
8847

Brahmaputra

Assam

Chittagong

4th Cat.

5th Cat.

6th Cat.

Kordofan

Khartoum

Atbara

Blue Nile

White Nile

Sudan

Asmara

Ras Dashan
4620

L.Tana

Danakil Basin

Addis Ababa

Ethiopian Highlands
4340

t.Abuya

Hadhramaut

Aden

Bab el Mandeb

Djibouti

G.of Aden

Socotra

Ras Hafun

Arabian Sea

Kuria Muria Is.

W.Masila
3217

Sana
2380

Riyadh

Lakshadweep Is.

Aravalli Ra.

Vindhya Mts.

Satpura Ra.

Narmada

Nagpur

Mahanadi

Bombay

Godavari

Hyderabad

Krishna

Western Ghats

Eastern Ghats

Deccan

Malabar Coast

Coromandel Coast

Bengal

Calcutta

Ganges Delta

Arakan Yoma

Burma

Rangoon

Bay of Bengal

Chittagong

Bahr el-Ghazal

Bahr el Jebel

Somali Plateau

Somali Peninsula

L.Kyoga

L.Turkana
4321

Lugh Ganane

Hargeisa

Mogadishu

Shebelle

I N D I A N   O C E A N

Maldive Islands

5826

C.Comorin
2695

Sri Lanka
2524
Pidurutalagala

Dondra Head

Andaman Sea

Andaman Is.

Isthmus of Kra
4360

Phuket

Nicobar Is.

L.Victoria
1134

Mt.Kenya
5199

Nairobi

Kilimanjaro
5895

Juba

Tana

L.Malawi

Rungwe
2960

Pemba

Zanzibar

Dar es Salaam

Equator

Ten Degree Channel

Nenlahi

3466

Simeulue

Nias
5400

Suvadiva Atoll

Scale 1:34 000 000

0   250   500   750   1000   1250   1500 km

0   250   500   750   1000 St.mls.

East from 80 Greenwich

40   50   60   70   80   90

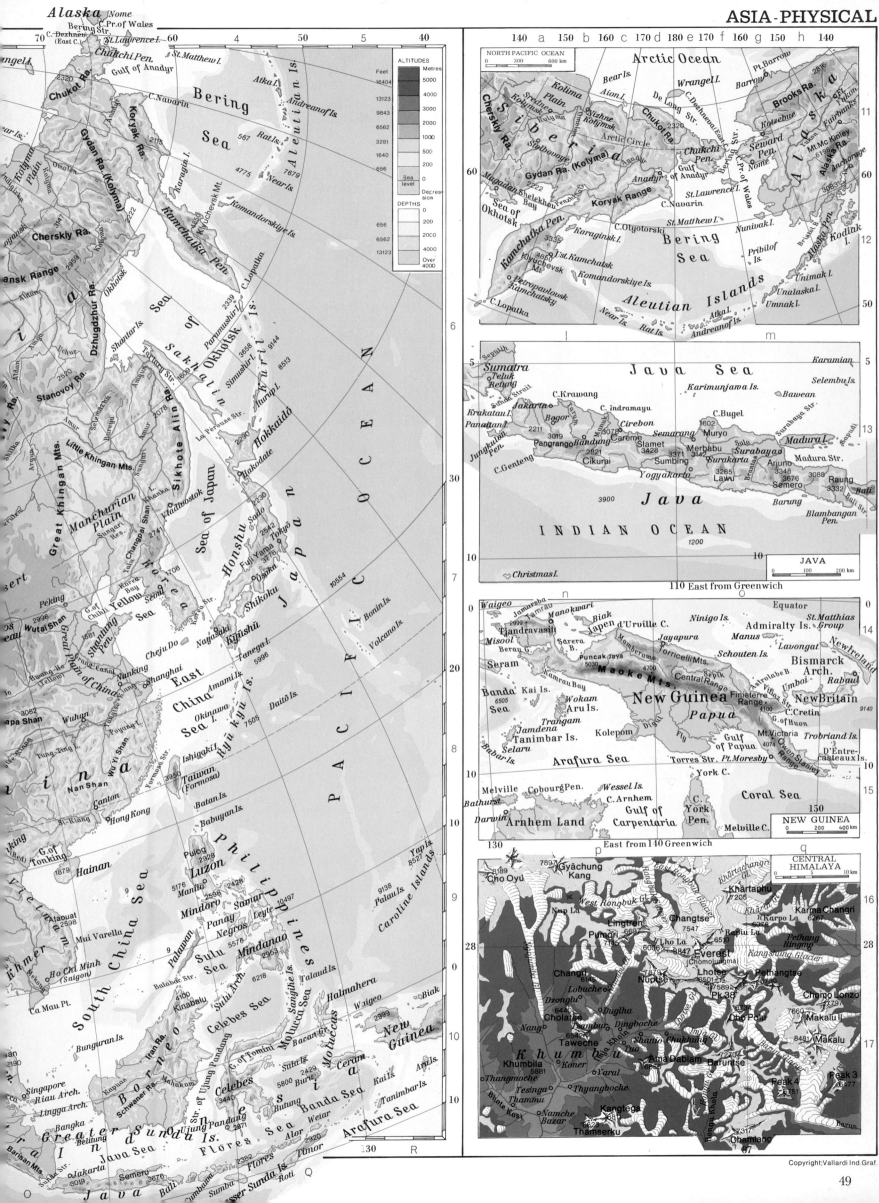

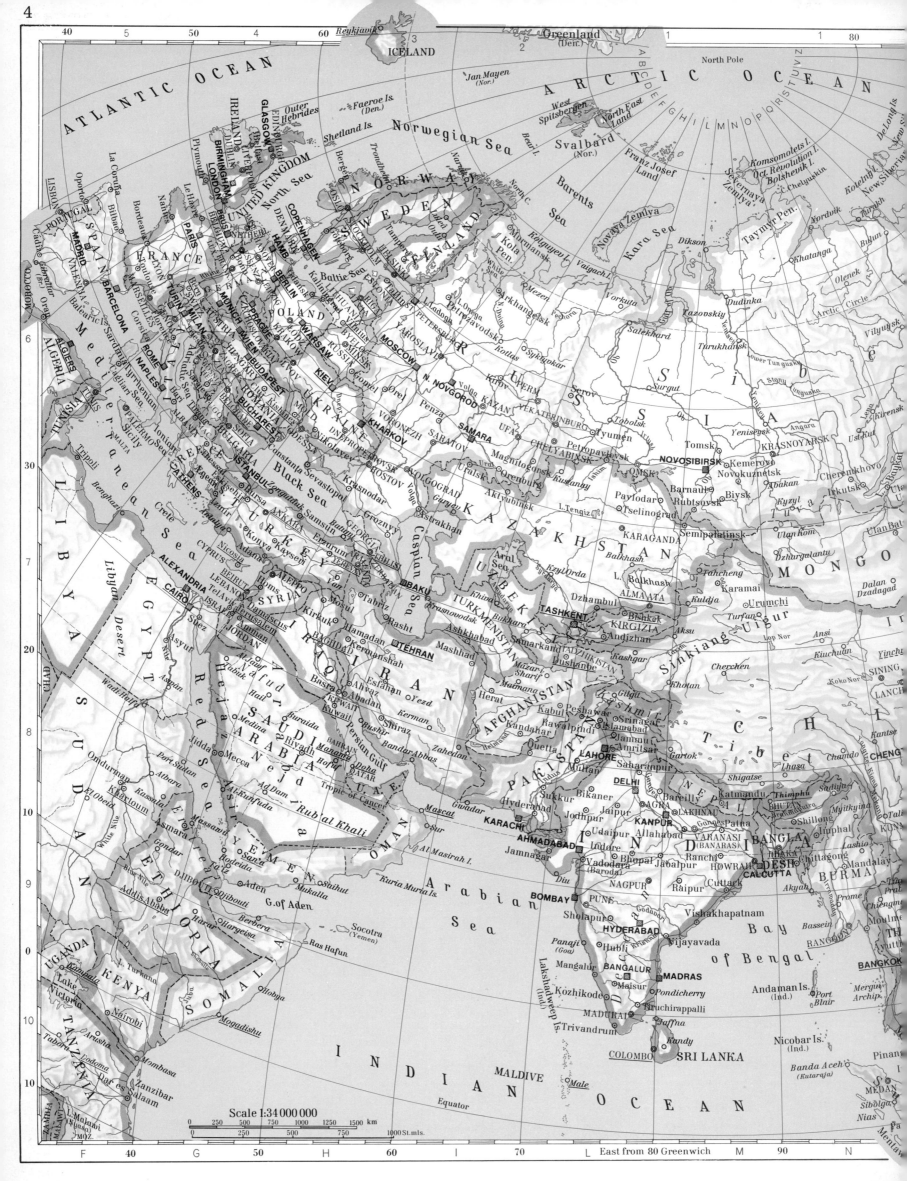

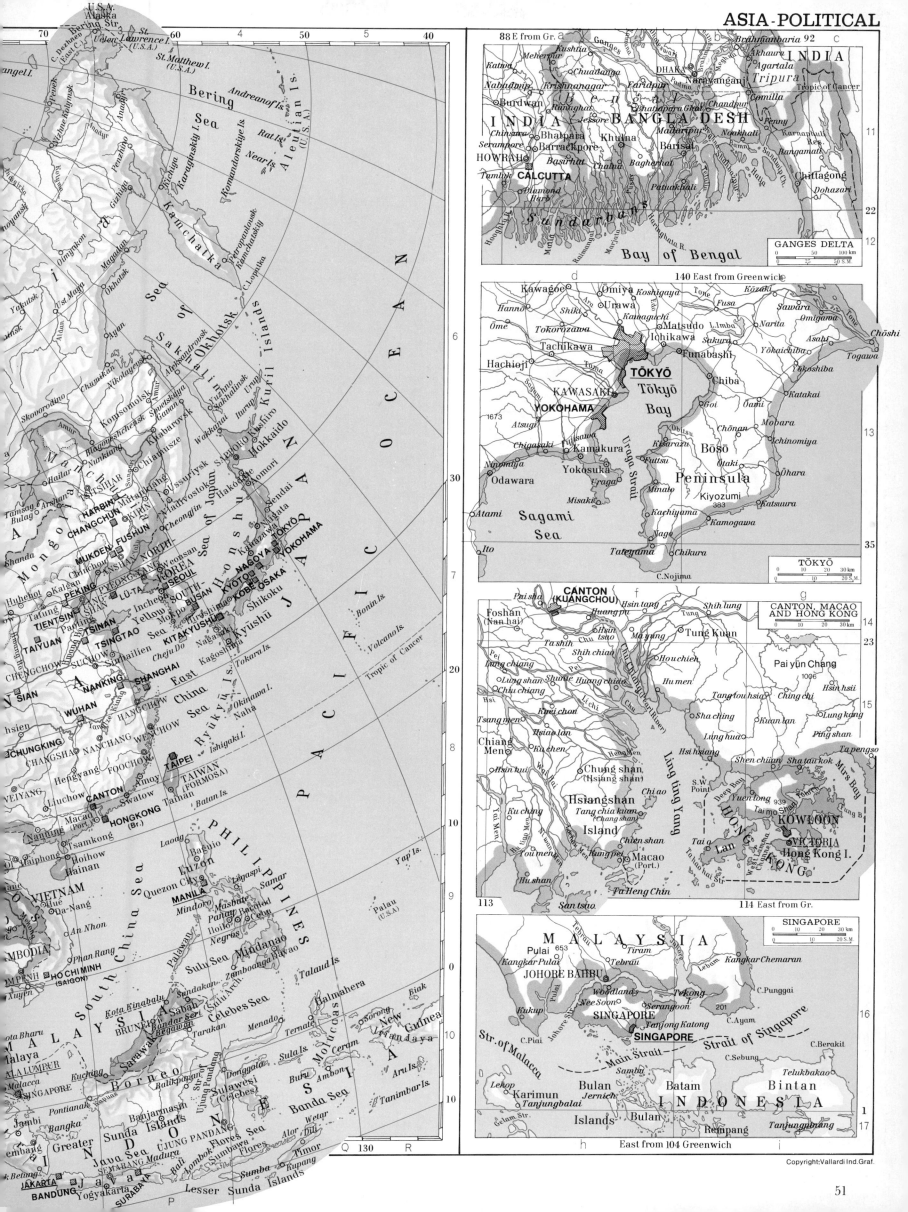

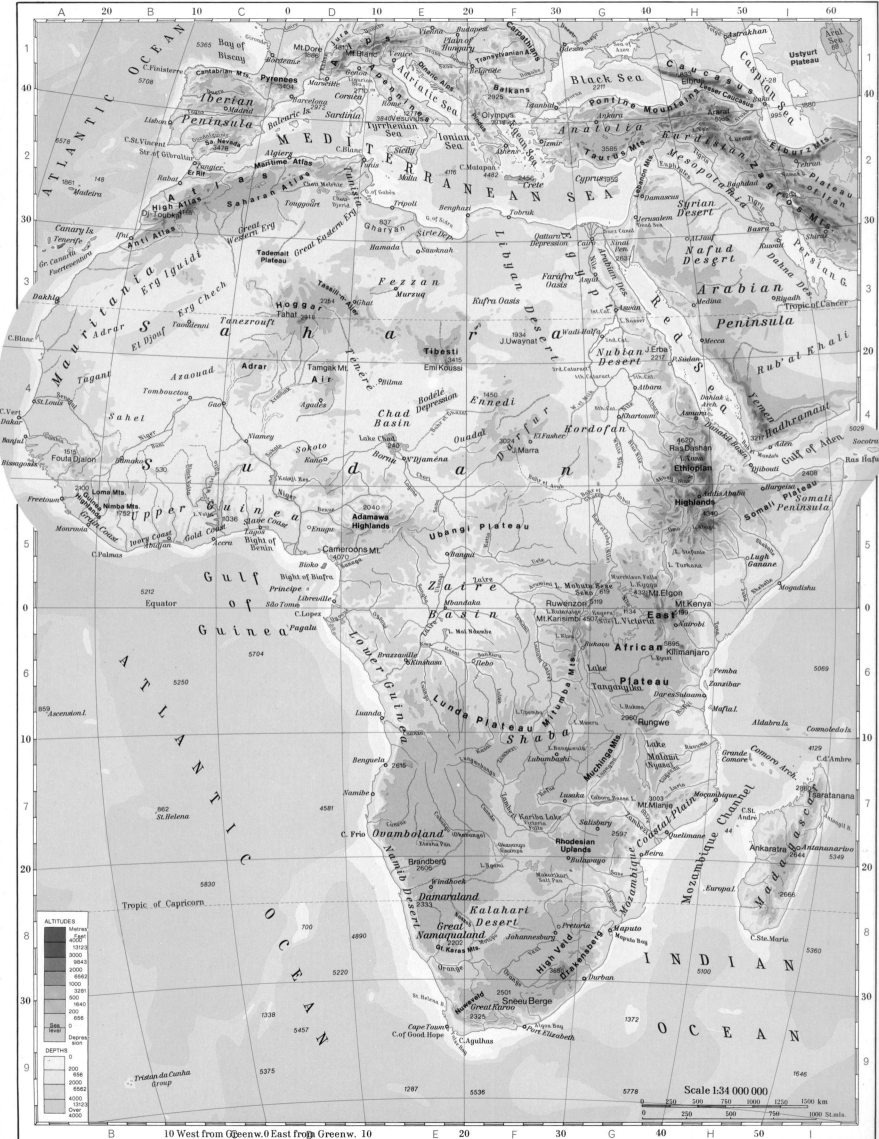

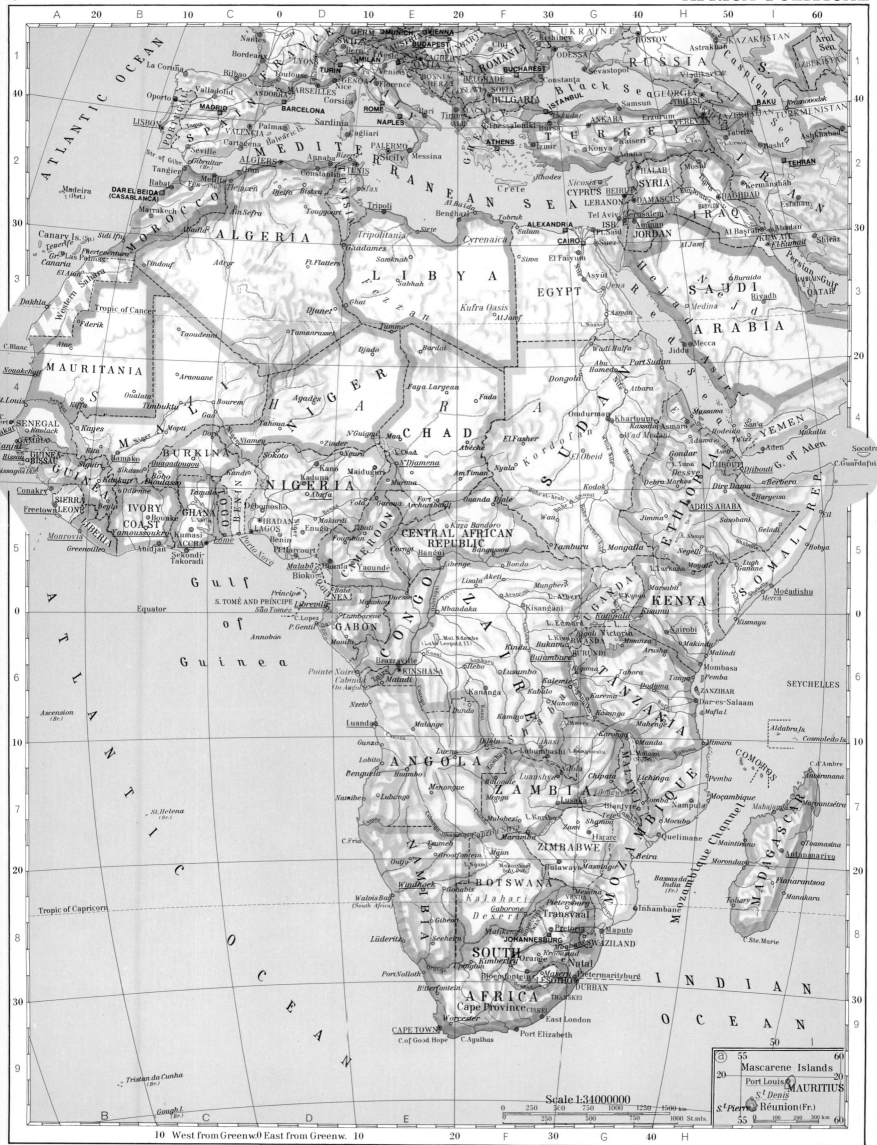

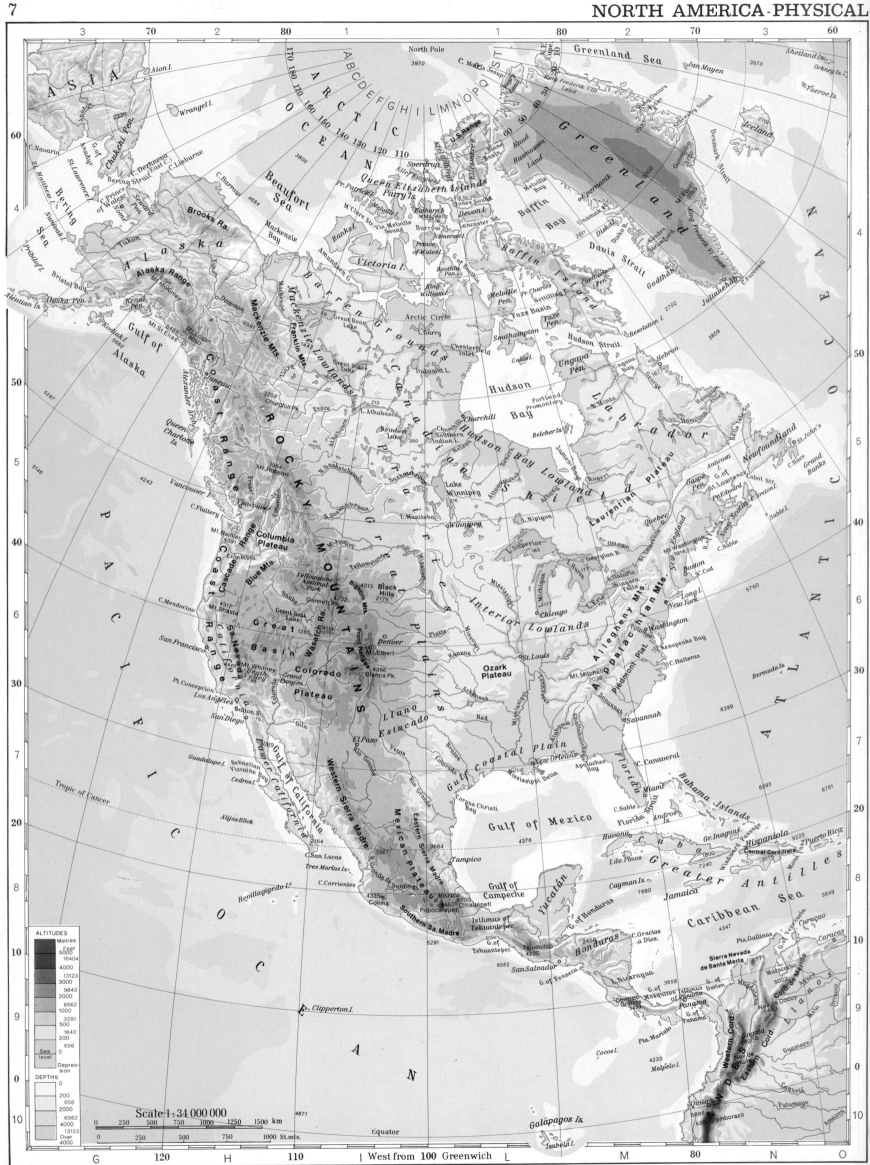

Scale 1:34 000 000

Scale 1:34 000 000

Scale 1:34 000 000

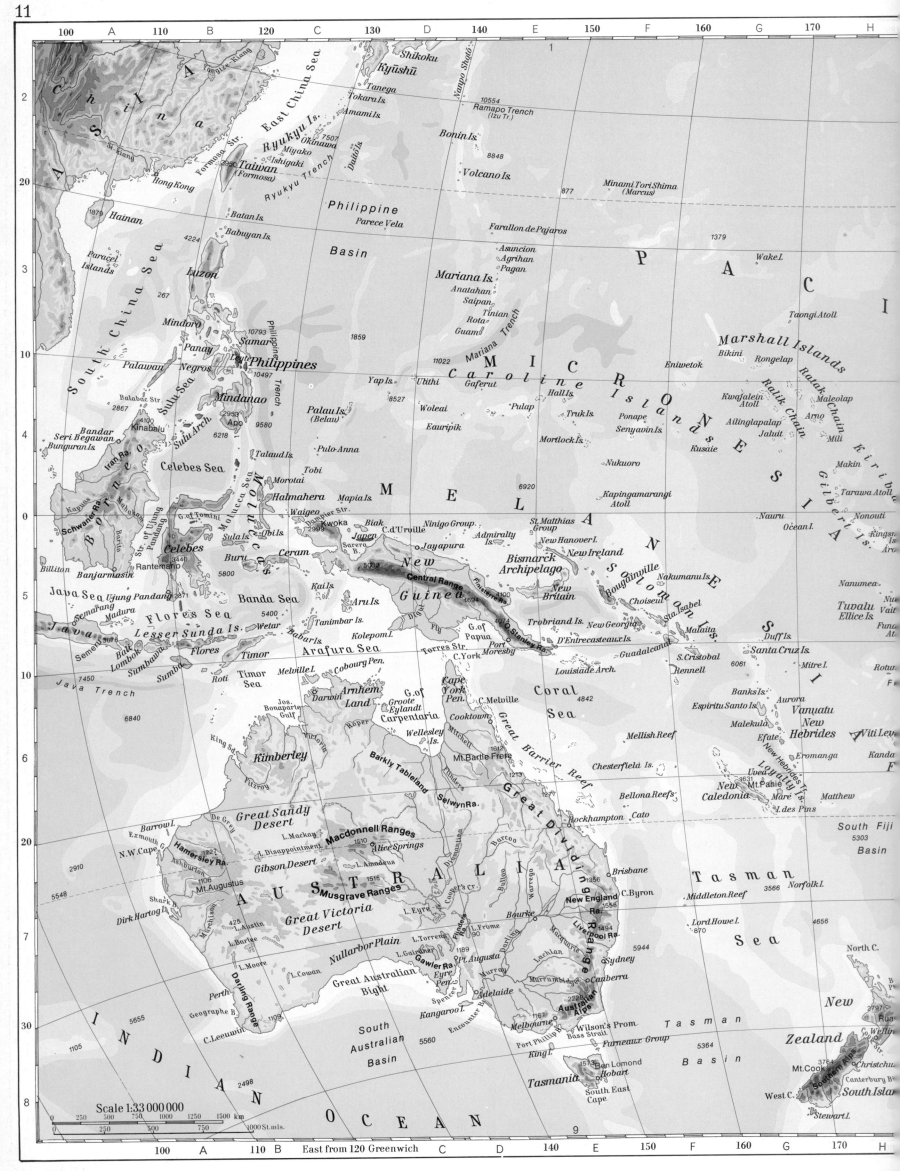

Scale 1:33 000 000

East from 120 Greenwich

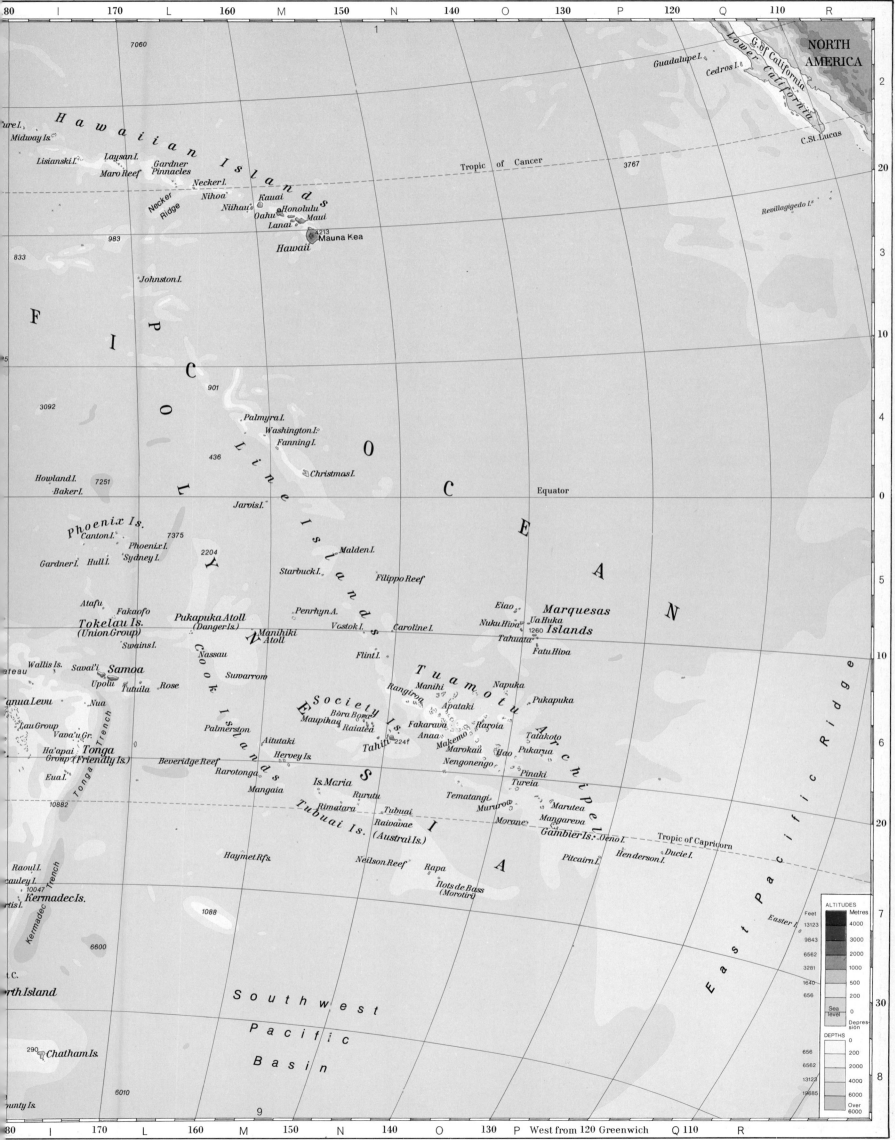

SURABAYA
Pasuruan
Malang 3676 *Banyuwangi*
Semeru
Java
3332
Singaraja 3142 *Lombok*
Bali 3775
Mataram

Sumbawa
2851
Raba
Flores
2382 *Ruteng*
Maumere *Lembata*
Sawu Sea
Alor
Dili 2920
Ramelau
Ocussi

INDONESIA

Arafura Sea

Waingapu
Sumba 1225
2345
Timor
Kupang
Sawu
Roti

Melville I.
Bathurst I. Dundas Str.
Pt. Hurd
Clarence Str.
Van Diemen Gulf
Croker I.
Cobourg Pen.
Wessel Is.

Timor Sea

Darwin
Anson B.
Adelaide River
Pine Creek
Katherine

Arnhem Aboriginal Reserve Land

INDIAN

C. Talbot
Admiralty G.
Joseph Bonaparte Gulf
Aboriginal Reserve
Daly
Mataranka
Limmen Bight

Sandy I. Scott Reef
Bonaparte Archip.
Brunswick B.
Wyndham
Ord
Victoria
Birdum
Daly Waters
Borroloo

King Sound
Collier B.
Kimberley
Durack
Victoria River Downs
Newcastle Waters
L. Woods
Anthony Lagoon

OCEAN

Dampier Land
Derby
1936
King Leopold Ranges
Inverway
Wave Hill
Powell Creek

Broome
Fitzroy
Fitzroy Crossing
Hall's Creek
Gordon Downs

NORTHERN

Alexand

Rowley Shoals
La Grange
Kura Soak
Tanami
Tennant Creek

Eighty Mile Beach
Joanna Spring
Gregory Salt Sea
The Granites
TERRITORY
Elkedra

Dampier Archipelago
Port Hedland De Grey
Great Sandy Desert
Percival Lakes
Barrow Creek
Sandover

Barrow I.
Roebourne
Marble Bar
L. Dora
L. Mackay
Aileron
Marshal

North West C.
Exmouth G.
Onslow
Fortescue
Roy Hill
L. Blanche
Patience Well
L. Macdonald
Macdonnell Ranges 1510
Alice Springs

Yanrey
Hamersley Ra. 1227
Ashburton
L. Disappointment
Gibson Desert
L. Hopkins
Aboriginal Reserve
Lake Amadeus
Simpso

Landor
Mundiwindi
1219
Mt. Deering
Fuke
Bundooma
Desert

Geographe Ch.
Salt Lake
Lyons
Mt. Augustus 1106
WESTERN
Weld Springs
Charlotte Wat

Gascoyne
Gascoyne
Carnarvon
Peak Hill
Carnegie
Aboriginal Reserve
Musgrave Ranges 1515
Alberga
Ilbunga

Naturaliste Ch.
Shark B.
Wooramel
L. Carnegie
L. Wright
Oodnadatta

Dirk Hartog I.
Hamelin Pool
Meekatharra
Wiluna
L. Wells
Wandunya
SOUTH
Warrina

Steep Pt.
Big Bell
AUSTRALIA
Yeo L.
L. Meramangye
Warrin

Ajana
Murchison
Cue
L. Austin
Lawlers
L. Carey
Serpentine Lakes
Coober Pedy
Strangways Springs

Northampton
Greenough
Mullewa
Mount Magnet
Morgans *Laverton*
Rason L.
Great Victoria Desert
Jubilee
AUSTRALI

Geraldton
Geelvink Ch.
Yalgoo
L. Bartee
L. Ballard
L. Carey
L. Minigwal
L. Dey-Dey
L. Maurice

Miling
L. Moore
Menzies
Forrest
Deakin
Ooldea
Tarcoola
Kingoonya
L. Woor

Kalannie
Broad Arrow
Rawlinna
Haig
Nullarbor Plain
L. Everard

Moora
Bullfinch *Kalgoorlie*
Boulder
Zanthus
Nullarbor
Colona
Penong
Ceduna

Northam
Southern Cross
L. Lefroy
Eucla
Eyre
Fowlers Bay
Streaky B.
Iron K

Perth
Merredin
L. Cowan
Norseman
Balladonia
Minnipa

Fremantle
Darling Ra.
The Johnston Lakes
L. Dundas
Great Australian Bight
Eyre
Kim

Geographe B.
1122
Narrogin
Newdegate
Port Lincoln
Elliston Pen

C. Naturaliste
Collie
Wagin
Ravensthorpe
Esperance
C. Catastrophe
C. Spencer

Augusta
Katanning
Ongerup
Hopetoun
Archip. of the Recherche
Kings

C. Leeuwin
Northcliffe *Albany* 1109
Kangaroo

Pt. D'Entrecasteaux
Nornalip Bald Hd.

INDIAN OCEAN

Scale 1:12 000 000

0 50 100   200   300   400   500 km

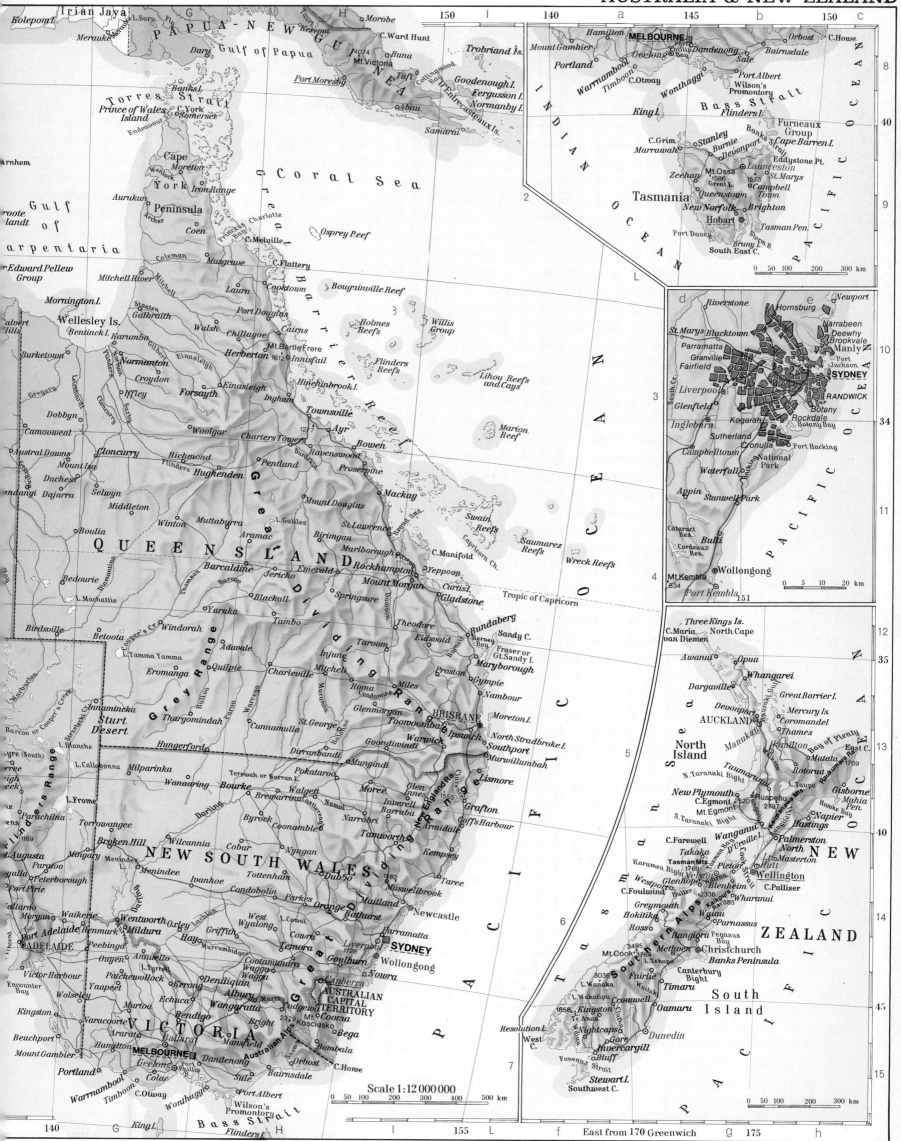

Scale 1:12 000 000

0 50 100 200 300 400 500 km

Tropic of Capricorn

East from 170 Greenwich

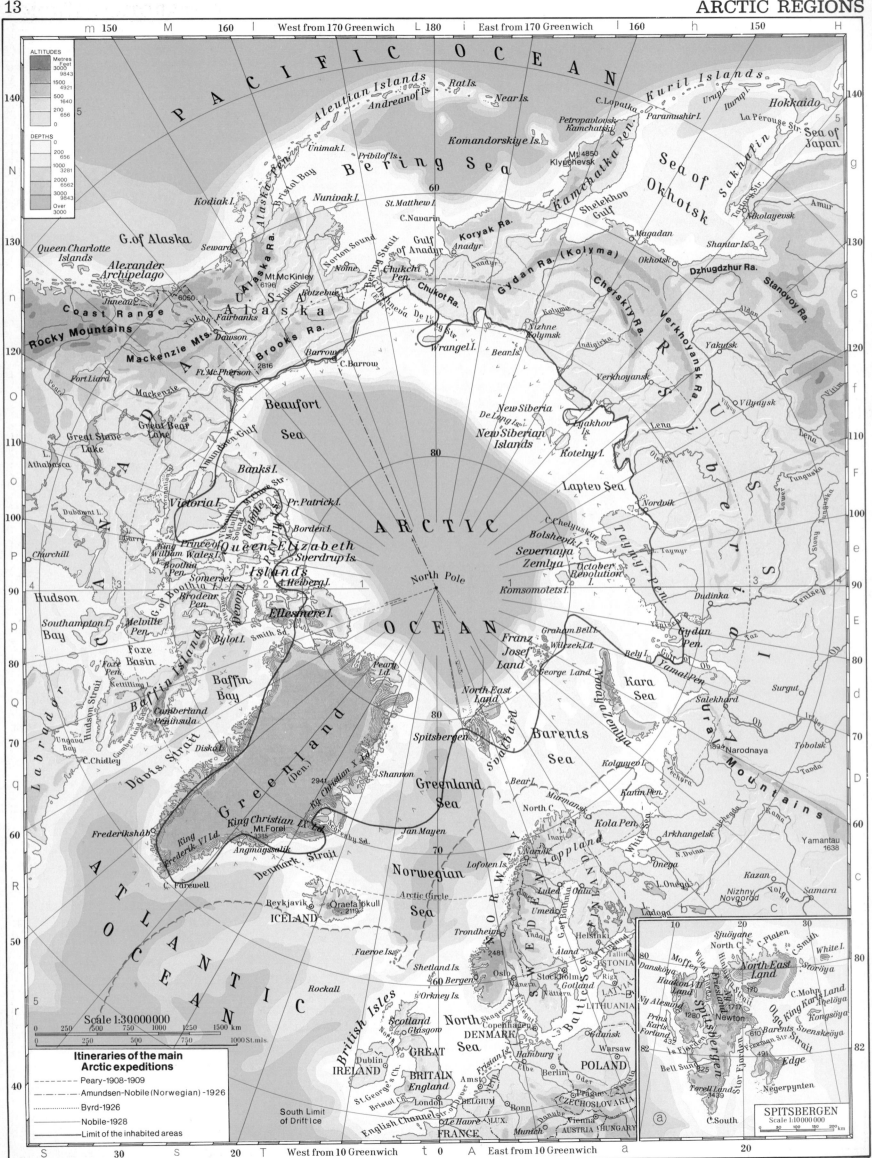

ALTITUDES
Metres	Feet
3000	9843
1500	4921
500	1640
200	656
0	

DEPTHS
0	0
200	656
1000	3281
2000	6562
3000	9843
Over 3000	

P A C I F I C   O C E A N

Aleutian Islands
Andreanof Is.
Rat Is.
Near Is.
Kuril Islands
C. Lopatka
Urup I.
Iturup I.
Hokkaido
Paramushir I.
La Pérouse Str.
Sea of Japan
Petropavlovsk
Kamchatski
Komandorskiye Is.
Mt 4850
Klyuchevsk
Sea of Sakhalin
Okhotsk
Amur
Nikolayevsk

Unimak I.
Bristol Bay
Nunivak I.
St. Matthew I.
B e r i n g   S e a
Kamchatka Pen.
Shelekhov Gulf
Magadan
Shantar Is.
Dzhugdzhur Ra.
Stanovoy Ra.

Kodiak I.
C. Navarin
Koryak Ra.
Anadyr
Okhotsk

Queen Charlotte Islands
G. of Alaska
Seward
Alaska Ra.
Norton Sound
Gulf of Anadyr
Anadyr
Gydan Ra. (Kolyma)
Cherskiy Ra.
Verkhoyansk Ra.

Alexander Archipelago
Mt McKinley 6196
Nome
Bering Strait
Chukchi Pen.
Chukot Ra.

Juneau
6050
Fairbanks
Kotzebue
Dezhneva (East C.)
De Long Str.
Nizhne Kolymsk
Kolyma
Indigirka
Verkhoyansk
Yakutsk
Aldan

Coast Range
U.   S.   A.
Alaska
Brooks Ra.
Wrangel I.
Bear Is.

Rocky Mountains
Mackenzie Mts.
Dawson
Barrow
C. Barrow
De Long Is.

Fort Liard
Ft. McPherson
2816
New Siberia
Lyakhov Is.
Vilyuysk

Peace
Mackenzie
Beaufort Sea
New Siberian Islands
Kotelny I.
Lena
Vilyuysk

Great Bear Lake
Amundsen Gulf
Banks I.
Laptev Sea
Olenek

Great Slave Lake
L. Athabasca
Dubawnt L.
Victoria I.
M'Clure Str.
Pr. Patrick I.
Nordvik
C. Chelyuskin
Bolshevik I.
Severnaya Zemlya
Tunguska

Garry
Melville I.
Borden I.
A R C T I C
October Revolution I.
Dudinka

Churchill
Prince of Wales I.
Queen Elizabeth Islands
Sverdrup Is.
A. Heiberg I.
North Pole
Komsomolets I.
Yenisey

Hudson
Boothia Pen.
Somerset I.
Brodeur Pen.
O C E A N
Franz Josef Land
Graham Bell I.
Wilczek Ld.
Gydan Pen.
Salekhard

Southampton I.
Melville Pen.
Ellesmere I.
Bylot I.
Smith Sd.
George Land
Novaya Zemlya
Kara Sea
Yamal Pen.
Surgut

Foxe Basin
Nettling L.
Baffin Island
Peary Ld.
North-East Land
Barents Sea
Narodnaya 1894

Labrador
Hudson Strait
Cumberland Peninsula
Baffin Bay
2941
Kg. Christian X Ld.
J. Shannon
Spitsbergen
Svalbard
Bear I.
Kolguyev I.
Kanin Pen.

Ungava Bay
C. Chidley
Davis Strait
Disko I.
Greenland (Den.)
Greenland Sea
Jan Mayen
Murmansk
North C.
Pechora

Frederikshåb
King Frederik VI Ld.
King Christian IX Ld.
Mt Forel 3385
Scoresby Sd.
Kola Pen.
White Sea
Arkhangelsk
N. Dvina
Onega
Kazan
Volga

Angmagssalik
Denmark Strait
Norwegian Sea
Inari
Narvik
Lofoten Is.
Lappland
Onega
L. Onega
Nizhny Novgorod
Kama
Samara

C. Farewell
Reykjavik
Oraefa Jokull 2119
Arctic Circle
Trondheim
Umeå
Ladoga

ICELAND
South Limit of Drift Ice
Faeroe Is.
2481
Luleå
Oulu
Helsinki
Tallinn
ESTONIA

A T L A N T I C
Rockall
Shetland Is.
60
Bergen
Oslo
Stockholm
Åland
Gotland
Riga
LATVIA
LITHUANIA

O C E A N
British Isles
Orkney Is.
Scotland
Glasgow
North Sea
Copenhagen
Gdansk
POLAND

Dublin
IRELAND
St. George's Ch.
Bristol Ch.
GREAT BRITAIN England
London
DENMARK
Amst.
Berlin
Warsaw

English Channel
Le Havre
BELGIUM
LUX.
Bonn
Elbe
Oder
Prague
CZECHOSLOVAKIA

FRANCE
Munich
Danube
Vienna
AUSTRIA HUNGARY

Scale 1:30000000
| 0 | 250 | 500 | 750 | 1000 | 1250 | 1500 km |
| 0 | 250 | 500 | 750 | 1000 St. mls. |

Itineraries of the main Arctic expeditions
- – – – – Peary - 1908-1909
- –·–·– Amundsen-Nobile (Norwegian) -1926
- ········ Byrd-1926
- –··–··– Nobile - 1928
- ──── Limit of the inhabited areas

SPITSBERGEN

Sjuøyane
North C.
C. Platen
White I.
C. Smith
Storøya
Moffen
Widjefjorden
Hinlopen Strait

Danskøya
Haakon VII Land
1717
North-East Land

Ny Ålesund
Newton 1280
C. Mohr
King Karls Land
Thelöya

Prins Karls Forland 432
Spitsbergen
Olga Barents Strait
Svenskøya
Kongsøya

Is. Fjorden
610
Freeman Str.
491
Edge

Bell Sund
825
Stor Fjorden
Edge

Forell Islands
1439
Negerpynten
C. South

SPITSBERGEN
Scale 1:10000000
| 0 | 50 | 100 | 150 | 200 km |

Copyright: Vallardi Ind. Graf.

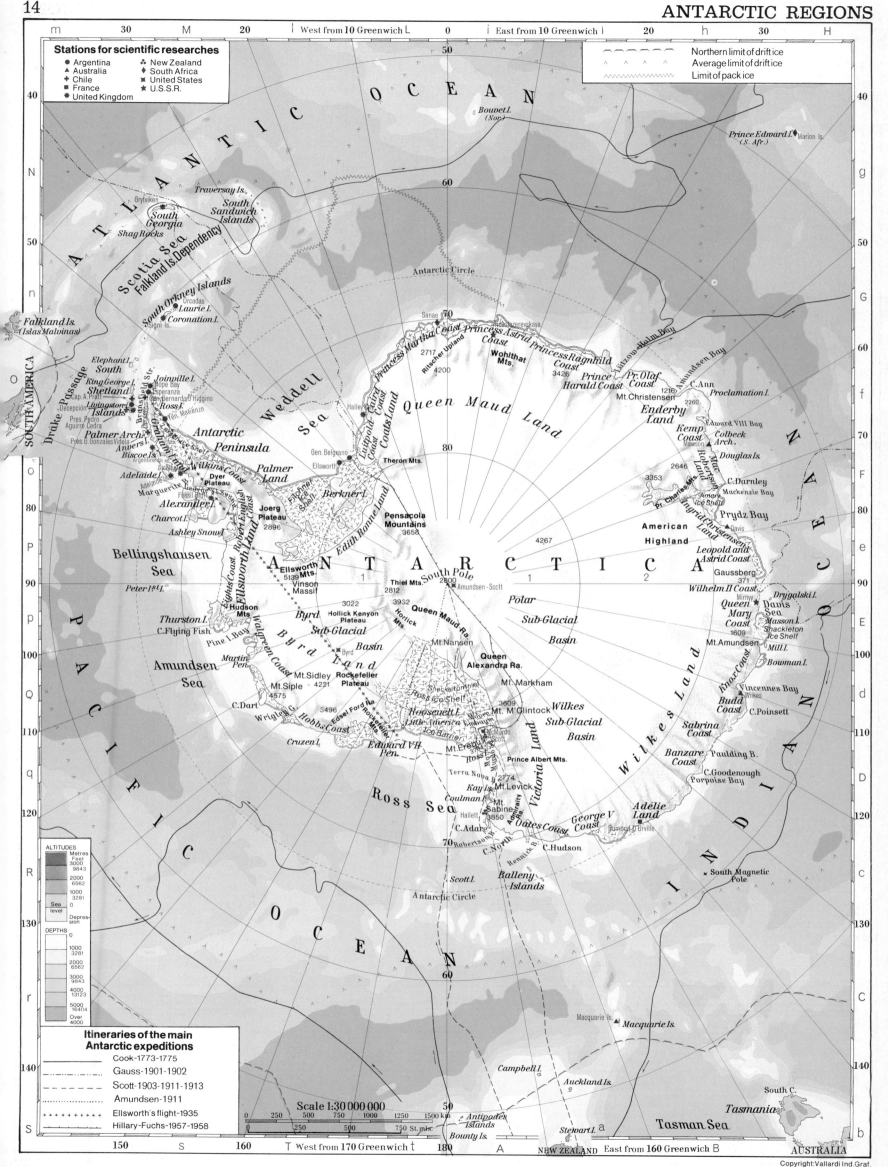

Stations for scientific researches
● Argentina
▲ Australia
✛ Chile
■ France
⬟ United Kingdom
♣ New Zealand
♦ South Africa
✕ United States
★ U.S.S.R.

Northern limit of drift ice
Average limit of drift ice
Limit of pack ice

Itineraries of the main Antarctic expeditions
Cook-1773-1775
Gauss-1901-1902
Scott-1903-1911-1913
Amundsen-1911
Ellsworth's flight-1935
Hillary-Fuchs-1957-1958

Scale 1:30 000 000

COUNTRIES AND COLONIAL DEPENDENCIES IN 1914

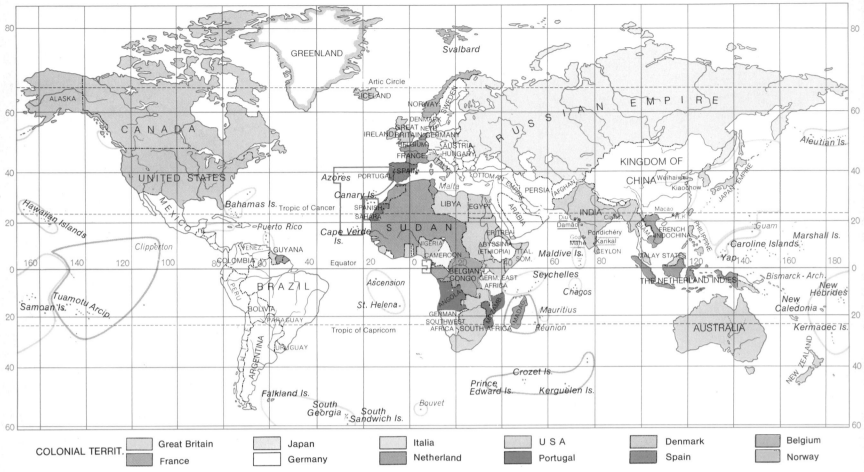

COLONIAL TERRIT.	Great Britain	Japan	Italia	USA	Denmark	Belgium
	France	Germany	Netherland	Portugal	Spain	Norway

WORLDWIDE POLITICAL AND ECONOMIC ORGANISATION

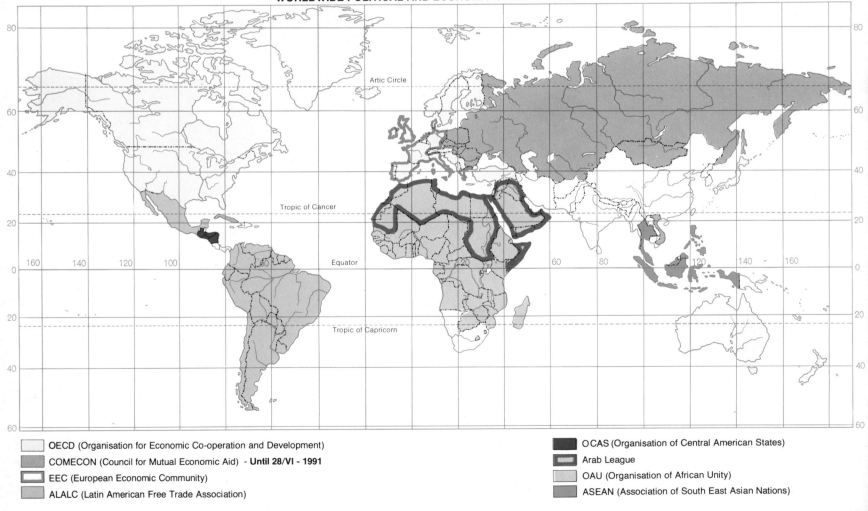

OECD (Organisation for Economic Co-operation and Development)

COMECON (Council for Mutual Economic Aid) - **Until 28/VI - 1991**

EEC (European Economic Community)

ALALC (Latin American Free Trade Association)

OCAS (Organisation of Central American States)

Arab League

OAU (Organisation of African Unity)

ASEAN (Association of South East Asian Nations)

Countries of Europe

ALBANIA - *Area 28,750 sq km; population 3,100,100; capital, Tirana (pop. 225,000); currency, lek (100 quindarka); official language, Albanian.*

Independent since 1912, formerly Turkish. A small republic, Albania lies to the south of Yugoslavia, with a western coastline on the Adriatic Sea. The country is mountainous, with lime soils and karst in the north. Grain and citrus fruits are grown, and sheep and goats are reared.

ANDORRA - *Area 455 sq km; population 47,000; capital, Andorra La Vella (pop. 15,000); currency, franc and peseta.*

A tiny state in the Pyrenees between France and Spain, Andorra consists of wild and rugged tree-covered mountains. Since 1278, the protecting powers have been France and the Spanish Bishopric of Urgel. The main product is tobacco. French and Spanish are spoken, as well as the native Catalan.

AUSTRIA - *Area 83,855 sq km; population 7,503,000; capital, Vienna (pop. 1,562,000); currency, schilling (100 groschen); official language, German.*

After the collapse of the Austro-Hungarian Monarchy, the first republic lasted from 1918 to 1938. Then came the *Anschluss* with the German Reich, lasting until 1945, when Austria again became a federal republic.

The south is mountainous, but to the north and north-east the land slopes gently down to the Danube. Cereal crops are cultivated there. The mountain forests produce wood that is used for export or goes to paper factories. Mineral products include iron, magnesium, lead, zinc, copper and oil. The metal processing and machine industries are prosperous.

BELGIUM - *Area 30,515 sq km; population 9,900,000; capital, Brussels (pop. 1,010,000); currency, franc (100 centimes); official languages, French (south), Flemish (north), Dutch, and German.*

An independent monarchy since 1830, formerly linked with the Netherlands, Belgium is thickly populated, with 325 people per sq km.

The country consists mainly of lowland. Agriculture has been developed to a high degree, and modern farming methods take advantage of the fertile soil and damp climate. Grain, sugarbeet, and potatoes are grown, and vegetables and flowers are cultivated under glass. Cattle and pigs are reared. The main industries are chemicals, textiles, and metals, and the production of glass for mirrors and windows.

BULGARIA - *Area 110,900 sq km; population 8,900,000; capital, Sofia (pop. 1,130,000); currency, lev (100 stotinki); official language, Bulgarian.*

Bulgaria won independence from Turkey in 1878, and in 1946 decided by plebiscite to become a Socialist People's Republic. It has been a democratic republic since 1990.

The country has a varying landscape, with mountain ranges (Balkans and Rhodope Alps) and lowland stretching away in the north to the River Danube. Cereals, fruit, vines, tobacco, sunflowers, and strawberries are cultivated. There are deposits of coal, petroleum, lead, and zinc.

CZECHOSLOVAKIA - *Area 127,880 sq km; population 15,600,000; capital, Prague (pop. 1,195,000); currency, koruna (100 haléru); official languages, Czech and Slovak.*

The state of Czechoslovakia was constituted in 1918 out of the union of Bohemia and Moravia (the inhabitants of both of which were known as 'Czechs') and Slovakia. A socialist federal republic after World War II, the country became a democratic federal republic in 1989.

Bohemia, in the northwest, is bordered by forests and mountains. The plains are well cultivated. Slovakia is mountainous, and has extensive meadowland and thick forestland. The country was highly industrialized even before the war, especially in Bohemia and Moravia.

DENMARK - *Area 43,070 sq km; population 5,125,000; capital, Copenhagen (pop. 1,343,000); currency, krone (100 øre); official language, Danish.*

Denmark has a monarchy dating back to before AD 1000.

The country consists of the peninsula of Jutland, which extends northwards from Germany, and 483 large and small islands. Danish agriculture is one of the most highly developed in the world. There is extensive pig and cattle rearing, and milk, butter, and cheese are exported.

ESTONIA - *Area 45,000 sq km; population 1,585,000; capital, Tallinn (pop. 485,000); currency, rouble (100 copecks); official language, Estonian.*

Originally one of the confederated republics of the USSR, it became an independent parliamentary republic in 1991.

The country is entirely low-lying, with modest resources of petroleum and methane. Fishing, with its related industries, is an important source of income.

FINLAND - *Area 337,010 sq km; population 4,940,000; capital, Helsinki (pop. 970,000); currency, markka (100 penniä); official languages, Finnish and Swedish.*

A parliamentary republic, Finland is a land of lakes and forests. There are some 55,000 lakes, which cover a tenth of the country, and forestland covers as much as two-thirds. The wood processing industry is of prime importance, and Finnish furniture and ready-made houses are highly prized everywhere. Cattle rearing and dairy produce also provide export surpluses, especially butter.

FRANCE - *Area 547,025 sq km; population 55,750,000; capital, Paris (pop. 10,210,000); currency, franc (100 centimes); official language, French.*

France is a parliamentary republic, which lies between the Atlantic and the Mediterranean; it is separated from Switzerland by the Jura Mountains, from Italy by the Alps, and from Spain by the Pyrenees. There are extensive plains along the Loire and the Garonne, and in the Paris basin. The climate is extremely favourable and agriculture is profitable. Cereals (especially wheat), vegetables, fruit, wine, and sugar-beet are the main crops. Cattle rearing is not quite as comprehensive, but the many varieties of delicious French cheeses are famous. The manufacture of machinery and cars, the aircraft industry, textile mills, and chemical works are all evidence of the country's increasing industrialization. France is a favourite tourist country by reason of its beautiful scenery and sea coasts, its excellent cuisine, its charming towns, and the wealth of its historical architecture.

GERMANY - *Area 356,970 sq km; population 79,100,000; capital, Berlin (3,308,000); currency, Deutsch Mark (100 pfennig); official language, German.*

A federal republic consisting of 16 *länder*, it was established on 23rd May 1949 on the territory occupied by the American, British and French armed forces. On 3rd October 1990 the German Democratic Republic, which had been established in 1949 on territory occupied by the Soviet armed forces, was dissolved and incorporated into Germany.

The country extends from the Alps to the North and the Baltic Seas and includes the southern part of the Jutland peninsula, which divides the two seas. From north to south the country divides into a vast plain in the north — part of the Great European Plain, a central highland area and a mountainous area in the south, which gradually rises to the Alps. It is fed by numerous navigable rivers, the most important being the Rhine, the Weser, the Elbe, and part of the Danube.

Cultivation includes cereals (barley, wheat, rye and oats), potatoes, vegetables, sugar-beet, hops, flax and animal fodder. Mineral resources include coal (particularly lignite, of which ex-East Germany is the biggest producer in the world), lead, zinc, potassium, radio-active minerals and natural gas from the bed of the North Sea. The most important industries are iron and steel in the Ruhr valley, engineering (particularly cars), chemicals (particularly pharmaceuticals), precision engineering and optical engineering. Industrial development has been facilitated by the excellent river network, and especially by the Rhine which carries most of the European river traffic.

GIBRALTAR - *Area 6 sq km; population 30,000; capital, Gibraltar (pop. 20,000); currency, pound (100 pence); official language, English.*

At the southern end of the Iberian Peninsula, the rocky promontory of Gibraltar occupies a strategic position at the entrance to the Mediterranean. It has been a British colony since 1713, and in a referendum held in 1967 the people voted almost unanimously to retain the link with Britain rather than return to Spain.

GREECE - *Area 131,945 sq km; population 9,700,000; capital, Athens (pop. 3,030,000; currency, drachma, (100 lepta); official language, Greek.*

This politically troubled land became a 'presidential parliamentary republic' in 1973, when the 'crowned democracy' was declared at an end.

Greece is a country of peninsulas and islands, reaching out from the Balkans into the eastern Mediterranean. Most of the country is mountainous. The mild climate is favourable for the cultivation of the vine, fruit, olives, and tobacco. Marble and emery are the most prized mineral products. Tourism is an important economic activity, for the products of the art of Ancient Greece attract visitors from all over the world.

HUNGARY - *Area 93,030 sq km; population 10,715,000; capital, Budapest (pop. 2,065.000); currency, forint (100 fillér); official language, Hungarian (Magyar).*
Until 1918, when it was proclaimed a republic, Hungary formed a joint monarchy with Austria. A People's Republic since 1949, it became a democratic republic in 1989.
Apart from the northern part of the country bordering on Czechoslovakia, Hungary is a tableland. Along the Danube (Duna) and the Tisza, the land is very fertile, but in the east it is dry and steppe-like. The main source of revenue is agriculture, and in the north vines are grown. Petroleum, brown coal, and rich bauxite deposits are exploited. There is considerable chemical and engineering industry around Budapest.

ICELAND - *Area 103,000 sq km; population 247,000; capital, Reykjavik (pop. 120,000); currency, króna (100 aurar); official language, Icelandic.*
Iceland formerly belonged to Denmark, but became an independent kingdom in 1918 and then, in 1944, a republic.
Most of the ground consists of solid lava, and there are still a few volcanic vents. Little land is left that can be used for agriculture. The most important source of revenue is fishing. The houses are heated by the numerous hot springs.

IRELAND, REPUBLIC OF - *Area 70,285 sq km; population 3,540,000; capital, Dublin (pop. 921,000); currency, pound (100 pence); official languages, English and Irish.*
Ireland lies west of Great Britain, across the Irish Sea, and consists of the Republic of Ireland, which has been independent since 1948, and the north-eastern part, Northern Ireland, which is part of the United Kingdom.
There is an extensive flat stretch of land with lakes, bordered on north and south by highland country. Ireland is called the 'Emerald Isle' because of its lush pastures — the essential raw material for the prosperous cattle rearing industry. The main agricultural products are cereals and potatoes. The manufacture of foodstuffs is an important industry.

ITALY - *Area 301,265 sq km; population 57,580,000; capital, Rome (pop. 2,830,000); currency, lira; official language, Italian.*
Italy as we know it today was not unified until 1861. It remained a monarchy until after World War II, when, in 1946, the people voted to make it a republic.
The Italian peninsula is bounded in the north by the Alps, and is traversed by the Apennines, running from north-west to south-east, for the whole of its length. In the north, south of the Alps, the fertile plain of the Po stretches to the Adriatic Sea. The most important agricultural products are wheat, rice, maize, vegetables, olives, citrus fruits, and the vine. Italy produces and exports more wine than any other country. There are abundant supplies of marble. Important industries include metal-working, mechanical engineering (especially motorcars), the processing of foodstuffs, and oil refining. Tourism is a major source of revenue, for no other country in the world possesses so many ancient art treasures.

LATVIA - *Area 64,000 sq km; population 2,690,000; capital, Riga (pop. 915,000); currency, rouble (100 copecks); official language, Latvian.*
Originally one of the confederated republics of the USSR, it became an independent parliamentary republic in 1991.
Facing onto the Baltic Sea, it consists of a gently undulating plain, crossed by the River Dvina. The economy is based principally on agriculture, forestry and livestock farming, with their related industries.

LIECHTENSTEIN - *Area 155 sq km; population 28,000; capital, Vaduz (pop. 5,000); currency, Swiss franc (100 rappen); official language, German.*
Liechtenstein has been a hereditary principality since the 1340s, and became an independent state in 1719.
It is a tiny country, consisting of nothing but mountains, between Austria and Switzerland. It is almost completely covered with forests.

LITHUANIA - *Area 65,000 sq km; population 3,725,000; capital, Vilnius (pop. 585,000); currency, rouble (100 copecks); official language, Lithuanian.*
One of the confederated republics of the Soviet Union since 1940, it became an independent parliamentary republic in 1991.
It consists of a large undulating plain crossed by the River Neman and surrounded to the East by about 4,000 lakes of glacial origin. It is mainly agricultural, its principal products being potatoes, animal fodder and flax. Cattle and pig farming are highly productive as is fishing on the lakes and rivers.

LUXEMBOURG - *Area 2,585 sq km; population 365,000; capital, Luxembourg (pop. 86,000); currency, franc (100 centimes); official languages, French, Luxembourgeois, and German.*
The Grand Duchy of Luxembourg has been independent since 1890.
It is a hilly country, and potatoes, cereals, and fruit are cultivated. The main source of revenue comes from the mining of iron ore.

MALTA - *Area 315 sq km; population 345,000; capital, Valletta (pop. 9,200); currency, pound (100 cents); official languages, Maltese and English.*
An island in the middle of the Mediterranean to the south of Sicily, Malta (which also includes the smaller islands of Gozo and Comino) became an independent country in 1964, after 150 years of British rule. The island has a mountainous landscape. Cereals, vines, and vegetables are cultivated.

MONACO - *Area 1.95 sq km; population 27,000; capital, Monaco (pop. 1,700); currency, French franc (100 centimes); official languages, French and Monégasque.*
This little hereditary constitutional principality lies on the French Mediterranean coast to the east of Nice.
Its favourable climate and the well-known Monte Carlo casino attract many tourists.

NETHERLANDS - *Area 40,845 sq km; population 14,000,000; currency, guilder (100 cents); official language, Dutch.*
After a period of domination by France, the Netherlands became an independent constitutional monarchy in 1815. At that time it also included what are now Belgium (broke away in 1830) and Luxembourg (1890).
The land is a plain, partly below sea level and protected by high dykes. The port of Rotterdam (pop. 1,025,000) has the largest turnover of merchandise in the world. The marine climate brings heavy rainfall, and the fertile soil bears rich crops of vegetables, flowers, and potatoes. Cereals are grown principally as fodder for the abundant cattle, which produce milk and cheese. The foodstuffs processing industry is highly developed. There are large margarine factories, electrical engineering works, and petroleum refineries.

NORWAY - *Area 324,220 sq km; population 4,220,000; capital, Oslo (pop. 460,000); currency, krone (100 öre); official languages, Bokmål (or Riksmål) and Nynorsk (or Landsmål).*
Norway was at various times united with Denmark or Sweden, and has a monarchy that goes back a thousand years.
Most of the country is mountainous, with deep fjords along the coast. The Gulf Stream provides a mild climate for the latitude, so that the Atlantic ports remain free of ice throughout the winter. The most important economic activity is fishing. Huge pine forests provide wood for the paper industry. In the tundra of the far north, there are 22,000 nomadic Lapps, who keep reindeer. Hydraulic power is drawn from the numerous waterfalls, and these provide even the smallest villages with electricity. Iron ore is mined, and oil began to be extracted from the North Sea fields in the 1970s.

POLAND - *Area 312,675 sq km; population 37,735,000; capital, Warsaw (pop. 1,580,000); currency, zloty (100 groszy); official language, Polish.*
Poland was once a monarchy, but its powerful neighbours several times forced it into accepting partial or total partitioning of its territory. After World War II, the victorious powers fixed Poland's new borders.
In 1947 it became a People's Republic, which it remained until 1989.
Most of Poland lies in the plain that stretches from Russia to northern Germany. Only towards the south does the land become at all mountainous. The most important economic activity is still agriculture, and the potato harvest is the second largest in the world. Cattle rearing provides meat exports as well as covering Poland's own needs. Slesia has rich mineral deposits, including considerable resources of coal, iron, lead, and zinc.

PORTUGAL - *Area 92,080 sq km; population 10,203,000; capital, Lisbon (pop. 2,010,000); currency, escudo (100 centavos); official language, Portuguese.*
Portugal was a monarchy until 1910, and has been an independent country since the 12th century. A military coup in 1974 saw the return of a multi-party system after a period of authoritarian rule.
The country occupies most of the western part of the Iberian Peninsula, and its traversed by mountain ranges and by rivers such as the Douro and Tagus (Tejo) that rise in Spain and flow into the Atlantic. Nearly half the people work on the land and in the forests. The mild climate is favourable to the cultivation of vegetables, cereal crops, olives, and, above all, the vine. Port, a fortified wine, is exported to countries all over the world. Fishing is an important industry, most of the catch (especially sardines and tuna) being canned. The harbour towns of Lisbon and Oporto have large industrial areas. Portugal has the most extensive cork forests in the world. The lovely coastline and picturesque forests attract large numbers of tourists.

ROMANIA - *Area 237,500 sq km; population 22,940,000; capital, Bucharest (pop. 2,190,000); currency, leu (100 bani); official language, Romanian.*

After being under Turkish control for a number of years, Romania became fully independent in 1878. It was a monarchy until 1947, and a year later a communist government was set up. It has been a democratic republic since December 1989.

The country is traversed by two crescent-shaped and wooded ranges of the Carpathians. Between them lies the Transylvanian plateau. The plains of Walachia and Moldavia extend towards the south and east, broken by the tributaries of the Danube and a number of lakes. In the south-east, the country reaches the Black Sea. Most workers are employed on the land, but the country's main wealth stems predominantly from industry and mining.

SAN MARINO - *Area 61 sq km; population 21,000; capital, San Marino (pop. 2,800); currency, Italian lira; official language, Italian.*

The independence of San Marino, the world's smallest republic, goes back to the 1200s, and it was founded about AD 350. Its status was recognized by Italy in 1862.

Entirely surrounded by Italy, the country lies on the eastern slopes of the Apennines. The main sources of revenue are agriculture, stock-breeding, and tourism.

SPAIN - *Area 504,780 sq km; population 38,870,000; capital, Madrid (pop. 3,100,000); currency, peseta (100 céntimos); official language, Castilian Spanish (Basque, Catalan, and Galician are spoken in their respective regions).*

A monarchy for many centuries, Spain became a republic in 1931. After the parties of the left had been successful in the 1936 elections, civil war broke out. It lasted three years, and the victorious General Franco became head of state. In 1947, he declared that Spain would revert to a monarchy, which it did when he died 28 years later.

Spain has two large plains—the Ebro basin in Aragon and the dry basin of the Guadalquivir in lower Andalusia. The rest of the country is mountainous, with, in the centre, the largely rainless Meseta plateau, which covers three-quarters of the country. Cereal crops, vines, and olives are grown there. A third of the work force is engaged in agriculture, either as labourers on private estates or as smallholders. One big problem is the migration of young people to the towns and tourist centres.

SWEDEN *Area 449,965 sq km; population 8,450,000; capital, Stockholm (pop. 1,470,000); currency, krona (100 öre); official language, Swedish.*

The Swedish monarchy has existed for nearly a thousand years. For more than the last 150 of these, Sweden has been involved in no wars. The social welfare and school systems are exemplary.

The eastern half of the Scandinavian mountain chain lies in Sweden. The land falls away gradually to the south-east until it reaches the Baltic. Numerous waterfalls are exploited for electric power. One-twelfth of the country is covered by lakes. In the plains, vast fields of wheat, sugar-beet, and potatoes are to be seen, and the forests of central Sweden provide immense quantities of timber. What is not exported is processed for furniture, cellulose, and paper. Sweden is a highly industrialized country, manufacturing, in particular, high-quality steel. Other important industries are ship-building, car and ball-bearing manufacture, and chemicals. The northern parts are peopled by several thousand Lapps, who live largely by rearing reindeer.

SWITZERLAND - *Area 41,295 sq km; population 6,630,000; capital, Bern (pop. 285,000); currency, franc (100 centimes or rappen); official languages, German, French, and Italian.*

The Federal Government consists of 22 basically independent *cantons*, whose parishes also enjoy the right to a considerable amount of self-administration. The country has been neutral for some 150 years.

Sandwiched between Austria and France in one direction, and between Italy and West Germany in another, Switzerland lies squarely in the Alps, and half of the country is higher than 1,000 metres. The northern part, the so-called *Mittelland* (the Swiss plateau), has a surface broken by many lakes and rivers. The main crop there is wheat, but on the mountain slopes cattle are reared and there is much dairy farming. Swiss industry is highly specialized, being concentrated on foodstuffs, pharmaceutical products, and precision engineering (especially watches and clocks). Tourism is very important, particularly in the many areas suitable for skiing.

UNITED KINGDOM *Area 244,045 sq km; population 56,930,000; capital, London (pop. 6,875,000); currency, pound (100 pence); official language, English.*

The United Kingdom of Great Britain and Northern Ireland is governed by a system of parliamentary democracy. The country is generally hilly, and Scotland and Wales are mountainous. The rivers are not very long, but they are for the most part navigable. The climate tends to be unsettled. Britain imports much food, especially from its former colonies, which today belong to the Commonwealth, of which Britain is the head. Sheep rearing is an important industry, producing meat and wool. Fishing is also important, and coal and other minerals produce considerable revenue. It was in Britain that the Industrial Revolution began in the 18th century, and this led to economic prosperity—textiles, engineering, motor-car and aeroplane manufacturing, and shipbuilding. Britain has also played a leading role in the development of rail traffic, and its merchant navy is one of the finest in the world. The country's insular situation, its many excellent river ports, and its frontage on the Atlantic Ocean, have made of the British a nation of mariners. Since the 1970's Britain, with its dwindling prosperity, has been trying to off-set its severe balance-of-trade deficit by the exploitation of its considerable North Sea oil resources.

ex-USSR - *Area 22,000,000 sq km (in Europe 5,443,000 sq km); population 278,000,000 (in Europe 206,600,000); capital, Moscow (pop. 8,800,000); currency, rouble (100 copecks); official language Russian.*

A socialist federal republic since 1922. With the dissolution of the People's Congress in September 1991 a new confederation of sovereign states was formed. There are 12 ex-Soviet republics: Russia, the Ukraine, White Russia, Kazakistan, Tadzhikistan, Khirghizia, Azerbaydzhan, Georgia, Turkmenistan, Uzbekistan, Moldavia, and Armenia.

In area, the Soviet Union is the largest country in the world, occupying more than half the continent of Europe and about a third of Asia. The centre and north of the European part is tableland. In the south, the frontier is formed by the Caucasus Mountains. The Volga is the longest river in Europe, and the most important in Russia. Beyond the Ural Mountains, the Asian part of the USSR consists of the western Siberian lowlands, the mountainous area of central and eastern Siberia, the flat and partially desert area of central Asia reaching as far as the Pamirs, and the Far East, bounded by the Sea of Okhotsk and the Sea of Japan.

As may be expected from the extent of the country, there is a wide range of climate. In the tundra of the extreme north, the ground never really thaws out, whereas vines and tea plants grow in the south. Inland, the summers are hot and the winters extremely cold.

Once an agricultural country, the Soviet Union is now an industrial world power. Even the extensive collectivized agriculture is largely automated. The country is rich in mineral resources, the conditions for the exploitation of which in the eastern areas are being constantly improved. Scientifically and technically, the USSR is one of the leading nations of the world.

VATICAN CITY STATE - *Area 0.44 sq km; population 1,000; capital, Vatican City; currency, Italian lira; official languages, Latin and Italian.*

The present-day frontiers of the Vatican, which lies wholly within Rome, were recognized by Italy in 1871, and the full and independent sovereignty of the Holy See was ratified in 1929. The museums of the Vatican are visited by hundreds of thousands of tourists every year.

YUGOSLAVIA - *Area 255,805 sq km; population, 23,560,000; capital, Belgrade (pop. 1,475,000); currency, dinar (100 paras); official languages, Serbo-Croatian, Slovene, and Macedonian.*

The present-day Socialist Federal Republic consists of six republics: Serbia, Slovenia, Croatia, Bosnia-Herzegovina, Montenegro, and Macedonia. Up to 1918, most of the country belonged to the Austro-Hungarian monarchy. Since 1991, profound political and institutional changes have been taking place.

Bare karst mountains fringe the Adriatic Sea. Inland, most of the agricultural exploitable plains lie along the Danube and its tributaries. The main crops are wheat, maize, tobacco, and vines, and stone fruits (plums, cherries) that are used in making highly popular alcoholic beverages. There are rich deposits of bauxite, lead, and zinc. The beautiful Adriatic coast has become an important centre of tourism.

Countries of Asia

AFGHANISTAN - *Area 652,900 sq km; population 15,900,000; capital, Kabul (pop. 1,297,000); currency, afghani (100 puls); official languages, Dari Persian and Pushtu.*

The country, a presidential republic since 1987, is entirely landlocked, lying between Iran, USSR, China and Pakistan. The great mountain range of the Hindu Kush extends north-east to south-west across the country, some of its peaks rising to about 7,600 m. The longest of the many rivers is the Helmand. Only some 12 per cent of the land is cultivated, and many people live as nomadic herdsmen, wandering over the mountain pastures with their herds of goats and karakul sheep. In the villages, cereals, sugar-beet, fruit, and cotton are grown. Exports include lambskins, carpets, and fruit. Manufacturing industries, especially textiles, are being developed.

BAHRAIN - *Area 670 sq km; population 421,000; capital, Manama (pop. 115,000); currency, dinar (1,000 fils); official language, Arabic.*

The state, a hereditary monarchy, independent since 1971, consists of several islands in the Persian Gulf, the largest of which is Bahrain Island. Once famous for its pearl fisheries, it has become rich by oil production. Its social services are highly developed.

BANGLADESH - *Area 144,000 sq km; population 102,800,000; capital, Dacca (pop. 4,500,000); currency, taka (100 poisha); official languages, Bengali and Bihari.*

Until 1971, the country was East Pakistan, but in that year it broke away from Pakistan after a bloody civil war, becoming a presidential republic. Its territory consists of part of Assam and the old province of East Bengal. Much of it is an alluvial plain formed by the Ganges and the Jamuna. The delta of the Ganges, on the Bay of Bengal, is the world's largest. The chief products are jute, rice, tea, and tobacco.

BHUTAN - *Area 46,000 sq km; population 1,300,000; capital, Thimphu (pop. 15,000); currency, ngultrum (100 chetrum); official language, Dzongka.*

Small kingdom in the Himalayas, lying between Tibet (China) and India, it is a hereditary monarchy. Most of its people live in the fertile valleys in the centre of the country. The south has forested lowlands, and the north is fringed by high mountain peaks. The way of life is very similar to that of Tibet. Most of the people live by farming; their chief crops are rice, wheat, and barley.

BRUNEI - *Area 5,765 sq km; population 230,000; capital, Bandar Seri Begawan (pop. 55,000); currency, dollar (100 cents); languages, Malay, Chinese, and English.*

Brunei, on the northern coast of Borneo, independent since 1983, is a hereditary monarchy ruled by a Sultan.

BURMA - *Area 676,550 sq km; population 35,300,000; capital, Rangoon (pop. 2,660,000); currency, kyat (100 pyas); official language, Burmese.*

The country became independent in 1948 after several generations of British rule.

The Arakan Mountains extend along the western side of the country, and the eastern half is a high plateau, the Shan Massif. Between the mountains and the plateau is a lowland drained by the Irrawaddy and Sittang rivers. Another great river, the Salween, flows near the eastern border. A narrow strip of land, the Tenasserim Coast, stretches southwards to the Malay Peninsula. Burma is rich in mineral resources—oil, precious stones, and metals. The chief crops are rice, wheat, millet, sugar-cane, ground-nuts, and tobacco. The forests yield teak and other woods. Most of the people are Burmans.

CHINA - *Area 9,560,980 sq km; population 1,057,210,000; capital, Peking (pop. 9,579,000); currency, yuan (10 chiao; 100 fen); official language, Chinese (Mandarin).*

The People's Republic of China, occupying more than one-fifth of Asia, is the home of about one-fifth of all the people in the world. Its history goes back nearly 4,000 years, and it has one of the oldest and most highly-developed civilizations. Vast areas of the country are almost uninhabited, but there are also many huge cities.

In the east, there is a 6,800-km coastline on the Pacific Ocean. The Formosa Strait separates China from another Chinese country, Taiwan. On the south, west, and north, lofty mountain ranges form natural frontiers. The high plateau of Tibet in the south-west lies between the Kunlun Mountains (to the north) and the Himalayas, the world's highest mountain range (to the south). Beyond the Kunlun Mountains is the Takla Makan Desert. In the north, in Inner Mongolia, is part of another great desert, the Gobi. The eastern part of China, the part where most of the people live, consists of two great river basins separated by the Chin Ling range. To the north of this range is the plain crossed by the Hwang Ho—the Yellow River, so called because of the yellow mud that colours its waters. To the south is the plain of the Yangtze-Kiang. These lowland regions are the historic China, the part of the country that the Great Wall was built to protect. In the north and in the mountains the winters are bitterly cold. In the south, the climate is tropical or sub-tropical. The south-eastern coast suffers from typhoons and other destructive storms. In the interior, the rainfall is irregular and droughts and floods have caused famine from time immemorial. Today, dams and irrigation give some measure of protection. Rice and wheat are the chief crops. In the Yangtze valley as many as three rice crops are harvested each year. The government has encouraged the development of industry, and, as a result, there are now thriving metallurgic and mechanical industries.

CYPRUS - *Area 9,250 sq km; population 680,000; capital, Nicosia (pop. 125,000); currency, pound (1,000 mils); official languages, Greek and Turkish.*

The island republic of Cyprus, in the Mediterranean Sea, was under British rule until 1960. Since independence it has suffered from conflict between the Greek majority (four-fifths of the population) and the Turkish minority.

The island, the third largest in the Mediterranean, has two mountain ranges: the Kyrenia Range in the north, and the Troodos Mountains in the centre and west. Between these ranges lies a fertile plain, the Mesaoria. The country is rich in minerals, including copper and asbestos. Agricultural products, such as cereals, wine, fruit, and tobacco, are the chief source of income.

HONG KONG - *Area 1,045 sq km; population 5,400,000; capital, Victoria (pop. 680,000); currency, dollar (100 cents); official languages, English and Chinese.*

The British crown colony of Hong Kong, on the southern coast of China, consists of Hong Kong Island, more than 200 other small islands, and Kowloon and the New Territories on the mainland. It is an important financial, industrial, and trading centre.

INDIA - *Area 3,287,780 sq km; population 685,184,000; capital, New Delhi (pop. 5,730,000); currency, rupeé (100 paise); official language, Hindi.*

Once 'the brightest jewel in the British crown', India has been an independent federal republic since 1947. It has more people than any other country except China. India's civilization is one of the world's oldest, dating back to at least 2500 BC.

The country occupies the greater part of the Indian Peninsula, its neighbours in the peninsula being Pakistan and Bangladesh. Its coastline on the Indian Ocean measures some 6,800 km. The terrain is very varied. Foothills of the Himalayas extend along 2,400 km of the northern border. To their south, the alluvial lowlands of the Northern Plains stretch right across the widest part of the peninsula. They have India's richest farming land, and are heavily populated. Still farther south is the Deccan Plateau, occupying the greater part of the peninsula. On both coastal edges it rises to mountain ranges called the *Ghats*. Almost all parts of the country are crossed by great rivers, but the most important are in the north: the Indus, the Ganges, and the Brahmaputra. In most areas, the south-west monsoon brings heavy rains each year from June to September. Much of the country is very hot, the coolest areas being in the hills and on the west coast. Rice and wheat are the most important crops. Other crops are millet, ground-nuts, bananas, cotton, rapeseed, linseed, and jute. There are great numbers of cattle, sheep, and goats; cattle are sacred to the Hindus and are not used for food. The most important manufactures are textiles, but the development of other industries is a major part of government planning. One of the country's most serious problems is over-population.

INDONESIA - *Area 1,904,345 sq km; population 172,244,000; capital, Djakarta (pop. 7,800,000); currency, rupiah (100 sen); official language, Bahasa Indonesia.*

The country, a presidential republic, independent since 1945, consists of about 3,000 islands grouped between the Indian and Pacific oceans. The largest are Sumatra, Celebes, and Java. Indonesia shares two other large islands: Borneo with Malaysia, and New Guinea with Papua New Guinea. Most of the larger islands are mountainous and volcanic. There are more than 200 volcanoes, of which about 60 are active and 125 more eject sulphur fumes. The most densely populated island is Java: more than half of all Indonesian live on it and it is the seat of the government. It has rich agricultural land in the north, and it is well known for its waxprinted fabric, called *batik*. Many of the other, lightly-populated islands are thickly forested, and some are swampy. The climate is generally humid and sultry, the hottest regions being on the islands that lie on the equator—

Sumatra and Kalimantan (the Indonesian part of Borneo), for example. All the islands are affected by the monsoons. Indonesia has rich mineral deposits, chiefly petroleum, tin, and bauxite. Rubber, tea, coffee, tobacco, and sugar are grown on plantations. The chief subsistence crops are rice and other cereals, bananas, spices, and beans.

IRAN - *Area 1,648,000 sq km; population 49,764,000; capital Tehran (pop. 6,000,000); currency, rial (100 dinars); official language, Farsi (Persian).*
The Islamic republic of Iran lies between the Caspian Sea in the north, and the Persian Gulf and Arabian Sea in the south. It was once called *Persia*. It is mostly a vast, mountain-fringed plateau, averaging some 1,200 m above sea-level. However, part of the Great Sand Desert, the Dasht-i-Lut, in the east-centre is some 250 m below sea-level. This desert is one of the hottest in the world. To its north is the Great Salt Desert, the Dasht-i-Kavir. The northern coastal strip is the only major agricultural area, and the chief crops are cereals, tea, fruit, and cotton. Several million people live nomadic lives as herdsmen. The rich mineral deposits include petroleum.

IRAQ - *Area 434,900 sq km; population 16,335,000; capital, Baghdad (pop. 3,810,000); currency, dinar (1,000 fils); official language, Arabic.*
The country, a presidential republic, has been independent since 1958; previously it had been under Turkish and, from 1920, British rule.
The lowlands in the centre of Iraq are the basins of the Tigris and Euphrates rivers. These great rivers are the frontiers of the historic region of *Mesopotamia*, 'the country between the rivers'. On the north, the lowlands are bordered by wooded hills, which are part of *Kurdistan*. The people of this region, the Kurds, look upon themselves as a separate nation. In the west of Iraq are the barren wastes of the Syrian Desert. The country's chief source of revenue is petroleum, and it has other minerals, too. Cereals, cotton, vegetables, and tobacco are the principal agricultural products.

ISRAEL - *Area 20,770 sq km; population 4,331,000; capital, Jerusalem (pop. 469,000); currency, shekel (100 agorots); official languages, Hebrew and Arabic.*
Since its foundation in 1948, Israel, a parliamentary republic, has fought a continuing war against various of its hostile Arab neighbours.
About half of the country is occupied by the Negev Desert, but the north is mountainous and there is also a low-lying coastal strip. Much desert land has been made arable by being cleared and irrigated. This pioneer work was carried out by *kibbutzim*, community settlements. Intensive agriculture is of major importance to the economy. The chief products are cereals, citrus fruits, grapes (for eating and for wine), and vegetables. There are textile, engineering, and chemical industries in addition to food processing. Mineral resources include potash, phosphates, oil, and natural gas.

JAPAN - *Area 372,839 sq km; population 122,779,000; capital Tokyo (pop. 12,000,000); currency, yen (100 sen); official language, Japanese.*
Nippon Koku, 'the Land of the Rising Sun', has an emperor who belongs to one of the world's oldest ruling dynasties.
The country consists of an archipelago in the Pacific Ocean, separated from the Asian mainland by the Sea of Japan. There are four main islands: Honshu, Hokkaido, Kyushu, and Shikoku. Among the more than 3,000 smaller islands there are two major groups: the Ryukyus and the Bonins. Most of the islands are mountainous, the highest peaks being on Honshu. Among them is Fujiyama, the highest mountain in Japan, which rises to 3,776 m. This snow-mantled peak is a volcano, but not active. There are nearly 200 other volcanoes, some of which erupt from time to time. Earthquakes are frequent, but generally they cause only minor damage. The islands have many rivers, some of which are very fastflowing, and are consequently suitable for the production of hydro-electricity. Most of Japan's farms are small. The chief crops are rice and other cereals, fruit, and vegetables. But because only a small part of the land can be cultivated, Japan has to import much of its food. It also has to import most of the raw materials that feed its industries. In spite of this the country has raised itself to the front rank of industrial powers, and has a leading place among producers of optical goods, cameras, radio and television equipment, and motor vehicles, including motorcycles. It is also a major shipbuilding country, and it has built up one of the world's largest fishing fleets. Japan is very densely populated but—in contrast to most other Asian countries—its population has risen slowly in recent years.

JORDAN - *Area 97,700 sq km; population 3,600,000; capital, Amman (pop. 972,000); currency, dinar (1,000 fils); official language, Arabic.*
The Hashemite Kingdom of the Jordan, a hereditary monarchy, is a mountainous country lying mainly to the east of the Jordan River. At the southern end of the river is the Dead Sea, the Earth's lowest surface point. The north-east of the country is part of the barren Syrian Desert. Only one-tenth of the land is agriculturally productive. The chief crops are cereals, olives, citrus fruits, and tomatoes. Phosphates and some other minerals are exported, and there are manufacturing industries and oil refining.

KAMPUCHEA - *Area 181,035 sq km; population 6,689,000; capital, Phnom Penh (pop. 750,000); currency, riel (100 sen); official language, Khmer.*
Kampuchea in Indochina was formerly the kingdom of Cambodia. Formerly a People's Republic, it has been a democratic republic since 1989.
Much of the country lies in the fertile alluvial basin of the Mekong River, but there are mountains in the north and south-west. Most people live by farming or fishing. The chief subsistence crop is rice, and other crops include cotton, pepper, tobacco, and rubber. Fish are taken from the Tonle Sap, the 'Great Lake', in the west.

KOREA, NORTH - *Area 120,540 sq km; population 18,450,000; capital, Pyongyang (pop. 2,639,000); currency, won (100 chon); official language, Korean.*
The peninsula of Korea on the north-east coast of China is separated from Japan by the Korea Strait. In 1910 it was annexed by Japan, and after World War II was occupied by Russian troops (in the north) and American troops (in the south). In 1948, the two occupation zones became separate states. A conflict between the two states from 1950 to 1953 involved several other countries, including the United States, China, Britain, and France. It ended with agreement that the 38° parallel should form the boundary between the two Koreas.
North Korea, the Democratic People's Republic of Korea, is mountainous and is very rich in minerals. It also has textile and engineering industries. The small amount of arable land is productive, the chief crops being cereals and cotton.

KOREA, SOUTH - *Area 99,143 sq km; population 40,467,000; capital Seoul (pop. 9,600,000); currency, won (100 chon); official language, Korean.*
The Republic of Korea occupies the southern part of the Korean Peninsula. It is generally mountainous, but the valleys and the southern plains are fertile. The chief crops are rice, vegetables, fruit, soya beans, and groundnuts. Manufactures include electrical goods and textiles, and there are some exports of minerals.

KUWAIT - *Area 17,800 sq km; population 2,048,000; capital, Kuwait City (pop. 168,000); currency, dinar (1,000 fils); official language, Arabic.*
The small, desert country of Kuwait—a hereditary constitutional monarchy, independent since 1961—has one of the world's highest *per capita* incomes as a result of its production of petroleum. It is believed to have about one-fifth of the world's known oil resources. It also produces natural gas. Much of its labour force consists of foreign workers from Saudi Arabia, Egypt, and other countries. There are highly-developed social services.

LAOS - *Area 236,800 sq km; population 3,720,000; capital, Vientiane (pop. 380,000); currency, new kip; official languages, Lao and French.*
Laos, fully independent since 1954 and now a People's Republic, was formerly part of French Indochina.
The country is landlocked, and its northern part is mountainous and heavily forested. In the south the land descends to the Mekong River; this regions is relatively fertile. The chief subsistence crops are rice and other cereals, but coffee, cotton, tea, and tobacco are also grown. The most important export is tin. Teak and other woods are exported, too.

LEBANON - *Area 10,400 sq km; population 2,200,000; capital, Beirut (pop. 900,000); currency, lira (100 piastres); official language, Arabic.*
Lebanon became an independent republic in 1944. Earlier, it had been part of the Ottoman Empire and, after World War I, a French mandated territory.
It has a narrow coastal strip on the eastern Mediterranean, behind which rise the Lebanon Mountains. Farther inland is the fertile Bekaa Valley, and then the heights of the Anti-Lebanon Mountains along the frontier with Syria. Only about one-third of the land is suitable for agriculture, the chief crops being citrus fruits, apples, grapes, olives, bananas, and tobacco. The country has many industries, and is an important financial and commercial centre. It is the only Arab state in which the Christian population is influential.

MACAO - *Area 16,9 sq km; population 275,000; capital, Macao (pop. 230,000); currency, pataca (100 avos); languages, Portuguese and Cantonese.*
Macao is an overseas province of Portugal. It consists of two small islands and a mainland

peninsula at the mouth of the Canton River in southern China. It is a popular tourist centre.

MALAYSIA - *Area 329,750 sq km; population 16,280,000; capital, Kuala Lumpur (pop. 1,100,000); currency, ringgit (100 sen); official language, Malay.*
The Federation of Malaysia became an independent country in 1963. Its territory consists of former British-ruled states in the southern part of the Malay Peninsula and the northern part of the island of Borneo. The peninsula regions are called *West Malaysia*, and those in Borneo *East Malaysia*. West Malaysia is separated by the Johore Strait from Singapore, which was part of the Federation until 1965. The peninsula has a mountain backbone; the western coastal plain is considerably wider than that in the east.
East Malaysia is extremely mountainous, its highest peak, Mount Kinabalu, rising to 4,100 m. About two-thirds of Malaysia is covered by thick rain forest. Rubber and timber are among the valuable forest products; Malaysia is the leading rubber producer in the world. There are rich deposits of tin, as well as mineral oils, iron, and bauxite. On the lowlands rice, peppers, and pineapples are grown.

MALDIVES - *Area 300 sq km; population 181,000; capital, Malé (pop. 55,000); currency, rupée (100 laari); official language, Maldivian.*
The Maldives, a former British protectorate and a presidential republic since 1968, consist of a chain of 12 atolls about 640 km south-west of Sri Lanka in the Indian Ocean. Altogether, there are about 2,000 coral islands of which some 200 are inhabited. No point is more than 2.4 m above sea-level.

MONGOLIA - *Area 1,565,000 sq km; population 1,900,000; capital Ulan Bator (pop. 500,000); currency, tugrik (100 mongo); official language, Khalkha Mongolian.*
From the 1600s to 1912, Mongolia was a Chinese province; its status was then in doubt until 1946 when China recognized its independence. It is now called the *Mongolian People's Republic*.
Most of the country consists of vast plateaux ringed by chains of mountains in the north and east. In the south-east is part of the Gobi Desert. Many of the people are herdsmen, but in recent years efforts have been made to develop agriculture. The country's mineral resources include coal, oil, and non-ferrous metals.

NEPAL - *Area 147,180 sq km; population 15,022,000; capital, Katmandu (pop. 393,000); currency, rupee (100 paisa); official language, Nepali.*
The Hindu kingdom of Nepal lies on the southern flank of the Himalayas, and Mount Everest (8,848 m) towers above its northern frontier. Most of the country is mountainous, and it has also thick jungles and swamps. The chief crops are rice and other cereals, and jute. In the villages, textiles and other woven goods are produced.

OMAN - *Area 212,500 sq km; population 1,370,000; capital, Muscat (pop. 50,000); currency, rial Omani (1,000 baiza); official language, Arabic.*
The sultanate of Oman, in the south-east of the Arabian Peninsula, has a long coastline on the Arabian Sea. The centre is low-lying but barren. In the north-east there are hills, and in the south-west the hot Dhofar Plateau. The chief exports are oil, dates, fish, and pearls.

PAKISTAN - *Area 803,945 sq km; population 89,740,000; capital Islamabad (pop. 200,000); currency, rupee (100 paisas); official language, Urdu.*
Until 1947, when it became an independent federal republic, the land that is now Pakistan was part of the British-ruled Indian Empire. In 1971, part of Pakistan—separated from the rest of the country by 1,500 km of Indian territory—broke away and formed the independent nation of Bangladesh after a bloody civil war.
Great mountain ranges rise along the north and north-west frontiers—the Himalaya, Hindu Kush, and Karakoram systems. On the boundary with Afghanistan is the Khyber Pass. About one-third of the country is a great plain, watered by the Indus. This plain was the site of one of the earliest civilizations. The climate is strongly affected by monsoons. Much of the country's agriculture depends on artificial irrigation. Cotton and rice are exported. There are textile, chemical, and other industries.

PHILIPPINES - *Area 300,000 sq km; population 48,070,000; capital, Manila (pop. 1,750,000); currency, peso (100 centavos); official language, Pilipino.*
The Philippines has been an independent republic since 1946. Before that, it was ruled by Spain for 300 years, and, after 1898, by the United States.
The country consists of more than 7,000 islands, extending for some 1,600 km between the Pacific Ocean and the South China Sea. The three largest islands are Luzon, Mindanao, and Palawan. About 700 islands are inhabited. Most of the islands are mountainous, and some have volcanoes. The chief crops are cereals, fruits, sugar, sweet potatoes, and hemp. There are valuable mineral deposits.

QATAR - *Area 11,000 sq km; population 370,000; capital, Doha (pop. 217,000); currency, riyal (100 dirhams); official language, Arabic.*
The sheikdom of Qatar occupies a 190-km long peninsula jutting northwards from the coast of Saudi Arabia into the Persian Gulf. Once a land of nomadic herdsmen, fishermen, and pearl divers, it has become a rich and important oil-producing state.

SAUDI ARABIA - *Area 2,149,700 sq km; population 7,200,000; capital, Riyadh (pop. 1,300,000); currency, riyal (20 qirshes); official language, Arabic.*
The kingdom of Saudi Arabia occupies the greater part of the Arabian Peninsula. The mountains of the Hejaz and Asir ranges extend along the west coast. Inland are rocky plateaux and deserts, the largest deserts being the An Nafud in the north, and the Rub'al Khali, the Empty Quarter, in the south. There are no permanent rivers. Many nomads roam the sandy wastes. The country has enormous revenues from oil production.

SINGAPORE - *Area 625 sq km; population 2,635,000; capital, Singapore (pop. 1,240,000); currency, dollar (100 cents); official languages, Malay, Chinese, Tamil, and English.*
The island country of Singapore, a parliamentary republic, is separated from the southern tip of the Malay Peninsula by the narrow Johore Strait. Until 1965 it was part of Malaysia, and before that was a British crown colony.
Most of the island is low-lying. It owes its importance to its fine harbour and its usefulness as a trade centre. In recent years it has greatly developed its industries. Its population is predominantly Chinese. The next largest group is Malay.

SRI LANKA - *Area 65,610 sq km; population 16,300,000; capital, Colombo (pop. 664,000); currency, rupee (100 cents); official language, Sinhala.*
A presidential republic since 1978, Sri Lanka is an island country in the Indian Ocean, off the southern tip of India. It was formerly called *Ceylon* and was British-ruled until 1948.
Most of the island is a fertile plain, but the southern part has mountains that rise to 2,550 m. Rice, tea, palms, and fruit grow in the tropical monsoon climate, and the forests provide rubber and valuable woods. Most of the people are Sinhalese, but there is a large Tamil minority. Unlike the Buddhist Sinhalese, the Tamils—who emigrated to Sri Lanka from southern India—are Hindus.

SYRIA - *Area 185,200 sq km; population 11,338,000; capital, Damascus (pop. 1,330,000); currency, pound (100 piastres); official language, Arabic.*
Syria, a presidential republic, became independent in 1946. Before that it had been ruled as a mandated territory by the French, and until 1919, as part of the Ottoman Empire.
The south of the country is in the Syrian Desert, to the north of which is the broad and fertile valley of the River Euphrates. Beyond the valley is a region of rough plains. The chief crops are wheat, barley, cotton, fruit, and tobacco. A number of cattle and sheep are also raised, and in the desert areas there are many nomadic herdsmen. Industries include food processing, and the manufacture of textiles and cement. Oil pipelines cross the desert from Iraq to the Mediterranean ports.

TAIWAN - *Area 35,980 sq km; population 19,672,000; capital, Taipei (pop. 2,637,000); currency, dollar (100 cents); official language, Chinese (Mandarin).*
The island of Taiwan, or Formosa, in the Pacific Ocean is separated from the Chinese mainland by the Formosa Strait. In 1895, it was ceded to Japan by treaty, but it was returned to China in 1945 after World War II. In 1949, Chiang Kai-shek withdrew to Taiwan after the civil war in which he and his supporters were defeated by the communists. He established a Chinese Nationalist republic with the military protection of the United States.
Two-thirds of the island is mountainous. The inhabitants live mainly on the fertile western coastal plain. The chief crops are rice, sugar, fruit, and vegetables. Fishing is important, and there are many manufacturing industries, such as textiles, chemicals, food processing, and the manufacture of electrical goods.

THAILAND - *Area 514,000 sq km; population 54,960,000; capital, Bangkok (pop. 5,716,000); currency, baht (100 stangs); official language, Thai.*
Thailand, a constitutional monarchy, was formerly known as *Siam*. The northern part of the country is on the Asian mainland, but a southern 'tail' stretches into the Malay Peninsula. In the far north, between the Mekong and Salween rivers, Thailand is mountainous. In the east is a high tableland. The centre heartland is the vast, fertile floodplain of the Chao Phraya (Menam) River. Rain and monsoon forests cover two-thirds of the country, and there are mangrove swamps along the wet southern coast. The most important crop is rice, the yield of which has been greatly increased by irrigation works. Rubber is the chief cash crop. Fishing is a major source of food. The country's natural resources include valuable woods, such as teak, from the forests, and tin, tungsten, and

other minerals. There are almost no roads; river and canal transport is widely used.

TURKEY - *Area 755,690 sq km; population 46,318,000; capital, Ankara (pop. 2,800,000); currency, lira (100 kurus); official language, Turkish.*
Formerly the centre of the Ottoman Empire, Turkey became a republic in 1923.
The greater part of the country is in Asia, but a small part is in Europe, across the Dardanelles, the Sea of Marmara, and the Bosporus. European Turkey is mainly low-lying, but the vast, broken Anatolian Plateau occupies much of the Asian section. To the north of the plateau are the Pontine Mountains, and to the south the Taurus Mountains. On the coasts the climate is mild. Crops include fruit, cereals, cotton, and tobacco. In the rugged highlands there are large flocks of sheep. Textiles and iron and steel are the two most important manufacturing industries in Turkey.

UNITED ARAB EMIRATES - *Area 83,600 sq km; population 1,622,000; capital, Abu Dhabi (pop. 243,000); currency, dirham (100 fils); official language, Arabic.*
The United Arab Emirates is a federation of seven sheikhdoms or emirates on the Persian Gulf, formerly known as the Trucial States. The seven emirates are Abu Dhabi, Dubai, Sharjah, Ajman, Umm al Qaiwain, Ras al Khaimah, and Fujairah.
The land is mostly low, flat desert, with some coastal hills. There are vast oil deposits in Abu Dhabi, and oil has also been found in Dubai and elsewhere. Many people live by herding or fishing, and dates are grown.

VIETNAM - *Area 329,555 sq km; population 58,770,000; chief cities, (north) Hanoi, the capital (pop. 2,870,000), (south) Ho Chi Minh City (Saigon, pop. 3,461,000); currency, dong (100 hao); official language, Vietnamese.*
Formerly part of French Indochina, Vietnam was divided from 1954 to 1975 into a communist state in the north and a non-communist state in the south. Then, a protracted and bloody war ended in a communist victory and the establishment of a People's Republic.

The country is about 1,600 km long, but is less than 80 km across at its narrowest point. The centre of Vietnam is a fertile coastal plain. In the north is the delta of the Red River, and in the south the delta of the Mekong River. There are many forests and marshes. The chief crop is rice, and other crops are coffee, tea, sugar, tobacco, and sweet potatoes. Rubber, quinine, and cinnamon are exported.

YEMEN - *Area 527,968 sq km; population 11,493,000; capital, Sana'a (pop. 427,000); currency, riyal (100 fils); official language, Arabic.*
It is a republic founded in 1990 from the union of ex-North Yemen and ex-South Yemen.
The country, which is found in the southernmost point of the Arabian peninsula, is largely mountainous along the edge, and a desert plain in the interior. Coffee, qat (from which a drug is produced), maize, sorghum wheat and barley are cultivated on the mountain slopes. Rice, tobacco, cane, cotton and dates are grown along the humid coastal areas between the mountains and the sea. Aden is an important commercial port.

Countries of Africa

ALGERIA - *Area 2,380,000 sq km; population 22,971,000; capital, Algiers (pop. 1,690,000); currency, dinar (100 centimes); official language, Arabic.*
Algeria has been an independent democratic People's Republic since 1962.
Nine-tenths of the country is in the Sahara, and is inhabited only around oases or by nomads. But the coastal strip between the Mediterranean Sea and the northern flank of the Atlas Mountains is fertile and thickly populated. Most of the towns are in this region, which has rich crops of cereals, vegetables, and early fruits. Wine is important too. Algeria has valuable deposits of petroleum, natural gas, and phosphates.

ANGOLA - *Area 1,247,000 sq km; population 9,385,000; capital, Luanda (pop. 1,134,000); currency, kwanza (100 lweis); official language, Portuguese.*
Until 1975, when it became a People's Republic, Angola was a Portuguese colony. Institutional changes are now in progress.
Apart from a long coastal plain, the country consists mainly of the vast Bié Plateau. Important crops include coffee, sugar-cane, cotton, and oil palms, and there are deposits of oil, iron, and other minerals.

BENIN - *Area 112,600 sq km; population 4,300,000; capital, Porto Novo (pop. 160,000); currency, franc (100 centimes); official language, French.*
Independent republic since 1960, Benin was previously a French colony and was called Dahomey. The centre of Benin is a high plateau, and there are lowlands in the north and south. The majority of the people live in the coastal region. Palm oil, coffee, tobacco, and cotton are exported.

BOTSWANA - *Area 600,400 sq km; population 1,127,000; capital, Gaborone (pop. 111,000); currency, pula (100 thebe); official language, English.*

The republic of Botswana, which became independent in 1966, was formerly the British protectorate of Bechuanaland.
The country is a plateau, the southern part of which is occupied by the Kalahari Desert, where Bushmen and small groups of Bantu live. The huge, swampy Okovango Basin in the north is formed by the Okovango River. Minerals and livestock are important.

BURKINA - *Area 274,000 sq km; population 7,900,000; capital, Ouagadougou (pop. 442,000); currency, franc (100 centimes); official language, French.*
The former French colony of Upper Volta became an independent republic in 1960, changing its name to Burkina in 1984.
It lies on a sloping plateau, and has the headstreams of the Volta River—the Black, White, and Red Voltas. Despite its rivers, the country has an acute shortage of water, and its soil is poor. The typical vegetation is savanna. Most people are subsistence farmers. The main exports are live cattle, cotton, hides and skins, groundnuts, and sesame.

BURUNDI - *Area 27,800 sq km; population 4,780,000; capital, Bujumbura (pop. 270,000); currency, franc (100 centimes); official languages, French and Kirundi.*
Burundi lies on the north-eastern bank of Lake Tanganyika. A former German colony, and later a Belgian mandated territory, it has been independent since 1962 and a republic since 1966.
Most of the country lies on a plateau, but there are mountains in the west; these mark the edge of the African Rift Valley, in which Lake Tanganyika lies. The savanna highlands have good pastures. Rice and other cereals are grown, as well as coffee and cotton.

CAMEROON - *Area 475,000 sq km; population 11,210,000; capital, Yaoundé (pop. 653,000); currency, franc (100 centimes); official languages, French and English.*

The Republic of Cameroon was formed in 1961 from French and British trust territories that had previously been part of the German colony of Kamerun.
The coastal plain on the Gulf of Guinea is marshy, and slopes upwards to the mountainous plateau that occupies most of the country. In the centre, the Adamawa Highlands rise to some 1,800 m. Half the country is thickly forested. Palm oil, rubber, and timber are important. The chief crops are cocoa and coffee.

CANARY ISLANDS - *Area 7,270 sq km; population 1,165,000; capital, Las Palmas (on Gran Canaria; pop. 287,000); currency, peseta; official language, Spanish.*
Group of thirteen islands some 100 km off the north-west coast of Africa, making up two provinces of Spain.

CAPE VERDE - *Area 4,035 sq km; population 325,000; capital, Praia (pop. 50,000); currency, escudo (100 centavos); official language, Portuguese.*
This archipelago off the west coast of Africa gained its independence from Portugal in 1975. The islands are mountainous and have a tropical climate, but droughts are common as the rainfall is uncertain. The main exports are fish, bananas and coffee.

CENTRAL AFRICAN REPUBLIC - *Area 623,000 sq km; population 2,900,000; capital, Bangui (pop. 596,000); currency, franc (100 centimes); official languages, French and Sango.*
The republic was a French colony before independence in 1960.
The country lies in the centre of the continent. It is mainly a hilly plateau, forested in the south. The chief rivers are the Ubangi and the Bomu. Cotton, coffee, and ground-nuts are exported. Minerals include gold and industrial diamonds.

CHAD - *Area 1,284,000 sq km; population 4,950,000; capital, N'djaména (Fort Lamy; pop.*

512,000); currency, franc (100 centimes); official language, French.

Chad, a former French colony, became independent in 1960. It is named after Lake Chad, on its western border.

The northern part of the country, in the Sahara, includes the high Tibesti Mountains. The south is savanna, some of it plateau country. Cotton and ground-nuts are exported.

COMOROS - *Area 1,862 sq km; population 355,000; capital, Moroni (pop. 20,000); currency, franc (100 centimes); official language, French.*
The Comoros Islands became an independent presidential republic in 1975. They are mainly mountainous, and densely forested. The main crops are coffee and sugar-cane, which are exported, and also vanilla, copra, and oils.

CONGO - *Area 342,000 sq km; population 1,912,000; capital, Brazzaville (pop. 595,000); currency, franc (100 centimes); official language, French.*
The People's Republic of the Congo was a French colony before independence in 1960.
It lies across the equator in western Africa, and has a short coastal plain on the Atlantic. Most of the country is high; the broad Batéké Plateau is savanna, but the northern region is covered with thick tropical forest. The Congo and Oubangui rivers form the eastern boundary. The chief crop is sugar-cane. There are various mineral resources.

DJIBOUTI - *Area 23,200 sq km; population 405,000; capital, Djibouti (pop. 200,000); currency, franc (100 centimes); official language, French.*
Formerly known as the French territory of Afars and Issas, it was renamed in 1967 and granted its independence in 1976.
It is an arid, hilly, desert land, but swampy in coastal districts. Farming is at a subsistence level, heavily dependent on livestock.

EGYPT - *Area 1,000,000 sq km; population 48,205,000; capital, Cairo (pop. 13,300,000); currency, pound (100 piastres); official language, Arabic.*
Egypt—now called the Arab Republic of Egypt—was a monarchy from 1923 to 1952. Earlier, it had been a British protectorate, and, until 1914, part of the Ottoman Empire.
Though most of Egypt's territory is in Africa, a small section, the Sinai Peninsula, is in Asia. The Suez Canal passes through Egypt, and by connecting the Mediterranean Sea with the Red Sea provides a short route for shipping between Europe and Asia. Most of the land is desert: the Libyan Desert in the west, and the Arabian Desert in the east, rising to the Red Sea Mountains. Between the deserts is the valley of the Nile, the world's longest river. The Nile has no tributaries during the whole of its 1,450-km course through Egypt. Agriculture is possible only in the valley, and, in particular, in the great delta of the Nile on the Mediterranean. The amount of arable land has been increased by building dams for irrigation. The most important dam, the Aswan High Dam, also provides hydro-electricity. Most of the people live in the valley; those in the desert live in oases or are nomads. Among the country's chief crops are cotton, sugar, citrus fruits, and rice.

EQUATORIAL GUINEA - *Area 28,000 sq km; population 300,000; capital, Malabo (pop. 40,000); currency, franc (100 centimes); official language, Spanish.*
The small country of Equatorial Guinea consists largely of the former Spanish possessions of Rio Muni and Bioko; it became an independent presidential republic in 1968. Rio Muni is on the African mainland. Fernando Pó (Macias Nguema) is a mountainous island in the Gulf of Guinea. Cocoa and coffee are exported.

ETHIOPIA - *Area 251,900 sq km; population 43,300,000; capital, Addis Ababa (pop. 1,423,000); currency, birr (100 cents); official language, Amharic.*
Until 1975, Ethiopia was ruled by an emperor who belonged to one of the oldest royal dynasties in the world; but in that year it became a republic. It was often called Abyssinia.
Most of the country consists of high and broken plateaux, divided into two regions by the African Rift Valley. To the west of the valley are the Ethiopian Highlands, which are wild and rugged and are cut by many river valleys. To the east is the Somali Plateau, which is generally more level. The country has little industry, though it has some mineral resources including gold, platinum, and potash. Cereals, coffee, cotton, sugar-cane, fruit, and tobacco are grown; coffee is exported.

GABON - *Area 267,000 sq km; population 1,300,000; capital, Libreville (pop. 255,000); currency, franc (100 centimes); official language, French.*
Gabon, a presidential republic, has been independent since 1960. Before that, it was a French colony.
Its coastal plain on the Atlantic is broad around the mouth of the River Ogooué. But most of the country is a mountainous plateau, which has extensive rain forests in which mahogany and other valuable timbers are cut. The most important crops are cocoa and coffee, and recently rice cultivation has begun. Gabon's mineral resources include deposits of oil, iron, and manganese.

GAMBIA - *Area 11,295 sq km; population 687,000; capital, Banjul (pop. 45,000); currency, dalasi (100 bututs); official language, English.*
The small country of Gambia was British-ruled before it became independent in 1965.
The country consists of a narrow strip of territory along the Gambia River. Some of the land is swampy or under water for part of the year. There are few mineral resources. The chief exports are ground-nuts and fruit.

GHANA - *Area 238,535 sq km; population 13,578,000; capital, Accra (pop. 1,580,000); currency, cedi (100 pesewas); official language, English.*
The former British colony of the Gold Coast, Ghana has been independent since 1957.
Most of eastern Ghana is in the basin of the Volta River and, like the coastal areas, is low-lying. But there are hills in the east, and a high escarpment extends across the country. The building of the Akosombo Dam on the Volta has produced the largest artificial lake in the world, covering more than 7,800 sq km. This project has aided irrigation and has provided much-needed electrical power. Gold, diamonds, manganese, and bauxite are mined, and there is an aluminium-smelting industry. The chief export crops are cocoa, coffee, and copra.

GUINEA - *Area 245,855 sq km; population 5,780,000; capital, Conakry (pop. 705,000); currency, syli (100 cauris); official language, French.*
Guinea, which became independent in 1958, was formerly a French colony.
The land rises from the broad, marshy coastal plain on the Atlantic to the Fouta Djallon, a rugged plateau. In the south-east, the thickly forested Nimba Mountains rise to some 1,800 m. The chief rivers are the Niger and the Gambia, both of which have their sources in Guinea. There are rich deposits of bauxite and iron. The chief export crops are bananas, pineapples, kola-nuts, and coffee.

GUINEA-BISSAU - *Area 36,125 sq km; population 768,000; capital, Bissau (pop. 110,000); currency, peso (100 centavos); official language, Portuguese.*
A former Portuguese possession (called Portuguese Guinea), Guinea-Bissau has been an independent republic since 1974.
The country consists of a mainland territory and a number of islands on the Atlantic coast of Africa. It is mostly low-lying, but the high plateau of the Fouta Djallon projects into the south-east. Crops are rice, ground-nuts, and palm oil.

IVORY COAST - *Area 322,465 sq km; population 6,898,000; capital, Abidjan (pop. 2,534,000); currency, franc (100 centimes); official language, French.*
Ivory Coast became an independent presidential republic in 1960; previously it was a French colony. The northern two-thirds of the country is a savanna-covered plateau. The coastal plain is broad and wooded. The most valuable export crops are cocoa and coffee; bananas and pineapples are also exported. Timber is an important source of revenue.

KENYA - *Area 582,600 sq km; population 19,540,000; capital, Nairobi (pop. 1,160,000); currency, shilling (100 cents); official languages, English and Swahili.*
Kenya became independent in 1963 and a republic in 1964; it had been a British colony since 1895.
Much of the northern part of the country is a plateau, a region of wide grasslands. In the south-west, the Kenya Highlands include Kenya's two highest mountains, Mount Kenya (5,199 m) and Mount Elgon (4,321 m). The Nyanza Plateau, which stretches from the highlands to Lake Victoria, is one of the most favoured agricultural regions. The African Rift Valley cuts through Kenya; Lake Turkana, in the north, lies within it. The lower parts of the country consist of dry and thorn savannas. The chief crops are sisal, cereals, pineapples, tea, pyrethrum, and coffee. Kenya is famous for its wild-life reserves.

LESOTHO - *Area 30,400 sq km; population 1,577,000; capital, Maseru (pop. 109,000); currency, loti (100 lisente); official languages, English, and Sesotho.*
Lesotho, the former British colony of Basutoland, is an enclave surrounded by the territory of South Africa. It became an independent constitutional monarchy in 1966. Nearly all of the country is high; the Drakensberg Mountains rise in the east. The Orange River has its source in Lesotho. The raising of livestock is important.

LIBERIA - *Area 111,400 sq km; population 2,211,000; capital, Monrovia (pop. 465,000); currency, dollar (100 cents); official language, English.*
The Liberian republic was founded in 1847, and is the oldest independent country in western Africa. It developed from a number of settlements for Blacks released from slavery in the United States.

The Guinea Highlands and Nimba Mountains in the north descend to savanna plateaux, and then to a marshy coastal plain. Iron and diamonds are mined. Crops include coffee and cocoa.

LIBYA - *Area 1,760,000 sq km; population 3,638,000; capital, Tripoli (pop. 989,000); currency, dinar (1,000 dirhams); official language, Arabic.*
Libya became an independent country in 1951, and has been a Socialist People's Republic since 1969. Earlier, it had been an Italian colony (from 1912) and, before that, part of the Ottoman Empire.
It is one of the largest countries in Africa, but nine-tenths of it is barren land, part of the Sahara. Most of the people live in the fertile lowlands along the Mediterranean coast. This region has groves of oranges and olives, and also grows cereals, tobacco, and vegetables. The country is rich because of huge deposits of petroleum.

MADAGASCAR - *Area 587,000 sq km; population 10,012,000; capital, Antananarivo (pop. 1,050,000); currency, Malagasy franc (100 centimes); official languages, Malagasy and French.*
The Democratic Republic of Madagascar occupies the island of Madagascar in the Indian Ocean, and a few small islands. It is some 400 km from the coast of the African mainland. France ruled it from 1885 to 1960. The centre of Madagascar is a high plateau, bounded by mountains in the north and south, and by a wide coastal plain on the west. Only one-tenth of the land is suitable for agriculture. Exports include sugar, coffee, pepper, vanilla, and cloves. Graphite, mica, and phosphates are mined.

MALAWI - *Area 118,500 sq km; population 7,982,000; capital, Lilongwe (pop. 220,000); currency, kwacha (100 tambala); official language, English.*
The former British protectorate of Nyasaland, Malawi became an independent country in 1964 and a presidential republic in 1966.
It lies along the western side of Lake Malawi (Lake Nyasa); which is in the African Rift Valley. Most of the people live by farming; and tea, tobacco, and tung-oil are exported. Cattle-rearing and fishing are important.

MALI - *Area 1,240,000 sq km; population 7,620,000; capital, Bamako (pop. 640,000); currency, franc (100 centimes); official language, French.*
Mali was formerly the French colony of Sudan. In 1959 it joined with Senegal to form the Federation of Mali; but the federation was dissolved after a year, and Mali and Senegal became separate countries. The loss of Senegal left Mali without an outlet to the sea.
The northern part of the country is in the Sahara and is inhabited only by nomads. The south is watered by the Niger and Senegal rivers. Cotton and ground-nuts are exported.

MAURITANIA - *Area 1,030,000 sq km; population 1,890,000; capital, Nouakchott (pop. 600,000); currency, ouguiya (5 khoums); official languages, Arabic and French.*
Mauritania became an independent country in 1960; it had been ruled by France since 1920. It is officially called the *Islamic Republic of Mauritania.*
Much of the country is in the western Sahara and consists of barren plateaux. Only in the south-west, the flood plain of the Senegal River, is the land fertile. Cereals and ground-

nuts are produced. The most important source of income is iron ore.

MAURITIUS - *Area 1,865 sq km; population 1,008,000; capital, Port Louis (pop. 145,000); currency, rupee (100 cents); official language, English. French and Creole are also spoken.*
The tiny country of Mauritius was a British crown colony until 1968, when it became an independent constitutional monarchy.
It consists of a group of islands in the Indian Ocean, the largest of which are Mauritius and Rodrigues. Mauritius Island is mountainous and is of volcanic origin. The main crop is sugar-cane.

MOROCCO - *Area 458,730 sq km; population 23,200,000; capital, Rabat (pop. 600,000); currency, dirham (100 centimes); official language, Arabic.*
Morocco, a constitutional monarchy, independent since 1956, is dominated by the Atlas Mountains, which rise to 4,164 m above sea-level in Mount Toubkal. To the east of the mountains are the wastes of the Sahara. Morocco's coastal plain on the Mediterranean, in the north, is hilly, but the western, Atlantic coast has sandy beaches. The country has rich mineral deposits, and supplies a third of the world demand for phosphates. Crops include cereals, oranges, olives, apricots, grapes (for wine as well as for eating), and nuts.

MOZAMBIQUE - *Area 799,380 sq km; population 14,372,000; capital, Maputo (pop. 1,007,000); currency, metical (100 centavos); official language, Portuguese.*
The Republic of Mozambique, independent since 1975, was formerly ruled by Portugal.
It has a coastline of some 2,400 km on the Indian Ocean, and the great Lake Malawi in the north. The country has a wide coastal plain, but most of it consists of highlands through which flow several rivers, including the Zambezi and Limpopo. Cane-sugar, coconuts, cotton, and tea are produced. Coal and iron are mined.

NAMIBIA - *Area 824,300 sq km; population 1,000,000; capital, Windhoek (pop. 115,000); currency, rand (100 cents); official languages, English and Afrikaans.*
Previously known as South-West Africa, Namibia has been an independent republic since 1990.
The coastal area, called the *Namib*, is desert. Inland is a vast plateau. Much of the country is too dry for crop cultivation, but there are large herds of livestock. Fishing is important and there are mineral deposits.

NIGER - *Area 1,186,000 sq km; population 7,250,000; capital, Niamey (pop. 400,000); currency, franc (100 centimes); official language, French.*
Niger, now a presidential republic, was ruled by France before independence in 1960.
It has no coastline, and most of it is an arid plateau. The northern part is in the Sahara. A few small rivers seep away into the desert; they provide water for scattered patches of green. The south of the country is savanna, and in the south-west there is fertile land around the Niger River. Cereals, coffee, and cotton are grown, and there are deposits of tin, iron, and uranium.

NIGERIA - *Area 923,800 sq km; population 112,260,000; capital, Lagos (pop. 1,250,000); currency, naira (100 kobo); official language, English.*
Nigeria, the most heavily-populated country in Africa, was a British colony and protectorate

until 1960, when it gained independence; it has been a federal republic since 1963.
The chief feature of the country is the great Niger River, which, with its tributaries, waters most of Nigeria. There are mangrove swamps and lagoons along the coast, particularly in the Niger delta. Some 80 km inland the rain forest begins; beyond this are the plateaux, and, still farther north, a semi-desert tract. Lake Chad is on the north-east frontier. Two-thirds of Nigeria's agricultural produce is exported. The country is the leading producer of ground-nuts in the world, and is among the leaders for cocoa. The rearing of stock is important. Petroleum, tin and coal are extracted. There are food-processing and oil-refining industries, and textiles, steel, and chemicals are manufactured.

RWANDA - *Area 26,300 sq km; population 5,660,000; capital, Kigali (pop. 180,000); currency, franc (100 centimes); official languages, French and Kinyarwanda.*
Until 1962, when it became an independent republic, Rwanda was part of the UN trust territory of Ruanda-Urundi, administered by Belgium. It is bounded on the west by Lake Kivu. Most of it occupies a hilly plateau. Mountains in the west, by the lake, divide the River Zaïre (Congo) basin from that of the Nile. Coffee, tea, and tobacco are exported.

SAO TOME AND PRINCIPE - *Area 965 sq km; population 117,000; capital, São Tomé (pop. 35,000); currency, dobra (100 centimos); official language, Portuguese.*
These islands in the Gulf of Guinea became independent from Portugal in 1975.
They are volcanic islands and are mountainous, over half the area being forested. The main exports are cacao, coffee, and rubber.

SENEGAL - *Area 197,000 sq km; population 7,188,000; capital Dakar (pop. 1,382,000); currency, franc (100 centimes); official language, French.*
Senegal, a former French colony, became part of the Federation of Mali in 1959; but one year later the Federation was dissolved, and Senegal and Mali became separate independent republics. Cape Vert in Senegal is the westernmost point in Africa. The country has a long, sandy coast on the Atlantic Ocean, and is mostly low-lying. But in the south-east it has hills of the Fouta Djallon. Its rivers include the Senegal and the Gambia. Much of the valley of the Gambia River forms a separate country, called the Gambia, which is an enclave within Senegalese territory. The chief crops are rice and groundnuts. Phosphates are mined.

SEYCHELLES - *Area 453 sq km; population 67,000; capital, Victoria (pop. 25,000); currency, rupee (100 cents); official language, English.*
The Seychelles, a former British colony, have been an independent presidential republic since 1976. The country consists of two groups of islands: one flat, the other mountainous. Coconut palms flourish on the fertile volcanic soils. The main exports are copra, vanilla, cinnamon, and guano.

SIERRA LEONE - *Area 71,700 sq km; population 3,820,000; capital, Freetown (pop. 470,000); currency, leone (100 cents); official language, English.*
Sierra Leone, which became independent in 1961 and a republic in 1971, was formerly a British colony; the colony was founded around a settlement at Freetown for escaped slaves.
Most of the country is high and mountainous, and consists of a broken plateau that rises to

the Fouta Djallon. Freetown is built on a hilly peninsula, but the rest of the coastal region is low-lying and marshy. Nearly three-quarters of the people live by agriculture: palm kernels, coffee, and cocoa are exported. Sierra Leone has useful mineral deposits. They include diamonds, iron, and bauxite.

SOMALIA - *Area 637,700 sq km; population 5,075,000; capital, Mogadishu (pop. 500,000); currency, shilling (100 cents); official language, Somali.*
Somalia became an independent country in 1960; it was formed from two British and Italian possessions. It lies on the 'horn' of Africa, and has coastlines on the north, and the east, where the coastal plain is broad. The interior of the country is a plateau, sloping upwards towards the Ethiopian Highlands in the west. Bananas are exported, and other crops are cereals, ground-nuts, and cotton.

SOUTH AFRICA - *Area 1,150,000 sq km; population 29,690,000; capitals, Cape Town (legislative capital, pop. 1,910,000) and Pretoria (administrative capital, pop. 822,000); currency, rand (100 cents); official languages, English and Afrikaans.*
South Africa is the richest and the most southerly country in Africa. A federal republic since 1961, it is governed by its white population, which, although large, is only about one-fifth of the country's total population. Since 1989 however the country has been moving towards the abolition of apartheid (the policy of racial segregation) and the extension to the black population of the vote and of a share in the government.
Most of the country consists of plateau land. The eastern plateau, the High Veld, is the most prosperous part of the country, with rich farmlands, highly-developed industry, and important mineral resources. To the south-east of the High Veld is the great mountain range of the Drakensbergs, and beyond that is a coastal plain. In the far north-east of the country is the *Transvaal*—the region 'beyond the Vaal River'. There are two other large rivers, the Limpopo and the Orange. South Africa's farms are among the most productive in the world. Their crops include cereals, vegetables, fruit, tobacco, and sugar-cane. Livestock, particularly sheep, are important. Vineyards produce fine wines. Textiles, steel, chemicals, and machinery are manufactured. More than one third of the gold mined in the world comes from South Africa. Diamonds, silver, iron, manganese, and chromium are also extracted.

SUDAN - *Area 2,510,000 sq km; population 26,250,000; capital, Khartoum (pop. 650,000); currency, pound (100 piastres); official language, Arabic.*
The Sudan, the largest country in Africa, was ruled by Egypt from 1820 to 1880, and was under joint British and Egyptian rule from 1898 to 1956. It gained independence in 1956 and it is now a presidential republic.
The Nile and its tributaries reach out into almost all parts of the country. The Blue Nile and the White Nile meet at Khartoum, and flow northwards to Egypt. Northern Sudan is desert. South of the desert are hills, and beyond them broad plains of scrubby grassland and savanna. The southern parts of the country, near the Equator, have rich vegetation, with alluvial grasslands, tropical forests, and swamp forests. Cotton and other crops are grown in the Nile valley and irrigation works have aided agriculture along the Atbara River. Cereals, fruits, ground-nuts, and sugar-cane are produced. In

the drier regions, cattle, sheep, goats, and camels are raised on a nomadic or semi-nomadic basis. Fishing is important, both in the Nile and its tributaries and also on the Red Sea coast.

SWAZILAND - *Area 17,400 sq km; population 716,000; capital, Mbabane (pop. 39,000); currency, lilangeni (100 cents); official languages, English and Siswati.*
Swaziland became an independent monarchy in 1968. At that time it was a British protectorate.
The Lebombo Mountains rise along the eastern side of the country. The rest of the terrain, except where cultivated, is veld, higher in the west than elsewhere. Crops include sugar-cane, citrus fruits, cotton, and rice. Iron, asbestos, and gold are mined.

TANZANIA - *Area 945,000 sq km; population 23,990,000; capital, Dodoma (pop. 140,000), de facto capital, Dar es Salaam; currency, shilling (100 cents); official languages, Swahili and English.*
The United Republic of Tanzania was formed in 1964, its territory being the former British trust territory of Tanganyika in eastern Africa, and some offshore islands of which the largest are Zanzibar and Pemba.
On the northern and western frontiers of continental Tanzania there are three great lakes; Victoria, Tanganyika, and Malawi (Nyasa). Most of the country is a hilly plateau, forested in places and covered with scrubby grassland in others. In the north-east of the plateau is Mount Kilimanjaro (5,895 m), Africa's highest mountain. The coastal plain is narrow at most points. About a quarter of the land area has been declared nature conservation territory. The mainland has poor soils. The chief exports from Tanzania are coffee, cloves, sisal, cotton, diamonds, and cashew nuts.

TOGO - *Area 56,000 sq km; population 2,900,000; capital, Lomé (pop. 400,000); currency, franc (100 centimes); official language, French.*
The small republic of Togo became independent in 1960; earlier it had been a French trusteeship territory, and, until 1919, a German protectorate.
Much of the country is mountainous and thickly forested, but there is savanna in the north-west. The coastal districts are swampy, with large land-locked lagoons. The people grow some cereals, cassava, and yams. Cocoa, citrus fruits, palm kernels, and coffee are the main crops produced for export.

TUNISIA - *Area 163,000 sq km; population 7,640,000; capital, Tunis (pop. 600,000); currency, dinar (1,000 millimes); official language, Arabic.*
A French protectorate from 1883, Tunisia became completely independent in 1956 and a presidential republic in 1957. It is one of the smallest countries of northern Africa, and has the continent's most northerly point, Cape Blanc.
The northern part of Tunisia is in the Atlas Mountains, which here rise to a maximum of some 1,500 m above sea-level. In the north-east there is a coastal plain. The southern region is in the Sahara. In the west is the vast salt pan called the *Chott Djerid*, which in the rainy season turns into a salty marsh. Vines, olives, vegetables, and citrus fruits grow in the Mediterranean region. In the desert, people live in the oases, where water is available, and nomads keep animals.

UGANDA - *Area 236,000 sq km; population 13,200,000; capital, Kampala (pop. 460,000); currency, shilling (100 cents); official language, English.*
The former British protectorate of Uganda became an independent country in 1962, and a republic the following year.
It is an inland country. In the south-east, it includes part of Lake Victoria, Africa's largest lake. Most of the country is a high plateau, bordered on the east and the west by mountains. In the east, Mount Elgon rises to 4,321 m; and in the west, the Ruwenzori Mountains rise to 5,119 m. The chief river is the White Nile. The leading exports are coffee, cotton, tea, copper, and hides and skins.

ZAIRE - *Area 2,350,000 sq km; population 29,600,000; capital, Kinshasa (pop. 2,700,000); currency, zaïre (100 makuta); official language, French.*
The country was formerly called the *Republic of the Congo*. It was a Belgian colony that became an independent presidential republic in 1960. Most of the country is a plateau, highest in the south-east, in Katanga. The eastern border, in the African Rift Valley, runs through several great lakes. This part is very mountainous, the Ruwenzori Mountains rising to 5,119 m. The Zaïre (Congo) River pursues a course of some 4,500 km through the country. Zaïre is rich in minerals, particularly in copper. Diamonds, cobalt, and iron are among the other minerals extracted. Agricultural exports include coffee, tea, sugar, cotton, rubber, and fruit. There are many manufacturing industries.

ZAMBIA - *Area 752,600 sq km; population 7,270,000; capital, Lusaka (pop. 870,000); currency, kwacha (100 ngwee); official language, English.*
Zambia, which became an independent presidential republic in 1964, was formerly the British protectorate of Northern Rhodesia.
The country is watered by one of Africa's great rivers, the Zambezi. Most of Zambia is a plateau, averaging some 1,200 m above sea-level. But some of the country is higher. The Muchinga Mountains in the eastern part rise to more than 2,130 m. There are many lakes, either in Zambia or on its borders. They include Lake Kariba, in the south, an artificial lake formed by the building of the Kariba Dam. This project supplies hydro-electricity to Zimbabwe as well as to Zambia. The country is rich in mineral resources, especially copper. The chief export crops are cereals, ground-nuts, tea, coffee, and cane sugar, but output is affected by high wages paid in mining.

ZIMBABWE - *Area 390,580 sq km; population 7,400,000; capital, Harare (pop. 660,000); currency, dollar (100 cents); official language, English.*
Zimbabwe was formerly the British colony of Southern Rhodesia, but in 1965 the colonial government declared the country independent. Britain declared this act to be illegal. In the 1970s, African nationalists waged a guerrilla war against the white government. The war ended in 1980 when legal independence was granted and the country became a republic.
It is a land-locked, mostly plateau region, lying between the basins of the Zambezi River in the north and the Limpopo River in the south-east. Lake Kariba on the border with Zambia is behind the Kariba Dam which was built across the Zambezi River. Hydro-electricity generated at the Dam is supplied to Zimbabwe and Zambia. Zimbabwe has rich mineral resources, including iron, copper, asbestos, and gold.

Countries of North and Central America

ANTIGUA AND BARBUDA - *Area 440 sq km; population 75,000; capital, Saint Johns (pop. 25,000); currency, East Caribbean dollar; official language, English.*
A former British colony, it became an independent state in 1991, remaining part of the British Commonwealth.
They are coral islands of volcanic origin in the Caribbean Sea. Cotton, sugar-cane, vegetables and fruit trees are cultivated. Tourism is highly developed.

BAHAMAS - *Area 13,935 sq km; population 240,000; capital, Nassau (pop. 135,000); currency, dollar (100 cents); official language, English.*
The Bahamas were a British colony from 1649 to 1964, when they became self-governing. They acquired their independence in 1973.
The whole group of islands is strung out between Florida and Haiti, and consists of some 700 islands, about 25 of which are inhabited, and over 2,000 reefs and keys. Thanks to the excellent climate, the Bahamas are a great attraction for foreign tourist traffic. The native population consists almost entirely of coloured peoples.

BARBADOS - *Area 430 sq km; population 250,000; capital, Bridgetown (pop. 7,600); currency, dollar (100 cents); official language, English.*
Barbados became a British colony in 1652, attained self-government in 1961, and won its independence in 1966.
It is the most easterly island of the Lesser Antilles, and has a tropical and humid climate. The fertile soil is given over almost exclusively to the production of sugar-cane. Tourism is the second most important industry.

BELIZE - *Area 22,965 sq km; population 166,500; capital, Belmopan (pop. 5,000); currency, dollar (100 cents); official language, English.*
Formerly called British Honduras, it was a British colony from 1884 till 1964, when it became the self-governing dependency of Belize. It gained independence in 1981.
It lies on the Caribbean coast of Central America, to the east of Guatemala. The population is made up largely of Blacks and people of mixed blood, along with about 3,000 Whites and several thousand American Indians. Wood, sugar, and citrus fruits are the most important exports.

BERMUDA - *Area 55 sq km; population 60,000; capital, Hamilton (pop. 1,700); currency, dollar (100 cents); official language, English.*
Bermuda, a group of some 350 small islands in the Atlantic, 930 km from the United States, became a British colony in 1684, and a self-governing dependency in 1968. About 20 of the islands are inhabited, and tourism is the most important source of income.

CANADA - *Area 9,976,140 sq km; population 26,000,000; capital, Ottawa (pop. 833,000); currency, dollar (100 cents); official languages, English and French.*
After the USSR, Canada is the next largest country in the world. It is, however, relatively thinly populated, and still welcomes immigration. For more than a hundred years, the English and French fought over the possession of this land. The last battle was won by the British in 1759, and in 1763 France resigned all her claims. The French settlers were, however, permitted to remain in the country and retain their own language. In the province of Quebec, the French Canadians still constitute a closed racial group. Canada has been a member of the British Empire and Commonwealth since 1867, but although the British monarch reigns as monarch of Canada, the country is completely independent and self-governing.
In a north-south direction, Canada stretches for some 4,670 km. As a result, the climate is extremely varied. A narrow coastal strip in the west has a mild maritime climate, whereas in the interior there is a dry and cold continental climate. North of the Arctic Circle, snow lies on the ground almost the whole year through, whereas in Ontario, on Canada's southern border, the vine is cultivated.
About half of Canada is taken up by a land region known as the Canadian Shield. Sparsely populated and made up of hard, ancient rocks, this horseshoe-shaped region stretches down central Canada from the Northwest Territories, round Hudson Bay to the northern coast of Quebec. A swampy, forested lowland separates the Shield from the southern shores of Hudson Bay, and to the east there are the Appalachian regions (Newfoundland, Nova Scotia etc.) and the St Lawrence-Great Lakes lowlands. The latter is a comparatively small region, but more than half the country's people live there. Its flat and rolling land is extremely fertile. West of the Shield are the interior plains (the prairies, where Canada's vast output of wheat is grown), and the western mountain region, which contains the Canadian Rockies and the Coast Mountains. Canada also has a number of very large islands, which lie almost entirely within the Arctic Circle.
Canada has vast mineral resources in the west, and more recently, oil and natural gas have been found, principally in the centre of the south-west. But although industry is in a leading position in the economy, Canada still remains a land of fishermen, hunters, and farmers. Almost half the land area is covered with forest. Thus, in addition to the trapping and farming of fur-bearing animals, the timber, furniture, and paper industries are very highly developed. Three-quarters of Canada's people live in the towns. Only small groups of the original inhabitants of the country are still extant: some 20,000 Eskimoes and 250,000 American Indians (most of whom live on reservations). All others are descendants of immigrants.

COSTA RICA - *Area 51,100 sq km; population 2,820,000; capital, San José (pop. 280,000); currency, colón (100 centimos); official language, Spanish.*
Originally a colony of Spain, Costa Rica has been an independent republic since 1821.
The country lies on the land bridge between North and South America, bordering in the north-east on the Caribbean and in the south-west on the Pacific. Its main products are coffee, sugar, and bananas.

CUBA - *Area 110,920 sq km; population 10,420,000; capital, Havana (pop. 2,000,000); currency, peso (100 centavos); official language, Spanish.*
Discovered by Christopher Columbus in 1492, Cuba was a Spanish possession until it became an independent republic in 1898. A revolution in the 1950s saw the communist Fidel Castro come to power in 1959, when he created a Socialist republic.
A beautiful island, the largest in the Greater Antilles, Cuba lies between Florida and Jamaica. Three-quarters of its inhabitants are Whites, mostly of Spanish descent, while the rest are Blacks or of mixed blood. The 3,400-km coastline has many small bays, and numbers of minor islands and coral reefs lie just off it. The eastern part of the island is mountainous, the maximum height being 2,000 metres. The rest is flat or rolling land. Cuba is the world's third largest producer of sugar-cane. Tobacco is also an important crop and there are large reserves of nickel.

DOMINICA - *Area 750 sq km; population 87,800; capital, Roseau (pop. 10,000); currency, dollar (100 cents); official language, English.*
A mountainous republic in the Lesser Antilles, Dominica has spectacular scenery and considerable volcanic activity. Cacao, limes, bananas, mangoes, oranges, avocado pears and vanilla are cultivated. The main exports are rum, lime juice and copra. Most of the population are Blacks.

DOMINICAN REPUBLIC - *Area 48,735 sq km; population 6,860,000; capital, Santo Domingo (pop. 1,410,000); currency, peso (100 centavos); official language, Spanish.*
The Dominican Republic has been independent since 1844, after periods of Spanish and French possession. It was, from 1915 to 1934, under the control of the United States.
It occupies the eastern two-third of the island of Hispaniola. The majority of the population is of mixed blood. The country is undulating, with mountains rising to over 3,000 metres in the Central Cordillera. The western coast is rugged and mountainous and the eastern low-lying with sandy beaches. The main agricultural product is sugar cane, which is also the main export.

EL SALVADOR - *Area 21,041 sq km; population 5,107,000; capital, San Salvador (pop. 500,000); currency, colón (100 centavos); official language, Spanish.*
The smallest but the most thickly populated of the Central American states, El Salvador has been an independent republic since 1841.
From a narrow, hot and humid coastal strip, the land rises to a volcanic mountain region, a 600-metre plateau, and another mountain range. Rice, maize, and coffee are the most important agricultural products. About three-quarters of the people are of mixed White/American Indian blood and a fifth are American Indians.

GREENLAND - *Area 2,175,600 sq km; population 54,600; capital, Godthåb (pop. 11,600); currency, krone (100 øre); official languages, Danish, and Greenlandic.*
Greenland, which lies to the north-east of North America, is the largest island in the world. Colonized at various times by Denmark and Norway, it became a province of Denmark in 1953 with equal rights with the rest of the country.

About 85 per cent of its surface is covered by a permanent layer of thick ice. After Antarctica, it is the largest frozen expanse of land in the world. A mountainous coastal strip surrounding the ice-cap is free of ice, and has been strongly indented by fjords to form a number of small islands and peninsulas. The highest peak rises 3,700 metres. Most Greenlanders have both Eskimo and Danish ancestry. They speak Greenlandic, a form of Eskimo language. Many speak Danish. The main occupations are fishing and fish processing. Internal autonomy was granted in 1979.

GRENADA - *Area 345 sq km; population 106,000; capital, St George's (pop. 8,000); currency, dollar (100 cents); official language, English.*
An island of the Lesser Antilles group, Grenada became an independent nation within the Commonwealth in 1974.

GUATEMALA - *Area 108,890 sq km; population 8,680,000; capital, Guatemala (pop. 1,300,000); currency, quetzal (100 centavos); official language, Spanish.*
The most populous of the Central American states, Guatemala, once a Spanish colony, has been independent since 1821. It has a long history of political troubles.
The land is volcanic, and has a tropical climate. Coffee is grown in the fertile mountain districts, and bananas and cotton are also important. About 45 per cent of the people are American Indians.

HAITI - *Area 27,750 sq km; population 5,550,000; capital, Port au Prince (pop. 750,000); currency, gourde (100 centimes); official language, French.*
Haiti, today an independent republic, has been a Spanish and French colony in turn, and was, from 1915 to 1934, under the control of the United States. It occupies the western third of the island of Hispaniola. It has a long history of uprisings and revolutions. The majority of the inhabitants are Blacks, the descendants of slaves. They speak a Creole dialect and practise voodoo. The small ruling class is made up largely of people of mixed blood.
The land is mountainous, only a third of it being arable. Coffee and sugar are the most important farm products. Bauxite is the most valuable export after coffee.

HONDURAS - *Area 112,090 sq km; population 4,800,000; capital, Tegucigalpa (pop. 640,000); currency, lempira (100 centavos); official language, Spanish.*
Formerly under Spanish control, Honduras declared its independence in 1822, and is today a presidential republic.
It lies in northern Central America, on the Caribbean, with a short Pacific coastline in the south. The interior is mountainous, and much of the coastal area is swamp and jungle. Most of the people are of mixed blood, and earn their living on the land. The most important products are bananas and coffee.

JAMAICA - *Area 10,990 sq km; population 2,350,000; capital, Kingston (pop. 615,000); currency, dollar (100 cents); official language, English.*
A former British colony, Jamaica became independent in 1962.
It is the southernmost island of the Greater Antilles group. The interior is mountainous, and the Blue Mountains in the east rise to a height of 2,256 metres. There are frequent earthquakes, one of which almost wholly destroyed

the capital in 1907. In the fertile coastal plain to the west of Kingston, the principal crop grown is sugar-cane. Jamaica is the world's third largest producer of bauxite (aluminium ore), and its rum is regarded as the finest in the world.

MEXICO - *Area 1,972,545 sq km; population 82,735,000; capital, Mexico City (pop. 8,240,000); currency, peso (100 centavos); official language, Spanish.*
Mexico was a Spanish possession until its independence in 1821. Today it is a republic consisting of 31 federal states.
The largest Central American country, it lies between the Pacific and the Gulf of Mexico, and borders the United States in the north. The Sierra Madre, an extension of the Rocky Mountains, stretches down from the north in two long chains through the whole of Mexico. Between them lies an elevated plateau, where most of the people live. On the southern edge of this plateau lie a series of volcanoes, some still active. The highest peak is Orizaba, which rises 5,700 metres. The long arm of Lower California extends in the west, separated from the rest of the country by the Gulf of California. In the east of Mexico is the Yucatán Peninsula, a low limestone plateau. Many famous ruins of the ancient Maya Indian civilization are located there.
Mexico still has some three million pureblooded American Indians, but most of the people are of mixed blood. About three-quarters of the working population is engaged in agriculture, although only an eighth of the land is arable. The country has rich mineral resources. Gold and silver have always been found there, and there are also iron, copper, lead, uranium, and, above all, oil and natural gas. These, of course, form the foundation for the developing manufacturing industries.

NETHERLANDS ANTILLES - *Area 800 sq km; population 190,000; capital, Willemstad (pop. 125,000); currency, Dutch guilder (100 cents); official language, Dutch.*
These islands, also known as the Dutch West Indies, have independence of administration and enjoy equal rights with the Netherlands themselves.
They consist of Bonaire and Curaçao off the Venezuelan coast, and three smaller islands of the Windward group. The inhabitants are principally Blacks and of mixed blood. The economy is based on the refining of oil imported from Venezuela to Curaçao.

NICARAGUA - *Area 130,680 sq km; population 3,620,000; capital, Managua (pop. 685,000); currency, córdoba (100 centavos); official language, Spanish.*
Nicaragua was a Spanish colony until 1821, and became an independent republic in 1838. It lies between Honduras and Costa Rica, and is the most thinly populated state in Central America. About 70 per cent of the inhabitants are of mixed blood, and the rest are Whites, Blacks, or American Indians.
The volcanic mountain region of the interior rises to a height of some 2,100 metres. The swampy land on the Caribbean is known as the 'Mosquito Coast'. Forests cover four-fifths of the land, and only about a tenth is used for agriculture. The main crops are cotton, coffee, and sugar. Meat is also exported, and there are important deposits of gold and silver.

PANAMA - *Area 77,080 sq km; population 2,320,000; capital, Panama City (pop. 550,000);*

currency, balboa (100 centésimos); official language, Spanish.
A small country that forms the narrow land bridge between North and South America, Panama is mountainous, with tropical rain forests, and is divided in two by the Panama Canal. Until 1903, Panama formed part of Colombia, but, with the support of the United States, it declared its independence once the Canal had been built. Much of the population finds employment in connection with the Canal. Important products include bananas and rice.

PUERTO RICO - *Area 9,103 sq km; population 3,350,000; capital, San Juan (pop. 850,000); currency, US dollar (100 cents); official languages, Spanish and English.*
An island of the Greater Antilles group, Puerto Rico belonged to Spain for nearly 400 years before being ceded to the United States in 1898. Formally independent, it is closely associated with the United States, and its inhabitants, who speak Spanish, have the rights of US citizens.
The island is thickly populated and poor, which means that many emigrate to the United States. The economy is based on manufacturing and tourism as well as on agriculture.

SAINT KITTS AND NEVIS - *Area 269 sq km; population 43,200; capital, Basseterre (pop. 185,000); currency, East Caribbean dollar (100 cents); official language, English.*
It has been an independent state since 1983, remaining part of the British Commonwealth.
They are volcanic coral islands to the southeast of Puerto Rico. They produce a modest amount of sugar cane.

ST LUCIA - *Area 610 sq km; population 145,780; capital, Castries (pop. 53,000); currency, dollar; official language, English.*
St Lucia gained its independence from Britain in 1979. It is a volcanic island, and its economy is based on farming and tourism.

ST VINCENT AND GRENADINES - *Area 390 sq km; population 120,000; capital, Kingstown (pop. 29,000); currency, dollar; official language, English.*
St Vincent also became independent from Britain in 1979, and its economy has a similar base to St Lucia.

THE UNITED STATES OF AMERICA
Areas in square kilometres

Alabama	131,333	**Montana**	377,069
Alaska	1,467,052	**Nebraska**	198,090
Arizona	293,749	**Nevada**	284,611
Arkansas	134,537	**New Hampshire**	23,380
California	404,973	**New Jersey**	19,479
Colorado	268,753	**New Mexico**	314,457
Connecticut	12,593	**New York**	123,882
Delaware	5,133	**North Carolina**	126,386
Florida	140,092	**North Dakota**	179,416
Georgia	150,408	**Ohio**	106,125
Hawaii	16,641	**Oklahoma**	178,145
Idaho	214,132	**Oregon**	249,115
Illinois	144,387	**Pennsylvania**	116,461
Indiana	93,491	**Rhode Island**	2,717
Iowa	144,887	**South Carolina**	78,282
Kansas	211,827	**South Dakota**	196,723
Kentucky	102,693	**Tennessee**	107,039
Louisiana	116,368	**Texas**	678,924
Maine	80,082	**Utah**	212,628
Maryland	25,618	**Vermont**	24,025
Massachusetts	20,269	**Virginia**	103,030
Michigan	147,155	**Washington**	172,416
Minnesota	205,358	**West Virginia**	62,341
Mississippi	122,496	**Wisconsin**	141,061
Missouri	178,696	**Wyoming**	251,755

UNITED STATES OF AMERICA - *Area 9,372,600 sq km; population 245,800,000; capital, Washington DC (pop. 3,560,000); currency, dollar (100 cents); official language, English.*

The United States is a federation of 50 states. The first 13 declared their independence in 1776, after emerging victorious in wars against their colonial masters, Britain and France. The United States is one of the largest and most powerful countries in the world. In the north, it has a long frontier with Canada, the eastern boundary is the Atlantic Ocean, the Pacific Ocean forms the western boundary, and the southern border is with Mexico and on the Gulf of Mexico. Alaska, the 49th state, lies to the west of Canada, and Hawaii, the 50th, lies in the Pacific, some 3,800 km west of California. The mainland may be divided into five natural regions: (1) the Atlantic coastal plain, which gives way in the west to (2) a highland region—the long range of the Appalachians; the land then falls away again to (3) the broad interior plains crossed in a north-south direction by the Mississippi and the Missouri; (4) the western highlands consist of the Rocky Mountains, with their high plateaux and peaks of over 4,000 metres, the Sierra Nevada, and other ranges; and (5) the coastal strip along the Pacific, which descends to the Ocean. Despite the size and variety of the country, most parts of the United States have a moderate climate.

The population is about 87 per cent Whites (descendants of immigrants and new immigrants themselves from all the countries of Europe), 11 per cent Blacks (mostly descendants of African slaves), and the others include some half million American Indians, most of whom live on reservations.

The United States is the richest country in the world. A high average standard of living is aimed at, and much is done to provide equality of opportunity, but a small minority still live in varying degrees of poverty.

It is mainly in the north that are found America's giant industrial undertakings. Industrialization has also extended to agriculture, and the working of the frequently huge farms is extensively mechanized and specialized. Nowhere else on Earth is so much maize, tobacco, soya bean, and lemons produced as in the United States. High productivity is also recorded for wheat, barley, oats, cotton, and sugar-beet. The high level of technological development of the country is also seen in the harnessing of energy (coal, oil, or natural gas), and also in the exploitation of the rich mineral resources in the ground.

Countries of South America

ARGENTINA - *Area 2,766,890 sq km; population 32,000,000; capital, Buenos Aires (pop. 9,800,000); currency, austral (1,000 old pesos); official language, Spanish.*

Argentina has been independent since 1816, and a federal republic since 1853. The country is 3,700 km long from north to south, almost half the length of the continent. In the north-west, there is the hot bush and forest lowland of the Gran Chaco, to the south the steppe lowlands of the Pampas, which extend as far as the coast, and in the west the Andes, which contain the highest mountain in South America, the 6,960 metres high Aconcagua. The climate varies from almost tropical in the Gran Chaco to cool in the south. In the damp north-eastern marginal areas, there is tropical primeval forest, in which palms, lianas, bamboo, mimosa, and acacia grow.

Ninety per cent of Argentinians are white, mostly of Spanish or Italian descent. A small German minority, however, wields considerable economic influence. Some pure-blooded Amerindians live in the Gran Chaco.

The basis of the economy is agriculture, but huge herds of cattle graze on the Pampas, and beef is an important export. The Pampas merge into a crescent-shaped region, nearly 320 km broad, in which grain is cultivated. Cotton is planted in the Gran Chaco, and the province of Tucumán in the north-west is a sugar-cane growing region. The mountains have considerable mineral resources, but these are largely undeveloped.

BOLIVIA - *Area 1,098,580 sq km; population 6,740,000; capital, La Paz (pop. 553,000); currency, peso (100 centavos); official language, Spanish.*

Under the leadership of Simón Bolívar, from whom it took its name, the country declared its independence from Spain and Peru in 1825; today it is a presidential republic.

Bolivia is completely landlocked. In the west, ranges of the Andes (the Cordilleras), with peaks rising to 6,100 metres, border the Altiplano, a treeless plateau some 3,800 metres above sea level. Here, in an elevated basin, lies Lake Titicaca. The eastern lowlands have affinities with the grass steppes (llanos) of the Amazon Basin and with the Gran Chaco, and they are sparsely populated. More than half the people live in the Altipiano, particularly on the slopes falling away to the east. Only 15 per cent are Whites, but they constitute the ruling class. More than half are Indians, and the rest are of mixed blood. Two-thirds of the population, especially the South American Indians, are engaged in agriculture, but their primitive methods produce poor results, although the llanos are very fertile. The land has considerable mineral resources, especially of tin.

BRAZIL - *Area 506,671 sq km; population 150,053,000; capital, Brasília (pop. 1,803,000); currency, cruzeiro (100 centavos); official language, Portuguese.*

Brazil declared its independence from Portugal in 1822, and became a republic in 1889. It is the fifth largest country in the world, taking up almost half the South American continent. The main river is the Amazon, in the north, with some hundred navigable tributaries. The Amazon lowlands have a hot and humid climate and constitute the largest tropical primeval forest region in the world. To the north lie the largely unexplored Guiana Highlands, which are partly covered with primeval forest, partly with savanna vegetation. Rain forests lie along the central coastal regions, while in the south-east there are subtropical forests and savanna. Savanna also dominate extensive regions of the highlands in the interior.

Brazil has a larger population than any other South American country. Until the mid-1600s, there was considerable immigration of Portuguese and Spaniards, and from the end of the 1500s Black slaves were brought into the country. It was not until the 19th century that free immigration began from all the countries of Europe. Today, barely 60 per cent of the inhabitants are White. About 10 per cent are Blacks and 4 per cent Asian, but a third are of mixed blood and Amerindians. Most of the Amerindians live in small bands in the forested Amazon region.

Brazil's wealth comes from agriculture. More than half of the whole work force is engaged in agriculture and forestry. The main crop is maize. The country also has rich mineral resources, and industrialization is being actively promoted.

CHILE - *Area 756,625 sq km; population 12,750,000; capital, Santiago (pop. 4,913,000); currency, peso (100 centavos); official language, Spanish.*

A former Spanish colony, Chile has been independent since 1818. It is a long, mountainous country, stretching along the Pacific coast for more than half the length of South America. There are three distinct climatic zones: in the north, a dry, desert zone with a rainless coast; in the centre, a subtropical zone; and in the south, a zone with heavy rainfall and low summer temperatures.

Between the Andes—the High Cordilleras in the east and the Coastal Cordilleras in the west—runs a great longitudinal valley. There are earthquake zones, and active volcanoes rising to a height of 6,700 metres. Tierra del Fuego, the southern tip of the continent, is separated from the mainland by the stormy Strait of Magellan.

Most of the population are of mixed blood. Of the original Indian native population, only about 500,000 are left. The small ruling class comes from people of European descent. Almost three-quarters of the inhabitants live in the central area, for this is the only part of the country that is arable. Extensive regions require artificial irrigation. There are rich mineral resources, and of all exported products, more than the half are mined (copper, iron, titanium, nitrates).

COLOMBIA - *Area 1,141,748 sq km; population 30,660,000; capital, Bogotá (pop. 4,070,000); currency, peso (100 centavos); official language, Spanish.*

Colombia won independence from Spain in 1819, and became a republic in 1886. It lies in the north-west of South America, bordering on Panama, which, for some time, formed part of Colombia. The Eastern Cordilleras, a range of the Andes, reach a height of 5,500 metres. The lowlands of the Amazon valley and the Orinoco

occupy large portions of the country, on both the Pacific and Caribbean coasts.

More than two-thirds of the population are of mixed blood, a fifth are Whites, and the rest are of Black or Indian origin. The original Indian population is today represented by only about 7 per cent of the inhabitants.

Although Colombia is developing its industry, it is still largely an agricultural country. Very little of the land is under cultivation. There are large numbers of smallholders. The main product is coffee.

ECUADOR - *Area 283,560 sq km; population 9,850,000; capital Quito (pop. 1,140,000); currency, sucre (100 centavos); official language, Spanish.*

Ecuador has been an independent republic since 1830. It suffers from constant uprisings, revolutions, and putsches, under which the country's economic development has been retarded. As a result, it is amongst the poorest countries of South America.

The country lies on the west coast of the continent, between Peru and Colombia. The coastal lowlands are from 50 to 150 km wide. Through the centre of the country run two parallel mountain chains of the Andes, with heights of 3,000-6,000 metres. There are large numbers of active volcanoes in this region. Towards the east, the mountain slopes fall steeply away down to the lowlands of the Amazon valley. Over a third of the inhabitants are Amerindians, engaged in agriculture. The coastal region is inhabited by Blacks, and people of mixed blood. The 10 per cent of Whites, chiefly descendants of the Spaniards, constitute the ruling class. Two-thirds of the population are engaged in agriculture or cattle rearing.

FRENCH GUIANA - *Area 88,900 sq km; population 92,000; capital, Cayenne (pop. 38,000); currency, French franc (100 centimes); official language, French.*

The country, which lies on the northern coast of South America, became an overseas department of France in 1946. Most of the people are Blacks or Creoles, and about 10 per cent are American Indians.

Tropical rain forest covers almost nine-tenths of the total area, and is still unexplored. Gold is mined and there are large deposits of bauxite. Crops grown include sugar and maize.

GUYANA - *Area 214,970 sq km; population 750,000; capital, Georgetown (pop. 190,000); currency, dollar (100 cents); official language, English.*

Formerly British Guiana, the country became an independent member of the Commonwealth in 1966, the world's first Cooperative Republic. Guyana lies between Venezuela and Surinam on the Atlantic Ocean. The highland region in the west rises to a height of nearly 3,000 metres. The mountains in the east are much flatter and give way to tropical rain forests. Most of the population live on the coastal strip.

About half of them are Asians, many of whose ancestors came from India. The Whites and the American Indians constitute only small groups. There are, however, sizeable Black and mixed-blood communities. Bauxite, alumina, manganese ores, and diamonds are mined and exported. Sugar, rice, shrimps, timber, rum and molasses are also exported.

PARAGUAY - *Area 406,750 sq km; population 4,000,000; capital, Asunción (pop. 790,000); currency, guaraní (100 céntimos); official language, Spanish.*

Paraguay won its independence from Spain and became a republic in 1811.

The larger, western part of the country lies in the Gran Chaco, whereas the eastern part is bordered by the Paraná and constitutes an undulating tableland with subtropical rain forests. Between the Paraguay and Paraná rivers, there are large marshes. Some 95 per cent of the inhabitants are of mixed blood. More than half the people live in or around the capital. And more than half are engaged in agriculture.

PERU - *Area 1,285,215 sq km; population 21,790,000; capital, Lima (pop. 6,000,000); currency, sol (100 centavos); official language, Spanish.*

Peru declared its independence from Spain in 1821, and after many internal political troubles eventually became a republic.

It has a 2,250-km coastal strip on the Pacific Ocean, which is fertile only along the river banks. The country is traversed from north to south by the Cordilleras (Andes), the highest peak being Huascarán, at 6,768 metres. The eastern chain of the Cordilleras merges into the highland region of the Montana, and this, in turn, gives way to wooded lowlands. The main sources of the Amazon rise in the Peruvian Andes. Most of the inhabitants are descended from American Indians, but the Whites constitute the ruling class. Quechua and Aymara, American Indian languages, are widely spoken. Half of the working population are engaged in agriculture, forestry, and fishing. On the large arable areas of the coastal district, cotton, sugar-cane, rice, maize, and many other crops are grown on plantations. There are extensive irrigation systems. There is also a flourishing mining industry. Copper, lead, and zinc are particularly important.

SURINAM - *Area 163,820 sq km; population 425,000; capital, Paramaribo (pop. 67,000); currency, guilder (100 cents); official language, Dutch.*

Surinam, formerly known as Dutch Guiana, became independent in 1975.

It lies on the northern coast of South America. Three-quarters of the land area is covered in forest, still largely unexplored. Half the inhabitants are of mixed blood. Along the coast, sugar-cane, coffee, citrus fruits, and cacao are cultivated, and there are vast desposits of bauxite.

TRINIDAD AND TOBAGO - *Area 5,130 sq km; population 1,100,000; capital, Port of Spain (pop. 60,000); currency, dollar (100 cents); official language, English.*

These two islands, the most southerly of the Lesser Antilles, formed a British colony from 1889 until their independence in 1962. They lie off the coast of Venezuela. The population of Tobago, by far the smaller of the two islands, consists almost exclusively of Blacks. On Trinidad, more than a third of the people are Indians, but the majority are Blacks or people of mixed blood.

Trinidad is a mountainous island and has large stretches of rain forest. Half of the country is cultivated (sugar and cocoa), and there are rich deposits of oil and natural asphalt.

URUGUAY - *Area 175,215 sq km; population 2,980,000; capital, Montevideo (pop. 1,300,000); currency, peso (100 centésimos); official language, Spanish.*

Uruguay became an independent republic in 1828, having belonged first to Spain and then to Brazil. It is situated on the Atlantic Ocean and on the Rio de la Plata, between Brazil and Argentina. Hilly grassland merges in the south into the Argentinian Pampas. The population consists largely of the descendants of Spanish and Portuguese settlers. The main source of income is the rearing of animals. Meat, meat products, and wool are exported. More than two-thirds of the total area is pastureland, only 10 per cent being arable.

VENEZUELA - *Area 912,050 sq km; population 18,750,000; capital, Caracas (pop. 3,500,000); currency, bolívar (100 céntimos); official language, Spanish.*

Venezuela won its independence from Spain in 1821 and became a republic in 1830. It lies in the northernmost part of South America, between Colombia and Guyana. The main river is the Orinoco, which drains four-fifths of the country. Mountain systems break up Venezuela into four distinct regions: the Maracaibo lowlands, the highlands in the north and north-west, the vast Orinoco plains or *llanos*, and the Guiana Highlands. The llanos, in the south-east, cover a third of the country's area.

The population consists mainly of 65 per cent people of mixed blood, 20 per cent Whites, and 10 per cent Blacks. Only 1 per cent are pureblooded South American Indians. Half of the inhabitants live in the towns.

For years, agriculture was the only source of revenue, with exports of coffee and cocoa. Now, however, Venezuela has developed into an important supplier of raw materials for industry. It is the ninth largest oil-producing country in the world, its oil resources being found mainly in the Maracaibo basin. Its iron ore deposits are also among the largest in the world, and there are important gold and diamond mines. Along with the development of refineries, the country is also being increasingly industrialized.

Countries of Oceania

AUSTRALIA - *Area 7,685,000 sq km; population 16,470,000; capital, Canberra (pop. 300,000); currency, dollar (100 cents); official language, English.*

The Australian Commonwealth was founded in 1901, comprising New South Wales, Victoria, Queensland, South Australia, Western Australia, and Tasmania. The Northern Territory was transferred from South Australia 10 years later, at the same time as the Australian Capital Territory was acquired from New South Wales. Australia is a member of the British Commonwealth, and a parliamentary democracy. The head of state is the British monarch, represented by a governor-general, who formally appoints the prime minister and other ministers from the majority party in parliament. Parliament (the House of Representatives and the Senate) is the legislative body.

Australia is the smallest of the continents, but it is sometimes also regarded as the largest island in the world. The area of the mainland (i.e. without Tasmania) is 7,618,517 sq km. The eastern and more populated part of the country has a regular coastline, with good harbours and rivers flowing to the sea. The western half has a broken coastline, which is thinly-populated except in the south-west. The Great Barrier Reef, the world's largest coral reef, stretches for about 2,000 km parallel to the Queensland coast at a distance of 15-240 km. It covers an area of some 200,000 sq km. Much of Australia's interior, especially in the west, is desert. But in the east, particularly the south-east, and in the south-west around Perth, the land is fertile.

The country as a whole is generally low and flat, but there are highlands stretching right along the east coast and along most of Victoria on the southern coast, the highest point being Mount Kosciusko, which rises 2,230 metres in the Australian Alps, near Canberra. In the centre of the continent, lowlands extend from the Gulf of Carpentaria to the shores of the Great Australian Bight in the south. A vast plateau, with an average height of about 300 metres, covers most of the western two-thirds of Australia. A largely desert region, it includes Western Australia, the Northern Territory, and much of South Australia, extending even into Queensland and New South Wales.

Australia has a warm, dry climate, the northern third of the country lying in the tropics. Only about a third of the country receives enough rain for good forming. Nevertheless, what good pasture land and arable land there is makes Australia the leading wool producing nation in the world and one of the leading meat and wheat exporting countries. Most of the farms are family concerns covering large areas and run with the help of machinery and seasonal workers. In the Northern Territory, some ranches, or *stations* as they are called, cover several thousand square miles.

But Australia is not just an agricultural and farming country. Mining is becoming increasingly important. The gold deposits have long been known, but rich strata of iron ore have also been discovered, and Australia is second in the world in the production of lead. Other important minerals include hard and brown coal, bauxite, copper, and zinc. There are several oilfields in production (in Queensland, Western Australia, and offshore Victoria), which supply about two-thirds of the country's needs. Natural gas deposits are also being exploited.

Industry has grown enormously, but there is a shortage of manpower to develop all the possibilities offered by this vast country. Economists believe that Australia could support three times its present population.

Most of the inhabitants of Australia are European immigrants or descendants of immigrants. Only about 100,000 of the original native race, the Aborigines, remain, and most of these live on protected reserves. They used to wander through the country beach-combing and hunting. They used primitive implements and weapons (spears, clubs, boomerangs) made of bone, sea-shells, rock, or wood. The Aborigines have chocolate-brown skin and certain physical characteristics that do not place them easily into any of the major racial stocks. They probably lived originally in south-eastern Asia.

The native animal world of Australia is markedly different from that found in other countries of the world, and this phenomenon can be explained by the development undergone by the Earth's crust. Some 200 million years ago, the great land mass that existed then broke up. As it broke away, each continent naturally carried with it the varieties of animal that lived there. These then developed in isolation from the others. So it is that only in Australia do we find the duckbilled platypus and the spiny anteater (echidna), representing a primitive subspecies of mammals. These lay eggs, hatch them out, and then feed their young on breast milk. A special variety of mammal is also found in Australia, the marsupials. These give birth to living young, which are so small that they slip into the mother's pouch immediately after birth. There they are suckled until they are large enough to live an independent life. The best known of these is the kangaroo, but there are also koalas, wombats, bandicoots, dasyures, Tasmanian wolves, and the cuscus.

FIJI - *Area 18,270 sq km; population 745,000; capital, Suva (pop. 70,000); currency, dollar (100 cents); official languages, English and Fijian.*

A group of 322 islands in the South Pacific, some 1,770 km north of New Zealand, Fiji came under British control in 1874 and became an independent nation within the Commonwealth in 1970.

Only 106 of the islands are inhabited, and the largest two, Viti Levu and Vanua Levu, make up seven-eighths of the total area. About half the people are Indians and some 42 per cent are Fijians. The Indians are largely descended from plantation labourers brought from India between 1880 and 1914. The islands have a favourable oceanic climate, and the main agricultural products are sugar-cane and coconuts. Tourism is becoming an increasingly important source of revenue.

FRENCH POLYNESIA - *Area 4,000 sq km; population 160,000; capital, Papeete (pop. 65,000); currency, CFP franc (100 centimes); official language, French.*

An Overseas Territory of France since 1958, French Polynesia consists of a number of islands scattered over a wide area of the eastern Pacific. These include the Society Islands, the Leeward Isles, and the Marquesas. The capital is located on Tahiti, in the Society group. Most of the people are Polynesians. The most important product is copra.

GUAM - *Area 550 sq km; population 130,000; capital, Agaña (pop. 4,800); currency, US dollar (100 cents); official language, English.*

The largest of the Mariana Islands, in the North Pacific, Guam was acquired by the United States from Spain in 1898. It was granted statutory powers of self-government in 1950, and the people became US citizens. Most Guamanians are Chamorros (of Indonesian and Spanish descent). The island is of vital strategic importance as an air and naval base, and about a third of the inhabitants are military personnel and their families. The interior of Guam is mountainous, and coral reefs lie off the coast.

HAWAII - *Area 16,641 sq km; population 832,000; capital, Honolulu (pop. 325,000); currency, US dollar (100 cents); official language, English.*

A group of islands in the central Pacific, about 3,800 km) west of the US mainland, Hawaii was accepted as the 50th state of the United States in 1959. It had been a US territory since 1900. The group comprises a 2,591-km chain of 122 islands formed by volcanoes built up from the ocean floor. Of the eight main islands, located in the south-east, seven are inhabited. They have a mild climate and fertile soil. The largest island is called Hawaii and covers nearly two-thirds of the total area. It has two active volcanoes (Mauna Loa and Kilauea) and the highest peak in the state, Mauna Kea, which rises 4,205 metres. About 80 per cent of Hawaii's inhabitants live on Oahu, the third largest island on which Honolulu and Pearl Harbor are located.

The original inhabitants of these islands were Polynesians, and 15 per cent of today's population have predominant Hawaiian ancestry. About 40 per cent are of White descent, and 30 per cent have Japanese ancestry. The chief products are cane-sugar and tropical fruits. About 35 per cent of the world's tinned pineapple is produced in Hawaii. The tourist industry is one of the state's largest sources of income.

KIRIBATI REPUBLIC - *Area 850 sq km; population 68,200; capital, Tarawa (pop. 2,100); currency, Australian dollar (100 cents); official languages, English and Gilbertese.*

Formerly a British colony known as the Gilbert Islands, the Kiribati Republic became independent in 1979. Until 1975 it was linked with Tuvalu (Ellice Islands) which became independent in 1978. The Kiribati Republic contains the Gilbert, Phoenix and Line Islands, and also Ocean Island. Most of the atolls rise to no more than 3.5 metres above sea level, and are thickly wooded with coconut palms. A high proportion of the population is Micronesian. Ocean Island, to the west of the Gilbert group, has important phosphate deposits. The only other export from the islands is copra.

MARSHALL ISLANDS - *Area 180 sq km; population 42,000; capital, Jaluit; currency, US dollar (100 cents); official language, English.*

A semi-independent republic after the break-up of the Trust Territory of the Pacific Islands in 1986, the Marshall Islands gained full independence in 1991. Its defence and foreign policy are still the responsibility of the United States.

It is made up of an archipelago of atolls, the most famous being Bikini, divided into two long arcs, Ratak and Ralik, in Micronesia. Most of the people are Micronesian. The main agricultural products are coconuts, copra and fruit.

MICRONESIA - *Area 720 sq km; population 100,000; capital, Kolonia; currency, US dollar (100 cents); official language, English.*
Like the Marshall Islands, it became a semi-independent republic after the break-up of the Trust Territory of the Pacific Islands in 1986, gaining full independence in 1991. Its defence and foreign policy are still the responsibility of the United States.
The Federate States of Micronesia consist of the Eastern Caroline Islands, mostly coralline, the major ones being Ponhpei and Chuuk. Most of the people are Micronesian. The chief products are copra, coconuts and fruit.

NAURU - *Area 21.5 sq km; population 7,300; capital, Nauru; currency, Australian dollar (100 cents); official languages, Nauruan and English.*
A tiny island in the Pacific Ocean, Nauru became an independent republic in 1968, having a special relationship with the Commonwealth. It had been under German control from 1888 to 1914, when it surrendered to Australian forces. It was administered under a mandate until 1947 and then a trusteeship.
The country lies almost on the equator, north of New Zealand, and is surrounded by a coral reef. Its importance is due to its valuable deposits of phosphates. About half the people are Nauruans, a quarter are other Pacific islanders, and the rest are Chinese or European.

NEW CALEDONIA - *Area 19,060 sq km; population 132,000; capital, Nouméa (pop. 75,000); currency, CFP franc (100 centimes); official language, French.*
An island in the western Pacific 1,127 km east of Queensland, New Caledonia was annexed by France in 1853, and with its various island dependencies is an Overseas Territory of France. Nearly a half of the inhabitants are Melanesians, and a third are Europeans (mostly French).
The island is rich in mineral resources, and is the world's third largest nickel producer, after the USSR and Canada. Chrome, iron, and other minerals are mined.

NEW ZEALAND - *Area 268,675 sq km); population 3,350,000; capital, Wellington (pop. 350,000); currency, dollar (100 cents); official language, English.*
Like Australia, New Zealand is an independent parliamentary democracy on the British model. The head of state is the British monarch, represented by the governor-general. The country became a British colony in 1840 when the Maoris, the original native population, ceded sovereignty to the British Crown, and a dominion in 1907.
North and South Islands, which make up nearly 99 per cent of the territory of New Zealand, lie in the South Pacific, about 1,930 km east of Australia. There are a number of smaller islands, and New Zealand has responsibility for a large area in the Antarctic Ocean. North and South Islands are separated by Cook Strait, just 26 km wide. Much of the country is mountainous. The highest point, Mount Cook, rises 3,764 metres in the Southern Alps, which extend along the entire length of the South Island. There are several volcanoes, including two active ones, on the North Island, which is also noted for its hot springs and geysers. The countryside has great natural beauty and there are many lakes. The climate is temperate, with a narrow annual range of temperature.
About half of the country is used for agriculture, and 90 per cent of the farmland is used for rearing sheep and cattle. New Zealand is the world's fourth largest sheep-rearing and second largest wool-producing country. The main crops are wheat, barley, and oats. Apart from wool and meat, the chief exports are butter and cheese. New Zealand has few mineral resources, the main ones being coal and gold. The generation of energy is dependent on hydro-electric power.
The development of New Zealand since the 1870s has been marked by the successful integration of the native population with the European immigrants (mostly from Great Britain). The Maoris are a branch of the Polynesian race and make up about 8 per cent of the total population.

PALAU - *Area 485 sq km; population 14,700; capital, Koror (pop. 8,100); currency, US dollar (100 cents); official languages, English and Palauan.*
Formerly part of the Trust Territories of the Pacific Islands, it has been a semi-independent republic since 1986, still retaining its status of US trust territory.
It consists of the island of Palau in the western Pacific, east of the Philippines. The population is mostly Micronesian. The chief product is copra.

PAPUA NEW GUINEA - *Area 462,840 sq km; population 3,560,000; capital, Port Moresby (pop. 152,000); currency, kina (100 toea); official language, English.*
Formerly a dependency of Australia, Papua New Guinea became self-governing in 1973 and fully independent in 1975. The country comprises the eastern half of the island of New Guinea (West Irian, part of Indonesia, is the other half) and a number of islands off the northern and eastern coasts. Papua, the southern part of the eastern half of New Guinea, was annexed by Queensland in 1883 and became a British protectorate in 1884. The Germans took possession of the northern part in the same year. The British government handed over control of British New Guinea in 1906 to Australia, who renamed it Papua, and the Australians also gained control of the German territory in 1921. They established joint control of the Territory of Papua and New Guinea in 1949.
Papua New Guinea lies wholly within the tropics, separated from Australia by the Torres Strait. A massive chain of mountain ranges stretches across the mainland, reaching a height of 4,700 metres with Mount Wilhelm in the Bismarck Range. The land is varied, with deep, forested valleys, large rivers and hundreds of swiftly flowing streams, and, to the south, one of the most extensive areas of swamp land in the world.
Most of the people are Melanesians, but there are also large groups of Papuans and Negritos. Farming is the principal occupation, and the chief crops are coffee, copra, and cocoa. Rubber and timber are also leading exports, and there is an important copper mine on the island of Bougainville.

SAMOA, AMERICAN - *Area 197 sq km; population 38,000; capital, Pago Pago (pop. 3,100); currency, US dollar (100 cents); official languages, Samoan and English.*
This group of five volcanic islands and two coral atolls in the South Pacific has been a territory of the United States since 1900. The people are Polynesians and are US nationals. The chief products are tuna fish and copra.

SOLOMON ISLANDS - *Area 27,550 sq km; population 301,000; capital, Honiara (pop. 31,000); currency, dollar (100 cents); official language, English.*
Formerly a British protectorate, this island group in the South Pacific became fully independent in 1978.
The larger islands are mountainous and forested. The rivers tend to flood. The largest island is Guadalcanal. Most of the people are Melanesians. The chief exports are copra, timber, and fish.

TONGA - *Area 700 sq km; population 100,000; capital, Nuku'alofa (pop. 29,000); currency, pa'anga (100 seniti); official languages, English and Tongan.*
A British-protected state since 1900, Tonga became independent in 1970.
The kingdom consists of 169 islands, also known as the Friendly Islands. Most of the islands are coral, but some are volcanic. Farming is the main occupation of the people, who are Polynesians, and copra and bananas are the chief exports. Tourism is being developed.

TUVALU - *Area 25 sq km; population 9,000; capital, Vaiaku (pop. 3,000); currency, Australian dollar (100 cents); official languages, English and Tuvaluan.*
Formerly the Ellice Islands, Tuvalu became independent in 1978.
The islands are low, and large expanses are thickly wooded. Most of the people are Polynesians. The most important export is copra.

VANUATU REPUBLIC - *Area 14,765 sq km; population 150,000; capital, Port-Vila (pop. 15,000); currency, vatu; official languages, English, French, and Bislama.*
A group of islands in the South Pacific some 800 km west of Fiji, the Vanuatu Republic became independent in 1980.
There are many active volcanoes on the islands. Most of the people are Melanesians. The chief product is copra.

WESTERN SAMOA - *Area 2,840 sq km; population 162,000; capital, Apia (pop. 35,000); currency, tala (100 sene); official languages, English and Samoan.*
A German protectorate in the early 1900s, Western Samoa was administered by New Zealand from 1920 to 1961, before voting its own independence as from 1962.
The country comprises 9 of the 14 islands of the Samoan Archipelago (the others constituting American Samoa). The two large islands, Savaii and Upolu, make up 99.8 per cent of Western Samoa's land area. They are mountainous, with rugged interior. Most of the people, who are Polynesians, live on the coast. The chief exports are copra, cocoa, and bananas.

WEST IRIAN - *Area 421,900 sq km; population 1,556,000; capital, Jayapura (pop. 150,000); currency, Indonesian rupiah (100 sen); official language, Indonesian.*
Formerly a Dutch colony, it is now an Indonesian trust territory. Indonesia considers it a province, being part of its national territory.
West Irian—also known as Irian Jaya—occupies the western half of New Guinea. The main products are maize, coconuts and bananas.

Index to the maps of the British Isles

Rosehearty II F3
Rossan Point III BC2
Rosslare III E4
Ross-on-Wye I D5
Rothbury I E1
Rotherham I EF3
Rothes II E3
Rothesay II C5
Rousay II E1
Rugby I E4
Rushden 5 F4
Ruthin I C3
Ryde I EF6
Rye I G6

S

Saffron Walden I G4-5
Saint Abb's Head II FG5
Saint Albans I F5
Saint Andrews II F4
Saint Austell I B6
Saint Bee's Head II BC2
Saint David's Head I A5
Saint George's Channel III EF4-5
Saint Helens I D3
Saint Ives I aB
Saint Ives I A6
Saint Martin's I aA
Saint Mary's I aA
Saint Neots I F4
Salcombe I BC6
Salford I D3
Salisbury I DE5
Saltash I B6
Sanday II F1
Sandown I EF6
Sandringham I G4
Sawel Mountain III DE2
Saxmundham I H4
Scafell Pikes I C2
Scalloway II a
Scalpay II C3
Scarborough I F2
Scarinish II B4
Scilly, Isles of I aA
Scourie II C2
Scunthorpe I F3
Seaham I E2

Selby I F3
Selkirk II EF5
Sevenoaks I G5
Severn I D4
Shaftesbury I DE6
Shannon, River III B4
Shannon, River III C3
Shapinsay II F1
Sheffield I EF3
Sheppey, Isle of I GH5
Shepton Mallet I D5
Sheringham I H4
Shetland Isles II a
Shrewsbury I D4
Sidmouth I CD6
Sittingbourne I G5
Sixmilebridge III C4
Skegness I G3
Skibbereen III B5
Skipton I DE3
Skokholm Island I A5
Skomer Island I A5
Skye II B3
Slaney II E4
Sleaford I F3
Slea Head III A4
Slieve Donard III EF2
Sligo III C2
Slough I F5
Slyne Head III A3
Snaefell I B2
Snowdon I BC3
Solihull I E4
Solway Firth II E6
Solway Firth I C2
Somerset I C5
Southampton I E6
South Downs I F6
Southend-on-Sea I GH5
Southern Uplands II DF5
South Esk II EF4
South Molton I C5
Southport I C3
South Ronaldsay II F2
Southwold I H4
Spalding I F4
Spennymoor I E2
Sperrin Mountains III DE2
Spey II E3
Spurn Head I G3
Stafford I DE4
Staffordshire I DE4
Staines I F5

Stamford I F4
Start Point I C6
Stevenage I FG5
Stewarton II D5
Stirling II DE4
Stockport I DE3
Stockton-on-Tees I E2
Stoke-on-Trent I DE3-4
Stonehaven II FG4
Stornoway II B2
Stowmarket I H4
Stow-on-the-Wold I E5
Stour, River I G4-5
Stour, River I D6
Strabane III D2
Strangford Lough III F2
Stranraer II C6
Strathclyde II C4
Strathy Point II D2
Stromness II E2
Stronsay II F1
Stroud I D5
Suck III C3
Sudbury I G4
Sunderland I EF2
Suffolk I GH4
Sumburgh Head II a
Surrey I F5
Sussex, East I G6
Sussex, West I F6
Sutton-in-Ashfield I EF3
Swadlincote I E4
Swaffham I G4
Swale I E2
Swanage I E6
Swansea I B5
Swindon I E5
Swinford III C3
Swords III E3

T

Tain II D3
Tamar I B6
Tamworth I E4
Tarbert (Outer Hebrides) II B3
Tarbert (Strathclyde) II C5
Taunton I CD5

Tavistock I BC6
Taw I C6
Tay II E4
Tees I E2
Teifi I B4
Teignmouth I C6
Telford I D4
Templemore III D4
Test I E5
Tetbury I DE5
Teviot II F5
Tewkesbury I D5
Thames, River I E5
Thames, River I G5
Thetford I H4
Thomastown III DE4
Thornhill II E5
Thirsk I E2
Thurles III CD4
Thurso II E2
Tilbury I G5
Tipperary III C4
Tipperary, County III CD4
Tiree II AB4
Tiverton I C6
Tobercurry III C2
Tobermory II B4
Tonbridge I G5
Tongue II D2
Torbay I C6
Torridon II C3
Totnes I C6
Towcester I E4
Tralee III B4
Tramore III D4
Trent, River I E4
Trent, River I F3
Tresco I aA
Trim III E3
Troon II D5
Trowbridge I DE5
Truro I aB
Truro I AB6
Tuam III D3
Tullamore III D3
Tullow III E4
Tunbridge Wells I G5
Turriff II F3
Tyne I DE2
Tyne and Wear I E1-2
Tynemouth I E1
Tywi I C5
Tywyn I B4

U

Uig II B3
Uist, North II AB3
Uist, South II A3
Ullapool II CD3
Ullswater I D2
Ulverston I CD2
Unshin III C2
Unst II a
Upper Lough Erne III D2
Ure I E2

V

Valencia Island III A5
Ventnor I E6
Vyrnwy, Lake I C4

W

Wakefield I E3
Wallingford I E5
Walls II a
Walney, Isle of I C2
Walsall I E4
Warley I E4
Warminster I DE5
Warrenpoint III E2
Warrington I D3
Warwick I E4
Warwickshire I E4
Wash, The I G4
Waterford III DE4
Waterford, County III D4
Watford I F5
Waveney I H4
Wellingborough I F4
Wellington I CD6
Wells I D5
Wells-next-the-Sea I G4
Welshpool I C4
Welwyn Garden City I F5
West Bromwich I E4
Western Isles II AB3
Westmeath III D3
Weston-super-Mare I CD5
Westport III B3
Wexford III E4

Weymouth I D6
Whalsay II a
Wharfe I E3
Whernside I D2
Whitby I F2
Whitehaven I C2
Whithorn II D6
Whitstable I H5
Whittlesey I F4
Wick II EF2
Wicklow, County III E3
Wicklow III EF3
Wicklow Head III F4
Wicklow Mountains III E3-4
Widnes I D3
Wigan I D3
Wight, Isle of I EF6
Wigtown II D6
Wiltshire I DE5
Winchester I E5
Windermere, I CD2
Windermere I D2
Windsor I F5
Winsford I D3
Wisbech I FG4
Witham I G5
Witham, River I F3
Withernsea I G3
Witney I E5
Woking I F5
Wolverhampton I D4
Woodbridge I H4
Woodstock I E5
Worcester I DE4
Workington I C2
Worksop I E3
Worthing I F6
Wrexham I C3
Wye I D4-5
Wymondham I GH4

Y

Yare I H4
Yell II a
Yeovil I D6
York I EF2-3
Yorkshire, North I EF2
Yorkshire, South I E3
Yorkshire, West I E3

Index to maps

Brescia 2 H6
Brest, France 2 F6
Brest, U.S.S.R. 2 M5
Brewarrina 12 H6
Bright 12 H7
Brighton (Tasmania) 12 b9
Brindisi 2 L7
Brisbane 12 G5
Bristol 2 F5
Bristol Bay 7 D4
Bristol Channel 1 EF5
British Antarctic Terr. 14 Nm3
British Columbia 8 G4
British Isles 1 D5-4
Brittany 1 F6
Brno 2 L6
Broad Arrow 12 c6
Broad Sud 12 H4
Broken Hill 12 G6
Brooks Ra. 7 D3
Brookvale 12 e10
Broome 12 C3
Brunei 4 P9
Brunswick B. 12 C3
Bruny I. 12 b9
Brussels 2 G5
Bryansk 2 O5
Bucaramanga 10 C3
Bucharest 2 N7
Budapest 2 L6
Budd Coast 14 D3
Buenaventura 10 C3
Buenos Aires 10 DE7
Buenos Aires L9 CD8
Buffalo 8 M5
Bug 1 M5
Bug (S.) 1 O6
Bugel C. 3 m13
Bujumbura 6 F6
Bukavu 6 F6
Bulan 4 h16
Bulan Islands 4 h16
Bulawayo 6 F8
Bulgaria 2 MN6-7
Buller 12 g14
Bullfinch 12 I6
Bulli 12 d11
Bulloo 11 D7
Bulun 4 Q2
Bunbury 1 G6
Bundaberg 12 I4
Bundooma 12 E4
Bunguran Is. 3 O9
Buraida 4 G7
Burdekin 12 H4
Bureya 3 Q4
Burgas 2 N7
Burgos 2 F7
Burgundy 1 G6
Burketown 12 F3
Burkina Faso 6 C4
Burma 4 N7
Burnett 12 I5
Burnie 12 b8
Bursa 2 N8
Buru 4 Q10
Burundi 6 FG6
Bushir 4 H7
Butte 8 H5
Butung 3 Q10
Bydgoszcz 2 L5
Byrd Land 14 QS2
Byrd Sub-Glacial Basin 14 Qr1
Byrock 12 H6
Byron C. 11 F7
Byrranga Mts. 3 NO2

C
Caatingas 9 EF4
Cabinda (to Angola) 6 E6
Cabot Str. 7 P5
Caceres 2 E8
Cadiz 2 E8
Cadiz, Gulf of 1 E8
Caen 2 F6
Cagliari 2 G8
Caird Coast 14 M2
Cairns 12 H3
Cairo 6 FG2
Cajamarca 10 C4
Calais 2 G5
Calama 10 D6
Calcutta 4 M7
Calgary 8 H4
Cali 10 C3
California 8 G6
California, Gulf of 7 H7
Callao 10 C5
Callodouna L. 12 G5
Calvert Hill 12 F3
Camagüey 8 N7
Cambay, Gulf of 3 L8
Cambodia 4 O8
Cambrian Mts. 1 F5
Cameroon 6 E5
Cameroons Mt. 5 DE5
Camooweal 12 F4
Campbell I. 14 A4
Campbell Town 12 b9
Campbelltown 12 d11

Campeche 8 M8
Campeche, Gulf of 7 L7
Campina Grande 10 G4
Campinas 10 F6
Campo Grande 10 E6
Campos 9 E6
Campos Sertao 9 F5
Canada 8 FO4-5
Canada Basin II FH1
Canadian Shield 7 IO4
Canary Basin II M4
Canary Is. 6 B3
Canaveral C. 7 N7
Canberra 12 H7
Cantabrian Mts 1 E7
Cantin C. 1 E9
Canton 4 P7
Canton I. 11 I5
Cape Barren I 12 b9
Cape Basin II O7-8
Cape Breton, I. 7 P5
Cape Provincie 6 F9
Cape Rise II O8
Cape Town 6 E9
Cape Verde Is. II MN5
Cape Verde Rise II M5
Cape York Peninsula 12 G3
Capoeiras Falls 9 E4
Capricorn Ch. 12 I4
Caprivi Strip 6 F7
Caracas 10 D2
Caravelas 10 G5
Cardiff 2 F5
Careme 3 I13
Carey L. 12 C5
Carlisle 2 F5
Carlsberg Ridge II R5
Carnarvon 12 A5
Carnegie 12 C5
Carnegie L. 12 C5
Carnot 6 E5
Carolina 10 F4
Caroline Basin II CD5
Caroline I 11 M5
Caroline Islands 11 EG3-4
Carpathian Mts. 1 MN6
Carpentaria, Gulf of. 11 D6
Caribbean Sea 9 CD2
Cartagena (Sp.) 2 F8
Cartagena (Cd.) 10 C2
Casablanca 6 C2
Cascade Range 7 G5
Caspian Depression I RS6
Caspian Sea 1 RS78
Castlereagh 12 H6
Catalonia 1 G7
Catania 2 L8
Catanzaro 2 L8
Catamarca 10 D6
Cataract Res. 12 d11
Catastrophe C. 12 F7
Cato 11 F7
Caxias 10 F4
Cayambe, Volc. 9 C3
Cayenne 10 F3
Cayman Is. 8 M8
Cebu 4 Q8
Cedros I. 7 H7
Ceduna 12 E6
Celebes 2 PQ10
Celebes Sea 3 P9
Central African Empire 6 EF5
Central Cord 9 C3
Central Cordillera 7 N8
Central German Highlands 1 H5
Central Pacific Basin II GH5
Central Plain 1 E5
Central Russian Uplands 1 OP4-5-6
Central Siberian Plateau 3 NO3
Ceram 4 Q10
Ceylon 3 M9
Ceylon (Sri Lanka) 4 M9
Chad 6 EF4
Chad Basin 5 E4
Chad, L. 5 E4
Chalna 4 a11
Châlon sur Saône 2 G6
Chamdo 4 N6
Chamlang 3 q17
Champagne 1 G6
Chandpur 4 b11
Changchun 4 Q5
Changpai Shan 3 Q5
Changri 3 p17
Changsha 4 OP7
Changtse 3 p16
Channel Is. 2 F6
Chany 3 L4
Charcot I 14 O3
Chari 5 E4
Charleston 8 N6
Charleville 12 H5
Charlotte 8 N6
Charlottetown 8 O5
Charlotte Waters 12 F4
Charters Towers 12 H3
Chatham Is. 11 I9
Chattahoochee 7 M6

Cheju Do 4 Q6
Chélif 1 G7
Chelkar L. 1 U6
Chelyabinsk 2 U4
Chelyuskin, C. 3 O2
Chengchow 4 P6
Chengtu 4 O6
Cheongjin 4 R6
Cheptsa 1 S4
Cher 1 G6
Cherbourg 2 F6
Cheremkhovo 4 O4
Cherepovets 2 N6
Chernovtsy 2 P4
Cherskiy Ra. 3 S3
Chesa Bay 1 R2
Chesapeake Bay 7 N6
Chesterfield Is. 11 F6
Chesterfield Inlet 7 L2
Cheyenne 8 I5
Chiamusze 4 R5
Chiang Men 4 f15
Chiao 4 g15
Chiba 4 e13
Chicago 8 M5
Chiclayo 10 C4
Chico 9 8D
Chicoutimi 8 N5
Chiengmai 4 N8
Chien shan 4 f15
Chigasaki 4 d13
Chihli, Gulf of 3 Q6
Chihuahua 8 I7
Chikura 4 e13
Chile 10 C8 D6
Chile Basin II K6-7
Chillagoe 12 G3
Chillan 10 C7
Chiloé I. 10 C8
Chimborazo 9 B4
China 4 M-P6
China, Plain of 3 P6
Chinchou 4 Q5
Ching chi 4 g15
Chinsura 4 a11
Chipata 6 G7
Chirripo Grande 7 M8-9
Chita 4 P4
Chittagong 4 N7
Chiu chiang 4 f15
Choiseul 11 F5
Cholatse 3 p17
Chomo Lenzo 3 q17
Chonan 4 e13
Chonos Arch. 10 C8
Cho Oyu 3 p16
Choshi 4 e13
Chott ech-Chergui 2 G9
Chott el Hodna 1 H8
Chott Djerid 5 D2
Chott Melrhir 5 D2
Christchurch 12 b14
Christensen Mt 14 g3
Christmas I. II M4
Chu 4 f14-15
Chuadanga 4 a11
Chubut 9 8D
Chu Chiang (Pearl R.) 4 f15
Chudskoye L. 1 N4
Chukchi Pen. 3 Z3
Chukchi Rise II F2
Chukot Ra 3 V3
Chumican 4 R4
Chungking 4 O7
Chung shan (Hsiang shan) 4 f15
Churchill 8 L4
Churchill Pk. 7 G4
Churchill (R.) 7 L4
Cikurai 3 I13
Cimone, Mte. 1 I7
Cincinnati 8 M6
Cinto, Mte 1 H7
Cirebon 3 I13
Citlaltepét 7 L8
Ciudad Bolivar 10 D3
Ciudad Juarez 8 I6
Ciudad Real 2 F8
Civitavecchia 2 I7
Clarence 12 I5
Clarence Str. 12 E2
Clarion Fracture Zone II H5
Clear, C. 1 DE5
Clermont Ferrand 2 G6
Cleveland 8 M5
Clipperton 8 J8
Clipperton Fracture Zone II HI5
Cloncurry 12 G4
Cloncurry R. 12 G3
Cluj 2 M6
Clutha 12 f15
Coast Range 7 FG4
Coast Range 7 G5-6
Coast Ranges 9 D3
Coast Ranges 9 C6-7
Coats I. 7 M3
Coats Land 14 IM2
Coatzacoalcos 8 L8
Cobar 12 H6
Cobourg Pen. 12 E2
Cochabamba 10 D5
Cochrane 8 M5
Cocos I. 8 M9

Cod C. 7 O5
Coen 12 G2
Coffs Harbour 12 I6
Coimbra 2 E7
Colac 12 G7
Colbeck Arch. 14 f3
Coleman 12 G2
Colima 7 I8
Collie 12 B6
Collier B. 12 C3
Collingwood Bay 12 HI1
Cologne 2 H5
Colombia 10 C3
Colombo 4 L9
Colon 8 M9
Colona 12 E6
Colorado 8 I6
Colorado Plateau 7 H6
Colorado R. 7 H6
Colorado R. 7 L6
Colorado R. 9 D7
Columbia Plateau 7 H5
Columbia R. 7 GH4-5
Columbus 8 M6
Comilla 4 b11
Commodoro Rivadavia 10 D8
Comorin C. 3 L9
Comoros 6 H7
Conakry 6 B5
Conceição do Araguaia 10 F4
Concepcion 10 C7
Concepcion 10 B6
Concepcion, Pt. 7 GH
Concordia 10 E7
Condamine 12 H5
Condobolin 12 H6
Congo 6 E5-6
Constance L. 1 H6
Constanta 2 N7
Constantine 6 D2
Coober Pedy 12 E5
Cook Islands 11 L6-7
Cook Mt. 12 g14
Cook Strait 12 g14
Cooktown 12 H3
Cooma 12 H7
Coonamble 12 H6
Cooper's Creek 12 F5
Cootamundra 12 H6
Copenhagen 2 I4
Copiapo 10 C6
Coppermine 8 GH3
Coqueta 9 C2-3
Coral Sea 11 EF6
Coral Sea Basin II D6
Cordeaux Res. 12 d11
Cordoba (Spain) 2 E8
Cordoba (Argentina) 10 D7
Cordoba, Sierra de 9 D7
Corfù 1 L8
Corinth, Gulf of. 1 M8
Cork 2 E5
Cornwall 1 F5
Coromandel 12 h13
Coromandel Coast 3 M8
Coronation I 14 N3
Corpus Christi 8 L7
Corpus Christi Bay 7 I7
Corrib, L. I DE5
Corrientes 10 E6
Corrientes C. 7 I7
Corsica 2 H7
Corumba 10 E5
Corunna 2 E7
Cosenza 2 L8
Cosmoledo Is. 5 H6
Costa Rica 8 M8
Cotopax 9 C4
Coulman I. 14 A2
Cowal L. 12 H6
Cowan L. 12 C6
Cowra 12 H6
Craiova 2 M7
Crete 2 MN
Creus, C. 1 G7
Crimea 2 O6
Croker I. 12 E2
Cromwell 12 g14
Cronulla 12 e11
Croydon 12 G3
Cruzeiro do Sol 10 C4
Cruzen I 14 S2
Cuando 5 F7
Cuango 5 E6
Cuanza 6 E7
Cuba 8 N7
Cubango (Okavango) 5 EF7
Cudgewa 12 H7
Cue 12 B5
Cuenca 2 F8
Cuenca 10 C4
Cuiaba 10 E5
Culiacan 8 I7
Cumana 10 D2
Cumberland Pen. 7 O3
Cunene 5 E7
Cunnamulla 12 H5
Curacao 9 D2
Curitiba 10 E6
Curtis I. 11 I8

Curtis I. 12 I4
Cuttack 4 M7
Cylades 1 M8
Cyprus 2 O9
Cyrenaica 6 F2
Czechoslovakia 2 IM5-6

D
Dacca 4 MN7
Dagestan 1 R7
Dahlak Arch. 5 GH4
Dahna Des. 3 G7
Dajarra 12 F4
Dakar 6 B4
Dakhla 6 B3
Dal 1 L3
Dalan Dzadagad 4 O5
Daleswari 4 a11
Dallas 8 L6
Dalmatia 1 IL7
Daly 12 E2
Daly Waters 12 E3
Damaraland 5 E8
Damascus 2 P8
Dampier Arch. 12 B4
Dampier Land 12 C3
Damson 12 H4
Danakil Basin 5 H4
Da - Nang 4 O8
Dandenong 12 H7
Danube 1 MN7 I6
Dar el Beida (Casablanca) 6 C2
Dar es Salaam 6 GH6
Darfur 5 F4
Dargaville 12 g13
Darling 11 E8
Darnley C. 14 F3
Dart C. 14 g2
Daru 12 G1
Darvaza 2 T7
Darwin 12 E2
Dasht - i - Kavir 3 H6
Dato Is. 3 R7
Daugavpils 2 N4
Davao 4 Q9
Davis Sea 14 E3
Davis Strait 7 OP3
Dawson 8 F3
Dawson Creek 8 G4
Dayr az Zawr 2 Q8
Dead Sea 3 F6
Deakin 12 D6
Death Valley 7 H6
Debrecen 2 M6
Debra Markos 6 G4
Deccan 3 L8
Deep Bay 4 f15
Deering, Mount 12 D5
Deewhy 12 e10
De Grey 12 BC4
Delhi 4 L7
Demavend 3 H6
Deniliquin 12 H7
Denmark 2 H4
Denmark Strait 7 S3
D'Entrecasteaux Is. 11 F5
D'Entrecasteaux, Pt. 12 B6
Denver 8 I5
Derby 12 C3
Des Moines 8 L5
Desna 1 O5
Desordem, Serra da 9 F4
Detroit 8 M5
Devon I. 8 M2
Devonport (Austr.) 12 b9
Devonport (N.Z.) 12 g13
Dey - Dey L. 12 E5
Dezful 2 R8
Dezhněv, C. (East C.) 3 Z3
Diamantina 10 F5
Diamantina 11 D7
Diamantina Trench II AB7
Diamond Harb 4 a11
Digul 11 DE5
Dijon 2 G6
Dikson 4 L2
Dili 4 Q10
Dilolo 6 F7
Dinaric Alps 1 L7
Dingboche 3 p17
Dire Dawa 6 GH4
Dirk Hartog I. 12 A5
Dirranbandi 12 H5
Disappointment L. 11 C7
Disappointment L. 12 C4
Disko B. 7 P3
Disko I. 7 p3
Diu 4 L7
Diyarbakir 2 Q8
Djado 6 E3
Djanet 6 D3
Djedi 1 G9
Djelfa 6 D2
Djerba I. 1 I9
Djibouti 6 H4
Dnepr 1 O5, O6
Dnepropetrovsk 2 OP6
Dnepr Uplands 1 NO6
Dnera 1 F7
Dnestr 1 N6

Dobbyn 12 F3
Dobruja 1 N6-7
Dodoma 6 G5
Doha 4 H7
Dohazari 4 b11
Dolomites 1 I6
Dominica 10 D2
Dominican Rep. 8 N8
Don 1 P5
Dondra Head 3 M9
Donegal B. 1 E5
Donets 1 Q6
Donets Ridge 1 P6
Donetsk 2 P6
Donggala 4 Q10
Dongola 6 F4
Dora L. 12 C4
Dore Mt. 1 G6
Dori 6 C4
Dortmund 2 H5
Douala 6 DE6
Douglas Is. 14 f3
Douro 1 E7
Dover 2 G5
Dover, Str of. 1 G5
Dovrefjell 1 H3
Drakensberg 5 FG8
Drake Passage 9 DE9
Drammen 2 H4
Drava 1 IL6
Dresden 2 I5
Drina 1 L7
Drubeta - Turnu Severin 2 M7
Drygalski I. 14 E3
Drysdale 12 D3
Dubawnt L. 7 IL3
Dubbo 12 H6
Dublin 2 E5
Dubrovnik 2 L7
Duchess 12 F4
Ducie I. 11 P7
Dudinka 4 M3
Duero 1 F7
Duff Is. 11 G5
Duglha 3 p17
Duluth 8 L5
Dundas L. 12 c6
Dundas Strait 12 E2
Dundee 2 F4
Dunedin 12 g15
Dunmore Hd 1 DE5
Durack 12 D3
Durango 8 I7
Durban 6 G9
Durmitor 1 L7
D'Urville I. 12 g14
Dushanbe 4 I6
Dusseldorf 2 H5
Dvina B 1 P2
Dyer Plateau 14 O2
Dzhambul 4 L5
Dzhargalantu 4 N5
Dzhugdzhur Ra. 3 R4
Dzonglu 3 p17
Dzungaria 3 MN5

E
East African Plateau 5 G6
East Australian Basin II D8
East Beskids I M6
East China Sea 3 Q7
East C. (Dezněv. C.) 3 Z3
East Cape 11 H8
East London 6 FG9
East Pacific-Antarctic Basin II IJ8-9
East Pacific Ridge II I6-7
East Ronglaek Glacier 3 p16
Eastern Cord. 9 C3
Eastern Cord. 9 C4-5
Eastern Ghats 3 LM8
Eastern Plateau II I7
Eastern Sayan 3 N4
Eastern Sierra Madre 7 I7
Eauripik 11 E4
Ebro 1 F7
Echuca 12 G7
Ecuador 10 C4
Eddiston Pt. 12 b9
Edinburgh 2 F5
Edirne 2 N7
Edith Ronne Land 14 om1
Edmonton 8 H4
Edo 4 d13
Edsel Ford Ra 14 S2
Edward VIII Bay 14 f3
Edward L. 5 F6
Edward V II Pen. 14 S2
Efate 11 G6
Egadi Is. 1 I8
Egmont Mt. 12 g13
Egridir L. 1 O8
Egypt, Arab Rep. of 4 E-F7
Eiao 11 N5
Eidsvold 12 I5
Eights Coast 14 Pp2
Eighty Mile Beach 12 BC3
Eil 6 HI5
Einasleigh 12 G3

Izmir 2 N8

J

Jabalpur 4 M7
Jackson 8 L6
Jackson, Port 12 e10
Jacksonville 8 N6
Jaffna 4 M9
Jaipur 4 L7
Jakarta 4 O10
Jaluit 11 G4
Jamaica 8 N8
Jambi 4 O10
James Bay 7 M4
Jamnagar 4 I7
Jammu 4 L6
Jan Mayen 3 B2
Japan 4 RS6
Japan Trench II D4
Japura 9 D4
Jaquaribe 9 G4
Jarvis I. 11 L5
Java 4 P10
Java Sea 3 O10
Java Trench 11 AB6
Jayapura 3 o14
Jequitinhonha 9 F5
Jericho 12 H4
Jernich 4 h16
Jerusalem 4 F6
Jessore 4 a11
Joanna Spring 12 C4
Joao Pessoa 10 G4
Jodhpur 4 L7
Joerg Plateau 14 O2
Johannesburg 6 G8
Johnston I. 11 G3
Johore Bahru 4 h16
Johore (R.) 4 i16
Johore Str. 4 h16
Joinville I. 14 n3
Jones Sound 7 M2
Jonkoping 2 L4
Joseph Bonaparte Gulf.
  12 D2
Juan Fernandez Is. 9 BC7
Juàzeiro 10 G4
Juba 5 H5
Jubilee L. 12 D5
Jucar 1 F8
Juiz de Fora 10 F6
Julian Alps 1 I6
Julianehab 8 PQ3
Juneau 8 F4
Jungkulon Pen. 3 I13
Jūra 1 H6
Juri 9 E4
Jurna 9 D4
Juruena 9 E4-5
Jutland 1 H4
Juventud, I. de la 7 M7

K

Kabalo 6 F6
Kabul 4 I6
Kachiyama 4 e13
Kaduna 6 D4
Kafue 5 F7
Kagera (Nile) 5 G6
Kagoshima 4 Q6
Kai Is 3 R10
Kaikoura Ra. 12 g14
Kaimanawa Mts. 12 h13
Kalahari Desert 5 F8
Kalamai 2 M8
Kalannie 12 B6
Kalemie 6 F6
Kalgan 4 P5
Kalgoorlie 12 C6
Kaliningrad 2 M5
Kalmar 2 L4
Kama 1 S4
Kama Reservoir 1 S4
Kamchatka Pen. 3 ST4
Kamina 8 P17
Kamogawa 4 e13
Kampala 6 G5
Kananga 6 F6
Kanazawa 4 R6
Kandahar 4 I6
Kandalaksha 2 O2
Kandalaksha B. 1 OP2
Kandavu 11 H6
Kandi 6 D4
Kandy 4 M9
Kane Basin 7 NO2
Kangaroo I 12 F6
Kangkar Chemaran 4 i16
Kangkar Pulai 4 h16
Kangshung Gl. 3 q17
Kangtega 3 p17
Kanin Nos, C. 1 Q2
Kanin Pen. 1 QR2
Kanka 1 S3
Kankan 6 C4
Kanpur 4 L7
Kansas (R.) 7 L6
Kansas St. 8 IL6
Kansas City 8 L6

Kantse 4 O6
Kaolack 6 B4
Kapalla 2 M7
Kapingamarangi Atoll
  11 F4
Kapuas 3 P9
Kara Bogaz Gol 1 T7
Karachi 4 I7
Karaganda 4 L5
Karaginskiy I. 4 UV4
Karakoram Ra. 3 L7
Karakum 3 HI6
Karamai 4 M5
Karamea Bight 12 g14
Karamian 3 m13
Kara Sea 3 I2
Karelia 2 OP3
Karema 6 G5
Kariba L. 5 F7
Karimun 4 h16
Karimunjawa Is. 3 m13
Karisumbi 5 F6
Karlskrona 2 L4
Karma Changri 3 q16
Karnaphuli Res. 4 b11
Karonga 6 G6
Karpatos 2 N8
Karpo La 3 q16
Karumba 12 G3
Kasai 5 E6
Kasanga 6 G5
Kashan 2 S8
Kashgar 4 L6
Kashmir 4 L6
Kassala 6 G4
Katakai 4 e13
Katanning 12 B6
Katherine 12 E2
Katmandu 4 M7
Katowice 2 L5
Kattegat 1 I4
Katwa 4 a11
Kaunas 2 M4
Kavala 2 MN7
Kavasaki 4 d13
Kawagoe 4 d13
Kawaguchi 4 d13
Kayes 6 B4
Kay Is. 14 A2
Kayseri 2 OP8
Kazakhstan 4 L5
Kazakh Upland 3 L5
Kazan 2 R4
Kazbek 1 QR7
Kazim 1 V3
Kebnekaise 1 L2
Kefallinia 2 L8
Ken 2 O3
Kembla Mt. 12 d11
Kemerovo 4 M4
Kemi 1 N2
Kemp Coast 14 G3
Kempsey 12 I6
Kenai Pen. 7 DE4
Kentucky 8 M6
Kenya 6 G5
Kenya Mt. 5 G5
Kerang 12 G7
Kerch 2 P6
Kerch Str. 1 P6
Kerema 12 H1
Kerguelen II R8
Kerguelen Gaussberg
  Ridge II R8
Kerkenna Is. 2 I9
Kermadec Is. 11 I8
Kermadec-Tonga Trench
  II F7
Kermadec Trench 11 I8
Kerman 4 H6
Kermanshah 4 G6
Kerulen 3 P5
Key West 8 M7
Khabarovsk 4 R5
Khalkis 2 M8
Khanty Mansiysk 2 Z3
Kharkov 2 P6
Kharta Gl. 3 q16
Khartachangri Gl. 3 p16
Khartapu 3 p16
Khartoum 6 G4
Khatanga 4 O2
Kherson 2 O6
Khios 2 N8
Khiuma 2 M4
Khoper 1 Q5
Khubumbu Gl. 3 p17
Khulna 4 a11
Khuma 1 M4
Khyber P. 3 L6
Kickiga 4 T4
Kiev 2 O5
Kiffa 6 B4
Kigali 6 G5
Kilimanjaro 5 G6
Kimba 5 F6
Kimberley 6 F8
Kimberley 12 D3
Kinabalu 3 P9
Kindu 6 F6
King Christian IX Land 8
  RS3
King Christian X Land 8
  S2

King Frederick VI Coast 7
  Q3
King Frederick VIII Land 7
  S2
King George I 14 n3
King I. 12 a8
King Leopold Range 12 D3
Kingoonya 12 F6
King Oscar Fjord 7 S2
Kingscot 12 F6
Kingsmill Is. 11 H5
King Sound 12 C3
Kingston (Australia) 12 F7
Kingston (Jamaica) 8 N8
Kingston (N.Z.) 12 f15
Kingston-upon Hull 2 G5
King William I 7 L3
Kinshasa 6 E6
Kirensk 4 O4
Kirgizia 4 L5
Kirgiz Steppe 3 HI5
Kirkuk 4 G6
Kirin 4 Q5
Kirov 2 R4
Kirovabad 2 R7
Kirthar Ra. 3 I7
Kisangani 6 F5
Kisarazu 4 d13
Kishinev 2 N6
Kisumu 6 G5
Kita 6 B4
Kitakyushu 4 Q6
Kivu, L. 5 F6
Kiyozumi 4 e13
Kizil 1 O7
Kizyl Arvat 2 T8
Klaipeda 2 M4
Klar 1 I3
Klyazma 1 PQ4
Klaipeda 2 M4
Klyuchevsk Mt. 3 U4
Knox Coast 14 Dd3
Knud Rasmussen Land 7
  OPQ2
Kobe 4 R6
Kodiak I. 7 D4
Kodok 6 G4
Kogarah 12 d10
Koko Nor 3 NO6-7
Kola Pen. 1 OPQ2
Kolepom 3 n14
Kolguyev Is. 2 O2
Kolyma (Gydan) Ra. 3 TV3
Kolyma Plain 3 T3
Kolyma R. 3 T3
Kommandorskiye Is. 4 T4
Komsomolets B-1 S6
Komsomolsk 4 R4
Koner 3 p17
Kono 6 D4
Konosha 2 Q3
Konotop 2 O5
Konya 2 O8
Konzhakovskiy Kam. I T4
Korab 1 M7
Korce 2 M7
Korea 4 Q6
Korea Bay 3 Q6
Korea Str. 3 Q6
Koryak Range 3 VZ3
Kosciusko Mt. 12 H7
Koshigaya 4 d13
Kota Bharu 4 O9
Kota Kinabalu 4 P9
Kotelny I 4 R2
Kotlas 2 R3
Kotto 5 F5
Kotuy 3 N3
Kotzebue 8 C3
Kowloon 4 g15
Kozaki 4 e13
Kozava 2 T3
Kra, Isthmus of 3 N8
Krakatau I. 3 I13
Krakow 2 L5
Krasnodar 2 P6
Krasnoe 2 V5
Krasnovodsk 2 S7
Krasnoyarsk 4 N4
Krawang C. 3 I13
Krios C. 1 M8
Krishna 3 L8
Krishnanagar 4 a11
Kristiansund 2 H4
Krivov Rog 2 O6
Kroonstad 6 F8
Kuala Lumpur 4 O9
Kuangchou 4 f14
Kuan tan 4 g15
Kuanza 5 E6-7
Kuban 1 P6-7
Kuban Steppe 1 PQ6
Kuchen 4 f15
Kuching 4 O9
Ku ching 4 g15
Kuei chou 4 f15
Kufra Oasis 5 F3
Kuybyshev Reservoir 1
  RS5
Kukup 4 h16
Kulaly 1 R7
Kuldja 4 M5
Kuma 1 R7
Kumasi 6 C5
Kumbila 3 p17
Kumbu 3 p17

Kung pei 4 g15
Kungrad 2 T7
Kunlun Shan 3 MN6
Kunming 4 O7
Kuopio 2 N3
Kupana 4 Q10
Kupang 12 C2
Kura 1 R7
Kura Soak 12 D3
Kure I. 11 I2
Kurgan 2 V5
Kuria Muria Is. 3 H8
Kuril Is. 4 ST5
Kuril-Kamchatka Trench II
  D3
Kusaie 11 G4
Kushiro 4 S5
Kustanay 2 U5
Kustia 4 a11
Kutaisi 2 Q7
Kuwait St. 4 G7
Kuybyshev 2 S5
Kwa 5 E6
Kwajalein Atoll 11 G4
Kweiyang 4 O7
Kyoga L. 5 G5
Kyoto 4 R6
Kyushu 4 R6
Kyzylkum 3 I5

L

Labrador 7 NO4
Labrador Basin II L3
Lachlan 11 F8
Lac des Volcans 5 F5
La Coruna 2 D-E7
Ladoga 1 O3
Laghouat 2 G9
Lagone 5 E4
Lagos 6 D5
La Grange 12 C3
Lahore 4 L6
Lakshadweep Is. 4 L8-9
Lambarene 6 E6
Lampedusa 1 I8
Lan 4 g15
Lanai 11 I2
Lancaster Sound 8 MN2
Lanchow 4 O6
Lands End 1 E5
Laoag 4 P8
Laos 4 NO8-7
La Paz (Bolivia) 10 D5
La Paz (Mexico) 8 I7
La Perousse Str. 3 S5
La Plata 10 E7
Lappland 2 MO2
Laptev Sea 3 Q2
L'Aquila 2 I7
Laredo 8 7L
La Rioja 10 D6
Larisa 2 M8
La Rochelle 2 F6
Larsen Ice Shelf 14 O3
La Sagra 2 F5
La Serena 10 C6
Lashio 4 N7
Las Palmas 6 B3
La Spezia 2 H7
Las Tablas 8 M9
Las Vegas 8 H6
Latvia 2 M4
Launceston 12 b9
Laura 12 G3
Laurentian Plateau 7 N5
Laurie I 14 N3
Laverton 12 C5
Lawlers 12 C5
Lawu 3 m13
Laysan I. 11 I2
Lebam 4 i17
Lebanon 2 P8
Leeds 2 F5
Leeuwin, C. 12 AB6
Leeward Is. 9 D2
Lefroy L. 12 C6
Legasri 4 Q8
Leghorn 2 I7
Le Havre 2 F6
Leichardt 12 F3
Leigh Greek 12 F6
Leipzig 2 I5
Lekop 4 h16
Le Mans 2 G6
Lena 3 OQ3-4
Leninakan 2 Q7
Lenkoran 2 R8
Lenvis 2 E4
Leon (Mexico) 8 I7
Léon,(Spain) 2 E7
Leopold and Astrid Coast
  14 e3
Lerida 2 G7
Lesotho 6 F8
Lesser Antilles 10 C3
Lesser Caucasus 1 QR7
Lesser Sunda Is. 3 Q10
Lésvos 2 N8
Lethbridge 8 H5
Leticia 10 C4
Levick Mt. 14 a2
Lewis 1 E4

Leyte 3 P8
Lhasa 4 N6
Lho La 3 p16
Lhotse 3 p17
Lhotse Gl. 3 p17
Liard 7 G3
Libenge 6 F5
Liberia 6 BC5
Libreville 6 D5
Libya 6 EF3
Libyan Desert 5 F3
Li chi 4 f15
Lichinga 6 G7
Liechtenstein 2 HI6
Liège 2 H5
Liepaja 2 LM4
Ligurian sea 1 H7
Lihou Reef and Cays 12 I3
Likasi 6 F7
Lille 2 G5
Lilongwe 6 G7
Lima 10 C5
Limburg 2 G5
Limerick 2 E5
Limmen Bight 12 F2
Limmen Bight (R.) 12 F3
Limoges 2 G6
Limpopo 5 G8
Linares 2 F8
Linchow 4 P7
Lindesnes 1 H4
Line Islands 11 M5
Lingga Arch. 3 O10
Ling ting Yang 4 f15
Lingtren 3 P16
Linosa 1 I8
Linz 2 I6
Lion, G. of 1 G7
Lipari Is. 1 I8
Lisala 6 F5
Lisbon 2 E8
Lisburne C. 7 C3
Lisianski I. 11 I2
Lismore 12 I5
Lithuania 2 M4
Little America 14 Tt2
Little Khingan Mts 3 Q4-5
Little Rock 8 L6
Liverpool (Eng.) 2 F5
Liverpool (Austr.) 12 I6
Liverpool Ra 11 E8
Livingston I. 14 O3
Llano Estacado 7 I6
Llanos 9 C-D3
Ljubljana 2 I5
Llullaillaco, V. 9 D6
Lobito 6 E7
Lobos Is. 9 B4
Lochou Men 4 g15
Lodz 2 L5
Lofoten Is. 2 I2
Logan Mt. 7 E3
Loir 1 G6
Loire 1 F6
Lolland 2 I5
Loma Mts. 5 BC5
Lomami 5 F6
Lomblen 12 C1
Lombok 4 P10
Lomé 6 D5
Lomonosov Ridge II C-D
  K-L1
London 2 F5
Londonderry 2 E4
Long Beach 8 G6
Long I. (Bahamas) 8 N7
Long I. (U.S.A.) 7 N5
Long Xuyen 4 O9
Lopatka C. 3 S4
Lopez C. 5 D6
Lop Nor 3 N5
Lord Howe I. 11 F8
Lorient 2 F6
Lorraine 1 H4
Los Angeles 8 G6
Louisiade Arch. 11 F6
Louisiana 8 L6
Lourdes 2 GF7
Lower California 8 H6-7
Lower Hutt 12 f14
Lower Tungusta 3 NO3
Loyalty Is. 1 G7
Lozva 1 V3
Lualaba 5 F6
Luanda 6 E6
Luang Prabang 4 O8
Luangwa 5 G7
Luanshya 6 F7
Lübeck 2 I5
Lübeck Bay 1 I5
Lubumbashi 6 F7
Lucknow 4 M7
Lüderitz 6 E8
Lugenda 5 G7
Lugh Ganane 6 H5
Lulea 2 M2
Lulua 5 F6
Lunda Plateau 5 EF6
Lung chiang 4 f15
Lung hua 4 f15
Lung Kang 4 g15
Lung shan 4 f15
Lungwebung 5 F7

Lurio 5 G7
Lusaka 6 F7
Lusambo 6 F6
Lü-ta 4 Q6
Lützow Holm Bay 14 H3
Lux 1 H6
Luxembourg 2 H6
Luzon 4 Q8
Lvov 2 M6
Lyndon 12 A4
Lyons 2 G6
Lyons (R) 12 B4

M

Maan Selka 1 N2
Macauley I. 11 I8
Macao 4 P6
Macapà 10 E3
Macdonald L. 12 D4
Macdonnell Range 12 E4
Macedonia 1 M7
Maceio 10 G4
Machattie L. 12 G4
Macias Nguema Biyoga
  6 D5
Mackay 12 H4
Mackay L. 12 D4
Mackenzie Bay (Antarc.)
  14 F3
Mackenzie Bay (Canada)
  7 F7
Mackenzie Lowlands 7
  GH3
Mackenzie Mts. 7 FG3
Mackenzie (R.) 7 G2
Macquarie 11 E8
Macquarie Is. 14 B4
Macquarie Ridge II D8
Mac Robertson Land 14 f3
Madagascar 6 H7-8
Madagascar Ridge II Q7
Madarepur 4 b11
Madeira 6 B2
Madeira (R.) 9 D4
Madras 4 M8
Madre de Dios 9 D5
Madrid 2 F7
Madura 4 I6
Madurai 4 L9
Madura I. 3 m13
Madura Str. 3 m13
Mafeking 6 F8
Mafia 1 H5
Magadan 4 S3
Magdalena 10 D5
Magdalena (R.) 9 C3
Magdeburg 2 I5
Magellan, Str. of 9 D9
Maggie's Spring 12 E4
Magnitogorsk 2 U5
Mangyshlak Pen. 1 S7
Mahakam 3 P10
Mahanadi 3 M7
Mahenge 6 G7
Mahia Pen. 12 g13
Maiduguri 6 E4
Maimana 4 I6
Main 1 I6
Mai Ndombe, L. 5 EF6
Maine 8 NO5
Mainland 1 F3
Main Strait 4 h16
Maintirano 6 H7
Maipo Vol. 9 CD7
Maitland 12 I6
Majorca 2 G8
Makalu V 3 q17
Makemo 11 N6
Makhachkala 2 R7
Makin 11 H4
Makokou 6 E5
Makran 3 HI7
Makurdi 6 D5
Malabar Coast 3 L8
Malacca 4 O9
Malacca Str. 3 O9
Maladeta 1 G7
Malaga 2 F8
Malaita 11 G5
Malang 12 A1
Malange 6 E6
Malaren L. 1 L4
Malargüe 10 D7
Malatya 2 OP8
Malawi 6 G7
Malawi L. (Nyasa) 5 G7
Malaya 4 O9
Malay Pen. 3 N9
Malaysia 4 OP9
Malden I. 11 M5
Maldive Is. 4 L9
Male 4 L9
Malea C. 1 M8
Malekula 11 G6
Maleolap 11 H4
Mali 6 C4
Malindi 6 H5
Mallorca 2 G8
Mallowa Well 12 C4
Malmö 2 I4
Malpelo 10 B3
Malta 2 I8
Mamoré 9 D5

Sarawak 4 P9
Sardinia 2 H7
Sarera B. 11 D5
Sarh 6 E5
Saru L. 12 G1
Saskatchewan 8 I4
Saskatchewan (R.) 7 I4
Saskatoon 8 I4
Sassari 2 H7
Satpura Ra. 3 L7
Saudi Arabia 4 G7
Saukuru 5 F6
Sava, R. (Chad) 5 E4
Sava, R. (Y-slav) I L7
Savai'i 11 I6
Save 5 G8
Savannah 8 N6
Savannah (R.) 7 M6
Sawara e13
Sawu 12 C2
Sawu Sea 12 C1
Saxby 12 G3
Sayn Shanda 4 O5
Scandinavia 1 M3
Scandinavian Mts. 1 H-M2-4
Schefferville 8 O4
Schwabian Jura 1 HI8
Schwaner Ra. 3 P10
Scilly Is. 2 E6
Scoresby Sound 7 S2
Scotia Basin II LM8
Scotland 2 F4
Scott I. 14 A3
Scott Reef 12 C2
Seattle 8 G5
Sebastian Vizcaino Bay 7 H7
Sebou 1 F9
Sebung C 4 i16
Seeheim 6 E8
Segre 1 G7
Seim 1 O5
Seine 1 G6
Sekondi-Takoradi 6 C5
Selembu Is. 3 m13
Selendzha 3 Q4
Selwyn 12 G4
Selwyn Ra. 11 D7
Semeru 3 m13
Semipalatinsk 4 M5
Sendai 4 S6
Senegal 6 B4
Senegal (R.) 5 B4
Senja 2 L2
Senyavin Is. 11 F4
Seoul 4 Q6
Sept Iles 8 O4
Seputih 3 I13
Serampore 4 a11
Serangoon 4 h16
Serbia 1 M7
Serov 4 I4
Serpentine Lakes 12 DE5
Setif 2 GH8
Setubal 2 E8
Sevan L. 1 R7
Sevastopol 2 O7
Sevilla 2 EF8
Severn 7 M4
Severnaya Zemlya 3 MN2
Seward 8 E3
Seward Pen. 7 7 C3
Seychelles 6 HI6
Shaba 5 6-7
Sha ching 4 f15
Shackleton Ice Shelf 14 E3
Shackleton Inlet 14 tA1
Shag Rocks 11 F9
Shahbazpur 4 b11
Shahrud 2 T8
Shakhty 2 Q6
Shanghai 4 Q6
Shenio 3 p17
Shannon 1 E5
Shantar Is. 3 R4
Shantung Pen. 3 P6
Shark B. 12 A5
Shasta Mt. 7 G5
Shatau Kok 4 g15
Shebelle 5 H5
Sheffield 2 F5
Shen chüan 4 g15
Shetland Is. 1 F3
Shibeli 5 H5
Shigatse 4 M7
Shih chiao 4 f15
Shikoku 4 R6
Shillong 4 N7
Shi lung 4 f14
Shiraz 4 H7
Shir Kuh 1 ST9
Shkoder 2 L7
Shkodër (L.) 1 L7
Shunte 4 f15
Siam, Gulf of O8-9
Sian 4 O6
Siberia 3 L3
Sibolga 4 N9
Sibiu M6

Sicily 2 I8
Sidi Bel Abbès 2 FG8
Sidi Ifni 6 B3
Sidley Mt. 14 R2
Sidra Gulf 5 E2
Sierra Leone 6 B5
Sierra Leone Basin II N5
Siguiri 6 B4
Sikasso 6 C4
Sikhote Alin Ra. 3 R5
Si-kiang 3 P7
Sila 1 L8
Silesia 1 L5
Simeulue 4 N9
Simferopol 2 O6
Simpson Desert 12 F4
Sinai Pen. 5 G3
Singapore 4 h16
Singapore, Strait of 4 i16
Singaraja 12 B1
Sinhailien 4 P6
Sining 4 O6
Sinkiang-Uigur 4 MN5
Sinop 2 P7
Sir Edward Pellew Group 12 F3
Siret 1 N6
Sirte 6 E6
Sirte Dep. 5 E2
Sirzelecki Cr. 12 F5
Sivas 21 P7
Siwa 6 F3
Skagen 1 I4
Skagerrak 1 H4
Skagway 8 F4
Skikda 2 H8
Skopje 2 M7
Skovorodino 4 Q4
Skye 2 E4
Slamet 3 I13
Slave 7 H4
Slave Coast 5 D5
Sligo 2 E5
Smolensk 2 O5
Snake 7 H7
Sneeu Berge 5 F9
Snowdon 1 F5
Snowy 12 H7
Socotra 4 H8
Sofia 2 M7
Sogne 1 H3
Sogne Fj. 2 H3
Sokna 6 E3
Sokoto 6 D4
Sokoto, (Reg.) 5 D4
Sokoto (R.) 5 D4
Solomon Is. 11 FG5
Somali Basin II Q5-6
Somali Peninsula 5 H5
Somali Plateau 5 H5
Somali Rep. 6 H5
Somerset 12 G2
Somerset I. 8 L2
Söndre Strömfjord 7 PQ3
Sorong 4 R10
Sörög 2 L1
Söröy 2 L1
Sous 1 E9
Sousse 2 I8
South Africa 6 E8-9
Southampton I. 8 M3
South Atlantic Ridge II N6-8
South Australia 12 EF5
South Australian Basin II BC8
South Carolina 8 M6
South China Sea 3 P8
South Dakota 8 IL5
South East Cape 11 E9
South-East Indian Basin II AB7
Southern Cross 12 B6
Southern Indian L. 7 L4
Southern Sierra Madre 7 IL8
South Fiji Basin 11 H7
South Georgia 10 G9
South Georgia Rise II M8
South Island 11 H9
South Korea 4 Q6
South Magnetic Pole 14 C3
South Orkney Islands 14 NM3
South Pacific Basin II FG8
South Pacific Ridge II FG8-9
South Pole 14 P1-E1
Southport 12 I5
South Sandwich Is. 14 M4
South Saskatchewan 7 H4
South Shetland Is. 14 nO3
South Taranaki Bight 12 g13
South West Africa 6 E8
Southwest C. 12 f15
South-West Indian Basin II R7-8
Southwest Pacific Basin 11 MN8-9
South Yemen 4 G8
Sovetskaya Gavan 4 R5
Spain 2 EF7
Spartivento C. 1 L8

Spencer C. 12 F7
Spencer Gulf 12 F6
Spitsbergen W. 4 D2
Split 2 L7
Spokane 8 H5
Sporades 1 N8
Spree 1 I5
Springsure 12 H4
Sredne Kolymsk 3 A11
Sri Lanka (Ceylon) 4 M9
Srinagar 4 L6
Staaten 12 G3
Stadlandet 1 G3
Stanley (Australia) 12 b8
Stanley (Falkland Is.) 10 E8
Stanovoy Ra. 3 Q4
Stanwell Park 12 d11
Starbuck I. 11 M5
Stavanger 2 G4
Stavropol 2 Q6
Steep Point 12 A5
Stefanie, L. 5 G5
Sterlitamak 2 T5
Stewart I. 12 f15
Stockholm 2 L4
Stolbovoye 3 b11
Stony Tunguska 3 NO3
Strangways Springs 12 F5
Strasbourg 2 H6
Streaky B. 12 E6
Strömo 1 E3
Stroms Vattudal I L3
Sturt Desert 12 G4
Stuttgart 2 H6
Styria 1 H18
Subotica 2 L6
Suchow 4 P6
Sucre 10 D5
Sudan 6 FG4-5
Sudan (Region) 5 CF4
Sudbury 8 M5
Sudeten Mts. 1 IL5
Suez 6 G2
Suez Canal 5 G2
Sukhona 1 R4-5
Sukkumi 2 Q7
Sukkur 4 I7
Sula Is. 4 Q10
Sulawesi (Celebes) 4 Q10
Sulu Arch. 4 PQ9
Sulu Sea 3 PQ9-10
Sumatra 4 NO9-10
Sumba 4 Q10
Sumbawa 4 P10
Sumbing 3 I13
Sunda Str. 3 O10
Sundarbans 4 a12
Sundsvall 2 L3
Sungari 3 R5
Sungari Res. 3 Q5
Superior, L. 7 M5
Sur 4 H7
Surabaya 4 P10
Surabaya Str. 3 m13
Surakarta 3 m13
Surgut 4 L3
Surinam 10 E3
Sutherland 12 d11
Suwadiva Atoll3 L9
Suwarrow 11 L6
Svalbard 4 E2
Svartisen 1 I2
Svir 1 Q3
Swain Reef 12 I4
Swains I. 11 IL6
Swatow 4 P6
Swaziland 6 F8
Sweden 2 L2 - L4
Switzerland 2 H6
Sydero 1 E3
Sydney (Australia) 12 I6
Sydney (Canada) 8 O5
Sydney I. 11 I5
Syktykar 2 S3
Sylt 1 H
Syracuse 2 L8
Syrcarya 3 I5
Syria 2 PQ9-10
Syrian Desert 3 FG6
Szeged 2 L6
Szczecin 2 L5

T

Tabriz 4 G6
Tachikawa 4 d13
Tacoma 8 G5
Tadzhikistan 4 IL6
Taganrog 2 P6
Tagant 5 B4
Tagus 1 E8
Tahan 3 O9
Ta hao hai Str. 4 g15
Tahat 5 D3
Tahcheng 4 M5
Ta Heng Chin 4 g15
Tahora 6 G5
Tahoua 6 D4
Tahuata 11 NO6
Tai o 4 g15
Tai mo shan 4 g15

Tainan 4 Q7
Taipei 4 Q7
Taitao Pen. 10 C8
Taiwan (Formosa) 4 Q5
Taiyuan 4 P6
Ta'iz 4 G8
Takaka 12 G14
Takla Makan Desert 3 M6
Taland Is.
Talbot C. 12 D2
Talca 10 C7
Tali 4 O7
Tallin 2 N4
Tamale 6 C5
Tamatave 6 H7
Tambo 12 H5
Tambura 6 F5
Tamgak Mt. 5 D4
Tamluk 4 a11
Tampere 2 M3
Tampico 8 L7
Tamworth 12 H6
Tama 5 GH6
Tana L. 5 G4
Tana R. (Finland) I N2
Tana R. (Kenya) 6 H6
Tanami 12 E3
Tanda 1 V3
Tandilo 10 D7
Tanega l. 3 Q6
Tanezrouft 5 D3
Tanga 6 G5
Tanganyika L. 5 G6
Tangier 2 E8
Tangtouhsia 4 f15
Tanimbar Is. 4 R10
Tanjong Katong 4 i17
Tanjungbalai 4 h16
Tanjungpinang 4 i17
Tanzania 6 G6
Tanzania St. 6 G6
Taongi Atoll 11 G3
Taonga 4 Q10
Taoudenni 6 C3
Tapajos 9 E4
Tapa Shan 3 O6
Tapengso 4 g15
Tara 2 Z4
Tarakan 4 P9
Taranto 2 L7
Taranto, Gulf of 1 L8
Tarawa Atoll 11 H4
Tarbes 2 F7
Tarcoola 12 E6
Tarim Basin 3 M5
Tarnów 2 M5
Taroom 12 H5
Tarragona 2 G7
Tartary Str. 3 S4
Tarum 3 I13
Tashauz 2 T7
Ta shin 4 f14
Tashkent 4 I5
Tasman Basin 11 FG9
Tasman Bay 12 g14
Tasmania 11 E9
Tasmania Ridge II D8
Tasman Mts. 12 G14
Tasman Sea 11 G7-8
Tassili-n-Ajjer 5 D3
Tatakoto 11 O6
Tateyama 4 e13
Tatra 1 L6
Tatung 4 P6
Tauri 12 H1
Taumarunui 12 g13
Taupo L. 12 h13
Taurus Mts. 1 O8
Tavda 2 U4
Taweche 3 p17
Taymyr Pen. 3 NO2
Taz 3 M3
Tazovskiy 4 LM3
Tbilisi 2 Q7
Te Anau L. 12 f15
Tekong l. 4 i17
Tekapo L. 12 g14
Tele-Pirez 9 E4
Telpos Iz 1 T3
Telukbakao 4 i16
Teluk Betung 4 O10
Tematangi 11 N7
Temora 12 H6
Temuco 10 C7
Ten Degree Channel 3 N9
Ténéré 5 DE3
Tenerife 6 B3
Tengiz L. 3 I4
Tennant Creek 12 E3
Tennessee 8 M6
Tennessee (R.) 7 M6
Teofilo Otoni 10 FG5
Terek 1 R7
Teresina 10 F4
Terewah L. 12 H5

Ternate 4 Q9
Ternel 2 F7
Terra Nova Bay 14 A2
Tesinga 3 p17
Tete 6 G7
Tetuan 2 F8
Teulada C. 1 H8
Texas 8 L6
Thailand 4 NO8
Thames 12 h13
Thames, R. 1 F5
Thammu 3 p17
Thamserku 3 p17
Thangmoche 3 p17
Thargomindah 12 G4
Thasos 1 N7
The Johnson Lakes 12 B6
Theodore 12 I4
Thessaloniki 2 M7
Thessaloniki, G. of 1 M7-8
Thessaly 1 M8
Thiel Mt. 14 Pp1
Thomson 12 G4
Thrace 1 N7
Three Kings Is. 12 f12
Thule 8 O2
Thunder Bay 8 LM5
Thurston 1 14 p2
Thyangboche 3 p17
Tiang-shan 4 P6
Tibati 6 E5
Tiber 1 I7
Tibet, Plateau of 3 MN6
Tibesti 5 E3
Tien Shan 3 LM5
Tientsin 4 P6
Tierra del Fuego 10 D9
Tigris 4 G7
Timan Ridge 1 RS3
Timaru 12 g14
Timboon 12 G7
Timor 4 Q10
Timor Sea 12 D2
Tinaku 1 M6
Tindouf 6 C3
Tinian 4 F4
Tinos 1 M8
Tirana 2 L7
Tiram 4 h16
Tiruchchirappalli 4 M8
Titicaca L. 9 D5
Titograd 2 L7
Tjandravasih 3 n14
Tlemcen 6 C2
Tobi 1 E3
Tobol 1 V4
Tobolsk 3 IL4
Tobruk 6 F2
Tocantins 9 G4-5
Tocorpuri 9 D6
Togawa 4 e13
Togo 6 D4-5
Tokara Is. 4 R7
Tokelau I. (Union Group) 11 I5
Tokyo 4 R6
Tokyo Bay 4 d13
Tolima 9 C3
Tolo Ch. 4 g15
Tombouctou 6 C4
Tomini, Gulf of 3 Q10
Tomsk 4 M4
Tone 4 e13
Tonga (Friendly Is.) 11 I6
Tonga Trench 11 I6-7
Tonking 3 O7
Tonking, Gulf of 3 O7
Tonle Sap 3 O8
Toowoomba 12 I5
Top L. 1 O2
Torne R. 1 M2
Tornio 2 MN2
Toronto 8 M5
Torozawa 4 d13
Torrens Lake 12 F6
Torreon 8 F7
Torres Strait 12 G2
Torrowangee 12 G6
Tottenham 12 H6
Toubkal, Djebel 5 C2
Tougqourt 6 D2
Toulon 2 H17
Toulouse 2 G7
Tou men 4 g15
Tours 2 G6
Townsville 12 H3
Tozeur 2 H9
Trabzon 2 P7
Transcaucasia 1 QR7
Trans-Himalaya 3 MN6-7
Transkei 6 FG9
Transvaal 6 G8
Transylvania 1 M6
Transylvanian Alps 1 MN6
Trapani 2 I8
Traversay Is. 14 M4
Tre Forcas C. 1 F8
Trento 2 I6
Tres Marias Is. 7 I7
Tres Puntas C 9 D8
Trieste 2 I6
Trikkala 2 M8

Trinidad (Bolivia) 10 D5
Trinidad (U.S.A.) 8 I6
Trinidad and Tobago 10 D2
Trindade I. 9 GH6
Tripoli 6 E2
Tripolitania 6 E2
Tripura 4 N7
Tristan da Cunha Is. 6 B9
Trivandrum 4 L9
Trobriand Is. 11 F5
Tromso 2 L2
Tronador 9 C8
Trondheim 2 HI3
Trondheim Fj. 1 I3
Tropical of Cancer 4 H7
Tropic of Capricorn 12 I4
Troves 2 G6
Trujillo 10 C4
Truk Is. 11 F4
Tsaidam 3 N6
Tsambur 3 p17
Tsamkong 4 P6
Tsang men 4 f15
Tsaratonana 5 H7
Tselinograd 2 Z5
Tsymlyansk Res 1 Q6
Tsinan 4 P6
Tsingtao 4 Q6
Tsitsihar 4 Q5
Tsumeb 6 E7
Tuamotu Arch. 11 NO6-7
Tuapse 2 P7
Tubuai Is. 11 N7
Tucson 8 H6
Tucuman 10 D6
Tufi 12 H1
Tulear 6 H8
Tulsa 8 L6
Tumaco 10 C3
Tummo 6 E3
Tumsag Bulay 4 P5
Tumucumuque, Sierra 9 E3
Tundra 1 ST2
Tung 4 f14
Tung Kuan 4 f14
Tung-Ting L. 3 P7
Tunis 6 DE2
Tunisia 6 DE2
Tunisi, Gulf of 1 I8
Tuo 3 p17
Tura 1 U3
Turanian Plain 3 HI5
Turath 4 G2
Tureia 11 O7
Turfan 4 M5
Turfan Depression 3 N5
Turgay 2 U6
Turin 2 H7
Turkana, L. 3 F9
Turkey 2 NQ8
Turkmenistan 4 GF5-6
Turku 2 M3
Turnu Severin 2 M7
Turrel L. 12 G7
Turukhansk 4 M3
Tutuila II IL6
Tuva 4 N4
Tuvalu II H5
Tver 2 P6
Tyrrhenian Sea 1 I7
Tyumen 2 V4

U

Ua Huka 11 O5
Uaupes 10 D3
Uaupes (R.) 9 D3
Ubangi 5 E5
Ubangi Plateau 5 EF5
Uberaba 10 F5
Ubithi A. 11 E4
Ubundu 6 F6
Ucayali 9 C4
Uchur 3 R4
Udaipur 4 L7
Uddjaur 1 L2
Udine 2 I6
Uele 5 F5
Uelen 4 Z3
Ufa 2 T5
Uganda 6 G5-6
Ugava Pen. 7 N3
Ujung Pandang 4 P10
Ujung Pandang, Str. of 3 P9-10
Ukhta 2 S3
Ukraine 2 MP6
Ulan-Bator 4 O5
Ulan Kom 4 N5
Ulan Ude 4 O4
Ulvanovsk 2 R5
Umea 1 L3
Umtata 6 F9
Una 1 L6
Ungava Bay 7 O4
United Arab Emirates 4 H7
United Kingdom 2 E4
United States 8 GO5-6
United States Ra. 7 MN1
Upemba L. 5 F6
Upernavik 8 P2
Upington 6 F8
Upolu 11 I6
Uppsala 2 L3

91